Columbo

Nelson Brenner/Steinmetz: "I think that I should warn you that I'm not an unworldly man. I have powerful and important friends, even in the police department. I respectfully request that you do not harass me."

Columbo: "Why, sir, I would never do that."

FIGURE 1: Screenshot: Peter Falk as Lieutenant Columbo and Patrick McGoohan as the villain Nelson Brenner. Patrick McGoohan (dir.), "Identity Crisis," *Columbo,* 1975. Universal Television.

Columbo

A Rhetoric of Inquiry with Resistant Responders

Christyne Berzsenyi

intellect

Bristol, UK / Chicago, USA

First published in the UK in 2021 by
Intellect, The Mill, Parnall Road, Fishponds, Bristol, BS16 3JG, UK

First published in the USA in 2021 by
Intellect, The University of Chicago Press, 1427 E. 60th Street,
Chicago, IL 60637, USA

Copyright © 2021 Intellect Ltd

All rights reserved. No part of this publication may be reproduced, stored in a retrieval system, or transmitted, in any form or by any means, electronic, mechanical, photocopying, recording, or otherwise, without written permission.

A catalogue record for this book is available from the British Library.

Copy editor: MPS Technologies
Cover designer: Aleksandra Szumlas
Cover photos:
1. Publicity photo of Peter Falk in the television program *Columbo*. 1974. NBC Television.
2. Publicity photo of Peter Falk at an awards dinner in Chicago. 1973. Margie Korshak Associates publicity agency.
3. Publicity photo of Peter Falk as TV character Columbo. 1973. NBC Television.
4. Photo of Peter Falk from the episode "Double Shock." 1973. NBC Television.
Production manager: Aimée Bates and Naomi Curston
Typesetting: Newgen KnowledgeWorks

Hardback ISBN 978-1-78320-985-9
Paperback ISBN 978-1-78938-325-6
ePDF ISBN 978-1-78938-319-5
ePUB ISBN 978-1-78938-320-1

Printed and bound by CPI.

To find out about all our publications, please visit our website.

There you can subscribe to our e-newsletter, browse or download our current catalogue, and buy any titles that are in print.

www.intellectbooks.com

This is a peer-reviewed publication.

For My Precious Beaus

Contents

List of Figures	ix
Preface	xiii
Acknowledgments and Gratitude	xvii

PART 1: UNDERSTANDING THE LIEUTENANT AND HIS VILLAINS	**1**

1. Introduction to Columbo and *Columbo*	2
A Snapshot of Television and Film History: Pre-*Columbo*	9
The Underestimated Detective (1910)	14
Scholarship and the Lieutenant	15
What Is to Come	18
2. *Columbo* and the Lieutenant: Literary Influences	22
The Firsts in Short and Long Detective Fiction in English (1841–62)	23
Fyodor Dostoevsky's Lieutenant Porfiry Petrovitch: Pretenses (1886)	24
Arthur Conan Doyle's Sherlock Holmes: Genius Detective (1887)	32
British Golden Age, Drawing Room Mysteries, the Cozy (1920–40)	33
3. Characterology and Character-Based Detective TV Shows	36
The Lieutenant with His Sergeants	39
Columbo: A Blend of Genres, Influences, and Deviations	44
4. Columbo, the Suspect Charmer	49
Suspects as Resistant Responders	49
Charming the Stinging Villains	50
Two Sides of Columbo Presented on a Case-by-Case Basis	60
Columbo and the Ancient Greek Virtue of *Sophrosyne*	66
Looking for the Right Word: Antipotency	71
The Underestimated Detective with the Intelligent Villains: Socrates and Columbo	72

5. The *Columbo* Killer	77
Classical Greek and Christian Villainy in *Columbo*	79
Rhetoric and Villainy	81
Villainy Embodied, Villainy Experienced	83
Audience–Villain Relationships: Antipathy, Ambipathy, and Sympathy	89
Villain Types and Audience–Villain Relationships Examined	92
6. Columbo, Women of His Investigations, and the Equal Rights Movement	103
Columbo's Female Villains: Ladylike but Lethal	105
Columbo-Femme Fatale	110
Female Accomplices	122
Columbo Plays the Underestimating, Traditional Male Chauvinist	127

PART 2: COLUMBO'S METHOD OF INVESTIGATION   133

7. Crime Scene Investigation and Ratiocination	134
8. The Working Cop's Habit of Asking Questions: A Rhetoric of Inquiry	138
Columbo's Leading and Misleading Questions in Rhetorical Inquiry	139
Elenchus and *Aporia* are Translations from the Greek	141
9. Killing Them Softly: Irritating the Suspects in Seven Modes	147
Obligating the Suspect with Appeasement Pressure and the Extrication of Any Threat	148
Irritating the Villains: Use of Excessive Flattery and False Modesty	150
Irritating the Villains: Repeated, Disingenuous Apologies	151
Irritating the Villains: Wasting the Suspect's Time	152
Irritating the Villains: Circumstantial Speech and Storytelling	155
Irritating the Villains: Doggedly Hounding Them for a Melt Down	156
Irritating the Villains: False Exits: "Oh, and One More Thing"	158
When Villains Realize that the Lieutenant is onto Them	160
Special Cases of Direct Confrontation: The Lieutenant Gets Mad	162
10. Columbo Closes the Case: Capture and Consequences	166
Columbo: Virtuous or Villainous?	169
Columbo: The Denouement	173

PART 3: *COLUMBO*'S LEGACY IN POPULAR CULTURE AND ACADEMIA — 175

11. Television Detectives Influenced by Lieutenant Columbo	179
Law and Order: Criminal Intent: Detective Robert Goren	180
Lieutenant Columbo's Possible Future	186
Spoofing the Lieutenant	188
12. Using Columbo's Method in Our Everyday Lives	192
13. "Just One More Thing": *Columbo* and Spectatorship	196

Works Cited	197
About the Author	209
Index	211

Figures

Figure 1	Screenshot: Peter Falk as Lieutenant Columbo and Patrick McGoohan as the villain Nelson Brenner. Patrick McGoohan (dir.), "Identity Crisis," *Columbo*, 1975. Universal Television.	ii
Figure 2	1973 publicity photo of Peter Falk, smiling as Columbo, *Columbo*, 1973. NBC Television. upload.wikimedia.org/wikipedia/commons/thumb/f/f9/Peter_Falk_Colombo_1973.jpg/250px-Peter_Falk_Colombo_1973.jpg	3
Figure 3	Screenshot: Peter Falk as Columbo and John Cassavetes as murdering maestro Alex Benedict. Cassavetes enters the room appalled. Nicolas Colasanto (dir.), "Etude in Black," *Columbo*, 1973. Universal Television.	4
Figure 4	Christyne Berzsenyi with "Columbo and Dog" sculpture by Géza Fekete, Miksa Falk Street, Budapest, Hungary. 2018. Ava Berzsenyi.	6
Figure 5	Homicide trends in the United States, 1950–2005. U.S. Bureau of Justice Statistics.	11
Figure 6	Screenshot: In the wildly popular television western *The Rifleman*, Chuck Connors plays Lucas McCain, a widowed fast-shooter and Civil War veteran with a Winchester rifle. He lives on a ranch outside the town of North Fork in the Mexican Territories and helps the marshal to bring justice and safety in the 1880s. Image from the show's opening credits. 1958–63, Four Star Productions, Four Star Television and Sussex Productions.	13
Figure 7	The book cover to *Crime and Punishment* by Fyodor Dostoevsky. Translated by Richard Pevear and Larissa Volokhonsky, London, Vintage Classics, Penguin Random House, 1993.	25
Figure 8	Screenshot: Sergeant Kramer (Bruce Kirby). Harvey Hart (dir.), "By Dawn's Early Light," *Columbo*, 1974. Universal Television. "The lovable but not-too-sharp Sergeant Kramer appears in six episodes." (Columbophile)	40

Figure 9	Screenshot: Columbo reluctantly mentoring earnest Sergeant Wilson (Bob Dishy) who teaches Columbo a modern investigative technology that helps solve the case. Boris Sagal (dir.), "The Greenhouse Jungle," *Columbo*, 1972. Universal Television.	41
Figure 10	Screenshot: Arrogant, double-murdering photographer Paul Galesko (Dick Van Dyke) jabs Columbo, "Need any help with your spelling, Lieutenant?" Clearly, the devoted Sergeant Hoffman (Michael Strong) is not pleased with the disrespect shown to the Lieutenant. Alf Kjellin (dir.), "Negative Reaction," *Columbo*, 1974. Universal Television.	41
Figure 11	Screenshot: Sergeant Young (Paul Shenar) assists his Lieutenant with a perplexing puzzle and learns a few tricks from the master. Robert Butler (dir.), "Publish or Perish," *Columbo*, 1974. Universal Television.	42
Figure 12	Screenshot: Fitness guru and murderer Milo Janus (Robert Conrad) shows the Lieutenant how to drink a healthy breakfast. Bernard L. Kowalski (dir.), "Exercise in Fatality," *Columbo*, 1974. Universal Television.	47
Figure 13	Screenshot: Gorgeous and glamorous Viveca Scott (Vera Miles) puts industry rival David Lang (Vincent Price) into his place by teasing him with odd sweetness about a secret new product. Jeannot Szwarc (dir.), "Lovely but Lethal," *Columbo*, 1973. Universal Television.	56
Figure 14	Screenshot: Columbo arrives underprepared Early Morning with Col. Lyle C. Rumford (Patrick McGoohan). Harvey Hart (dir.), "By Dawn's Early Light," *Columbo*, 1974. Universal Television.	57
Figure 15	Screenshot: Columbo with Dog. Harvey Hart (dir.), "Forgotten Lady," *Columbo*, 1975. Universal Television.	58
Figure 16	Screenshot: Wife-murdering psychiatrist Dr. Flemming (Gene Barry) smugly suggests a toast as he thinks he has defeated the Lieutenant, but is about to hear otherwise. Richard Irving (dir.), "Prescription Murder," *Columbo*, 1968. Universal Television.	69
Figure 17	Screenshot: Alex Benedict (John Cassavetes) in the act of murdering his demanding mistress Jenifer Welles (Anjanette Comer). Nicholas Colasanto (dir.), "Étude in Black," *Columbo*, 1972. Universal Television.	95
Figure 18	Screenshot: Columbo with Lauren Staton (Faye Dunaway), both cozy at a diner, playing their parts with some personal engagement. Vincent McEveety (dir.), "It's All in the Game," *Columbo*, 1993. Universal Television.	113

FIGURES

Figure 19 Screenshot: Beth Chadwick (Susan Clark) and Columbo soon after she mistakes her tyrannical brother for a burglar and fatally shoots him by accident. She is already irritated but has so much more questioning to endure. Everett Chambers (dir.), "Lady in Waiting," *Columbo*, 1971. Universal Television. 115

Figure 20 Screenshot: Husband-murderer Leslie Williams (Lee Grant) calls Columbo out on his folksy pretense. Richard Irving (dir.), "Ransom for a Dead Man," *Columbo*, 1971. Universal Television. 119

Figure 21 Screenshot: Viveca Scott (Vera Miles) as the glamorous beauty mogul and killer stifles the urge to dismiss the insulting working-class detective who just admits the cosmetic industry has "come a long way since hair curlers and face grease." Jeannot Szwarc (dir.), "Lovely but Lethal," *Columbo*, 1973. Universal Television. 130

Figure 22 Screenshot: Once again, Columbo is suffocating the celebrity suspect Nora Chandler (Anne Baxter) with exaggerated and unprofessional attention, which stresses the actress's overly polite demeanor with the investigating Lieutenant. Richard Quine (dir.), "Requiem for a Falling Star," *Columbo*, 1973. Universal Television. 135

Figure 23 Screenshot: Ken Franklin (Jack Cassidy) is a quintessential villain being annoyed by the ever-present and dutiful Lieutenant. Steven Spielberg (dir.), "Murder by the Book," *Columbo*, 1971. Universal Television. 148

Figure 24 Screenshot: Arrogant surgeon and killer Dr. Barry Mayfield (Leonard Nimoy) can barely tolerate Columbo's question. Hy Averback (dir.), "A Stitch in Crime," *Columbo*, 1973. Universal Television. 149

Figure 25 Screenshot: The murderous maestro Findlay Crawford (Billy Connolly) has just been through an ordeal, courtesy of the Antipotent Detective. Patrick McGoohan (dir.), "Murder in Too Many Notes," *Columbo*, 2001. Universal Television. 155

Figure 26 Screenshot: Columbo crowding suspect Charlie Clay (Robert Vaughn). Patrick McGoohan (dir.), "The Last Salute to the Commodore," *Columbo*, 1976. Universal Television. 157

Figure 27 Screenshot: Det. Robert Goren (Vincent D'Onofrio) and Det. Alexandra Eames (Kathryn Erbe) pretending to be coworker-friends of the deceased to get information from associate mothers watching their children at the park. Jean de Segonzac (dir.), "Privilege," *Law and Order: Criminal Intent*, 2007. Wolf Film, NBC Universal Television. 181

Figure 28 Screenshot: Paul Hanlon (Robert Culp) gets worn down by the persistent Lieutenant. Jeremy Kagan (dir.), "The Most Crucial Game," *Columbo*, 1972. Universal Pictures. 182

Figure 29 Mark Ruffalo in *Zodiac* and Peter Falk in *Columbo* look alike. Tom. "Mark Ruffalo As 'Columbo'?....Yes Please!!" *The Last Reel*, 17 July 2014, 4:24 p.m., thelastreel.blogspot.com/2014/07/mark-ruffalo-as-columboyes-please.html. 187

Figure 30 Screenshot: The Mighty Carson Art Players, Peter Leeds and Sandy deBruin, in a spoof skit "Columbo," bothering suspects until they are driven mad and desperate. *The Tonight Show with Johnny Carson*, 1975. Carson Production, NBC Productions. 189

Preface

I wasn't always a fan of Lieutenant Columbo, but I was always a fan of the show *Columbo*. I was drawn into the dark, dramatic, stately gothic sets of the old-money mansions, though not all of the episodes had such grand sets. Being able to witness the murderer's plans, motives, and execution of the serious transgression of murder and almost get away with it was intriguing. I wondered why the suspects didn't go somewhere to avoid the annoying detective, but now I realize that they were playing "cool," "normal," and "innocent." Their arrogant certitude convinced them that their façade of innocence would ensure their escape from punishment for their murderous deeds. The double edge of this sword is that their position as innocent and committed to finding the real killer is what enables Columbo to smother them with questions.

When I was a young viewer during the mid-1970s and early 1980s, I principally watched *Columbo* because my mother watched the show, along with many other crime and mystery shows: *FBI* (1965–74), *Adam-12* (1968–75), *Hawaii Five-O* (1968–80), *McMillan and Wife* (1971–77), *Police Story* (1973–77), *Police Woman* (1974–78), *Kojak* (1973–78, 1985–90), *The Streets of San Francisco* (1972–77), *Barnaby Jones*,(1973–80), *Rockford Files* (1974–80), *Ellery Queen* (1965–76), *Baretta* (1975–78), *Starsky and Hutch* (1975–79), *Charlie's Angels* (1976–81), *Hardy Boys and Nancy Drew Mysteries* (1977–79), *Cagney and Lacey* (1981–88), etc. Perhaps some of those were my viewing picks.

With *Columbo*, I mistakenly conflated two discrete characters: the Lieutenant of the Los Angeles Police Department and the less impressive detective that engages with the suspects. Unable to perceive this complex duality, I have to admit that I rooted for the villain to get away from the pesky, irritating, relentless detective who appeared simple, unpolished, and weird in contrast with the exciting, successful, and glamorous murderers. While most of the villains are characteristically irritating in their arrogance, dismissiveness, and murderous deeds, several victims are unsympathetic as they blackmail and betray others' trust, threatening personal or social losses for financial gain and other forms of compliance. Furthermore, some villains are sympathetic, having killed someone unintentionally or solely because the victims gave them no foreseeable alternatives. In many cases, the killers commit what could be argued as justifiable homicide or a crime of passion, making Columbo less sympathetic as he doggedly and dispassionately pursues evidence for arrest—just doing his job. Coupled with Columbo's vague character and ever-present claustrophobic investigative methods, I identified more with the celebrity guest villains than with the detective-hero. Perhaps as much as the guilty suspects, I didn't want to hear "just one more thing." I wanted many of the suspects to get away with the murder/manslaughter, though not all.

Certainly, I was not of the conviction that, in real-life, self-important murderers ought to get away with homicide. Instead, it was the fantasy of the villains' wealthy, privileged refinement that was so captivating, by design, no doubt. Of course, eventually, each killer goes too far, choosing desperate acts of violence to maintain "innocence" and self-preservation, blaming innocent, likeable people, or acting with insatiable greed. In response, I could not help but react with what the narrative demands of its spectators: desire for each villain's capture by the hero–detective.

As I got older, I continued to watch the show, reacting with a combination of intrigue and irritation until my doctoral education in rhetoric changed my point of view, as all education can and should do. Identifying communication tactics used by the Lieutenant in rhetorical action with the suspects became an intellectual pleasure. The uniqueness of his investigation, which relies on a folksy and nonthreatening persona and on the use of well-designed questions, uttered at the right times to get to the truth about each case, emerged as a rhetorical act of inquiry. Such inquiries relate to inconsistencies in narrative about a suspect's feelings for and relationship with the victim, crumbling or unprovable alibis, and knowledge or abilities relevant to the crime that were previously downplayed or denied. Through his method of disarming the hubris-engorged villains and strategically asking indirect inquiries, not direct interrogations, Columbo brings to light what the audience already knows—who committed the crime, how, and, to some extent, why. Certainly, the investigation and arrest of particularly unsavory characters—those who bribe in greed, power and lust, threaten others' ruin, and refuse to support others reasonably—is always deserved. Further, my previous fascination and identification with the clever and dazzling killers shifted to the strategically annoying Lieutenant of many rhetorically crafted questions and intrusions.

Over time, I realized differences of character between the duplicitous, persistent, polite, strategic Lieutenant and the unsophisticated, badgering, falsely self-effacing persona of the detective who investigates the homicide with the suspects' aid. Releasing my stubborn resistance to the detective, I realized the sophistication of Columbo's humble and unauthoritative approach with carefully phrased questions, enabling him to project the inferior social status, intellect, and efficacy that subsequently elicits his underestimation by the conceited villains.

Here is where the intersection between the study of rhetoric and fictional detectives' methods of investigation began. Humbly, I present my analyses of those successful and recurring habits of self-deprecation, strategic questions at opportune moments, and "just one more thing" that create an effect of under-competence and an effect of underratedness. As the book concludes, I suggest ways that Columbo's method may be applied in our daily interactions with resistant individuals (self-reflection, self-disclosure, collaboration, persuasion) across fields of professional and personal contexts. Sharing this work with television show enthusiasts and academic readers alike is my pleasure.

Acknowledgments and Gratitude

To my Mom, Ava, who has sacrificed so much of her life to help me along with mine; who exposed me to the intellectually stimulating, darkly creative, and morally satisfying pleasures of *Columbo* and other detective fictions; and who exemplifies, too effectively at times, Columbo-like investigative methods, discovering whatever truths she seeks.

To my father, Leslie, who died too young while I was in grad school, but left the legacy of hard work, whether circumstances feel pleasant, exciting, arduous, mundane, or stressful.

To my smart and practical brother, Laszlo, who exemplifies the courage and fortitude required to envision and complete big projects, reminding me regularly to "just keep going."

To my husband Philip, who picked up my slack mostly with patience, my mother-in-law Carolyn, who asked great questions and became my promotions team, and my father-in-law, Sam, who routinely asked, half-kidding, "Are you done with your book yet?" to push me along. To close friends and surprising new friends whose genuine inquiries and constructive input facilitated idea development, creative problem-solving, and a sense of audience. You have my sincerest gratitude for those thoughtful conversations.

To Pamela Genova, David Mair, David Chin, and Dr. Craig, whose successes, expectations, and support have inspired me to want to be more like them. For those stalwart and philanthropic intellects who offered their help, particularly in the arduous final stages of revision and editing, I humbly and repeatedly say, "Thank you! Thank you! Thank you!" (In alphabetical order): Ms. Lorna Chin, Ms. Susan Hales, and Ms. Janis Winter. Also, to my research assistants, Tyler Kazokas and Katie Kelch, who served during the critical early stages of this project. Of course, the reviewers and editors affiliated with Intellect worked hard on this project throughout the composing process to make the book a smoother read.

To Ronn Akins and all of my fellow art class participants who allowed me to use painting and words in both creative and therapeutic ways over the years of writing this book.

Last but not least, I thank Chancellor Vernon Dale Jones and his committee at Penn State University Wilkes-Barre, who awarded me a subvention grant to increase the book's accessibility to readers.

PART 1

UNDERSTANDING THE LIEUTENANT AND HIS VILLAINS

1

Introduction to Columbo and *Columbo*

Criminals always underestimate this bumbling detective—but he's no dumbo, he's Columbo!

(MeTV/*Columbo*)

In the hit television police drama *Columbo*, murderers repeatedly fall into underestimated detective Columbo's masquerade of bumbling and inept naïveté (NBC, ABC: 1968–2003, sixty-nine 90-minute+ film-length episodes). Nevertheless, by the end of each episode, the guest-star murderers know better. Infamously played by the New York-born actor Peter Falk (1927–2011), Lieutenant Columbo is a working-class, New York-accented import to the Los Angeles Police Department. Incongruously and exclusively, the detective wears a tan summer suit with white shirt, tie, worn brown lace ups, and beige trench coat in the arid Southern California climate. From the university studies and imaginations of the successful television writer-producer team of Richard Levinson and William Link, detective Columbo possesses several incongruities and unrealistic actions that are incommensurate with a Los Angeles Police Lieutenant: smoking cheap cigars that taint the pristine, elite suspects' mansions or work showrooms; refusing to carry a side arm out of dislike for them; recoiling from the sight of blood; driving an old Peugeot in disrepair; and sweetly partnering, on occasion, with his equally graceless but adorable Bassett Hound, "Dog."

Along with keen observations of irregularities in human behavior and the slightest of details, Lieutenant Columbo's constructs of a humble, simple, deferential persona mask his primary investigative method: making indirect inquiries of the suspects. The significance of the fictional Lieutenant's methods of inquiry is in the questions he asks, the seemingly trivial subjects about which he asks, the way he asks questions, when he asks them, and how they evolve with the stages of the investigation.

FIGURE 2: 1973 publicity photo of Peter Falk, smiling as Columbo, *Columbo*, 1973. NBC Television. upload.wikimedia.org/wikipedia/commons/thumb/f/f9/Peter_Falk_Colombo_1973.jpg/250px-Peter_Falk_Colombo_1973.jpg

Lieutenant Columbo solves murder cases by strategically conversing with the wealthy, powerful, and successful murderers as his primary investigative method. The deliberate, functional, and purpose-driven approach to asking for information and managing a relationship with each suspect can be defined as rhetorical inquiry. Borrowed from Aristotle, rhetoric is the study and practice of learning what aspects and tactics make interaction and communication most effective, achieving delineated purposes with clearly understood audience perspectives: trust and cooperation building, tension-relief with humor, persona-construction, information-sharing, information-solicitation, persuasion of a point of view, disarming a resistant persona, and the like. While the implementation of rhetoric is often done in the declarative mode of making statements, the Lieutenant relies on the interrogative mode of asking questions in a methodical inquiry to resolve homicide cases. As a special case of "resistant responders," these characteristically arrogant villains feign cooperation to avoid discovery, resist offering self-incriminating clues, and stave off inevitable arrest.

FIGURE 3: Screenshot: Peter Falk as Columbo and John Cassavetes as murdering maestro Alex Benedict. Cassavetes enters the room appalled. Nicolas Colasanto (dir.), "Etude in Black," *Columbo*, 1973. Universal Television.

Such an example can be seen in Figure 3. Here the crafty Lieutenant tests the resistant suspect's fortitude for maintaining a cooperative façade by laying his half-smoked, cheap cigar onto a priceless piano on which he bangs out "Chopsticks," an act of disrespect on multiple levels.

A structural difference between *Columbo* and other police dramas is its inverted mystery plot format, theorized by R. Austin Freeman (1912). The majority of crime and detective stories are of the mystery type, in which facts about who commits the crimes and how are the puzzles to be solved. A minority of crime stories immediately reveal the identity of "whodunit" and how in order to shift the focus of the inverted mystery to how the detective investigates the murder and, eventually, solves the case. In the "Preface" to his collection of short stories *The Singing Bone* (1912), Freeman explains the subgenre:

> Some years ago, I devised, as an experiment, an inverted detective story in two parts. The first part was a minute and detailed description of a crime, setting forth the antecedents, motives, and all attendant circumstances. The reader had seen the crime committed, knew all about the criminal, and was in possession of all the facts. It would have seemed that there was nothing left to tell. But I calculated that the reader would be so occupied with the crime that he would

overlook the evidence. And so it turned out. The second part, which described the investigation of the crime, had to most readers the effect of new matter.

The contrast between the puzzle mystery (whodunit) and the inverted mystery (howcatch'em) is in the type of attention on the investigative method and the spectator roles: the readers/viewers of the mystery are drawn into the narrative that builds toward conclusive revelation, while the intrigue of the inverted mystery lies in the detective's discovery of crime details, ratiocination of clues (Edgar Allan Poe's term for the application of logical analysis and reasoning of details within criminal investigation), and suspects interrogated, culminating in the detective's exposure of the criminal (Reilly 238–39). Contrary to the mystery, viewers are not invited to gather clues and try to solve the mystery along with the detective of the whodunit genre story. Instead, each story begins with the disclosed commission of the crime, positioning readers as informed observers of the detective's investigation into the incrimination process (Reilly 238). By opening each episode with 15–20 minutes of the known criminal executing a murder, Levinson and Link developed a television police series unlike other police procedurals broadcast at the time. Further, their success was evident in the show's consistent high ratings, attracting large viewership for 69 feature-film length episodes that originally broadcast over almost four decades (1968–2003), followed by their continuous syndication. Importantly, since the last original broadcast in 2003, the program has had continuous years of DVD sales and syndication in the United States and in 40 countries worldwide (*Daily Mail*).

In their 1983 nonfiction exposé *Stay Tuned: An Inside Look at Making Primetime Television,* Levinson and Link explain the show's history, starting with the first *Columbo:* "Prescription Murder" (1968), originally created as a single made-for-television film. When the film got such good ratings, NBC network approached Levinson and Link to consider developing a series built around the detective character. Rejecting the exhaustive and quality-inhibiting weekly series format, the producers and Falk agreed to a 90-minute "spoke" in the NBC Mystery Movie "wheel" concept: each week, one of four different series was shown on a rotating basis (1971–77). *Columbo* was interspersed with *McMillan & Wife* (starring Rock Hudson and Susan Saint James, 1971–77), *McCloud* (starring Dennis Weaver, 1970–77) and temporary entries rotating in and out of the schedule such as *Hec Ramsey* (Richard Boone, 1972–74), *Quincy, M.E.* (Jack Klugman, 1976), and others. The 90-minute program length also allowed each episode to be more intricate and substantial in production and content than the typical one-hour installment (44 minutes with commercial breaks), and intricacy was stock-in-trade for the character (Bounds). With this wheel format, the pilot *Columbo:* "Ransom for a Dead Man" aired in 1971.

FIGURE 4: Christyne Berzsenyi with "Columbo and Dog" sculpture by Géza Fekete, Miksa Falk Street, Budapest, Hungary. 2018. Ava Berzsenyi.

As a composite of several influences, the Lieutenant's popularity has continued unabated since *Columbo:* "Prescription Murder" (1968), bridging several generations of original and new audiences. In Frank Sanello's 1989 *Chicago Tribune* lifestyle article, even Peter Falk expresses puzzlement about the global reach of the show and the character.

Another indicator of icon status includes the presence of a statue of Peter Falk as Lieutenant Columbo with his occasional sidekick Basset Hound, "Dog," at his feet. Commemorating the actor's speculated ethnic ties to the nineteenth-century Hungarian politician Miksa Falk, the statue stands off of this Budapest street location bearing the historical figure's name. Besides this tenuous genealogical connection, the statue testifies to the show's popularity with Hungarians, as further evidenced by its noteworthy syndication, dubbed or subtitled with the Magyar language (Grundhauser). Sculpted in bronze by Géza Fekete, the *Columbo* tribute statue's location was determined by the public in a well-travelled part of the capital city: "When you leave the tram stop at Jászai Mari tér on Szent István körút, you will quickly meet the TV sleuth and 'Dog.' The sculpture is being photographed a lot (by tourists and locals alike), since almost everyone seems to like *Columbo*" (Weil). While there are no signs directing visitors to the sculpture, the statue has taken on semi-sacred status as a pilgrimage destination for the show's fans: "He invested the shabby, preoccupied detective with such depth that the show became one of the most successful detective series in the world" (Grundhauser).

Moreover, *Columbo* has inspired a variety of merchandise, creative works, fan club events, and collectible memorabilia that serve to extend fans' experience of the show beyond the episodes:

- Books and articles about *Columbo* (including this project), Peter Falk's autobiography, Levinson and Link's work autobiography, Mark Dawidziak's history of NBC *Columbo* episodes, and Sheldon Catz's complete series episode analysis, and numerous coffee table anthologies about prime time detective characters and their series
- The Milton Bradley *Columbo* detective board game
- *Columbo* postage stamps
- Original artwork by Peter Falk and those created for the show
- Original stories written by William Link after his creative partner, Richard Levinson, died.
- Auctioned series costumes and props
- Costumes to imitate the detective character
- Merchandise with his image and/or quotes
- Numerous social media fan pages in multiple languages
- Fan fiction of Columbo stories

- Training manuals and articles for sales professionals
- Professionals comparing Columbo's inquiry methods with their own interactions with clients, patients, congregational members/nonmembers, or supervisors, as if the iconic detective were a real person.

In addition, *Columbo* was nominated for numerous awards from various institutes: eleven Golden Globe nominations with two wins, nominated for three Edgar Allan Poe awards (1972, 1974, 1979) and won the last one, received an Online Television and Film Association award (2008), won two Bambi awards for Best Television Series International (1976 and 1993), eleven Primetime Emmy nominations for writing, direction, cinematography, and leading and supporting actors, winning five; and many other awards, including being inducted into the Emmy Hall of Fame (Emmy.com, IMDb.com). These are high distinctions for the series, its star Peter Falk, and the sixty-nine villains played by notable guest star actors. In light of *Columbo*'s critical success and sustained popularity, the lack of critical scholarship is peculiar.

In fact, entertainment and trade journalists continue to recognize Lieutenant Columbo as one of the "smartest" and "most memorable male" television detectives (Anderson). Directed by Steven Spielberg, "Murder by the Book" was ranked No. 16 on "*TV Guide*'s 100 Greatest Episodes of All-Time" and in 1999, the magazine ranked Lieutenant Columbo No. 7 on its list of "50 Greatest TV Characters of All Time." In 2012, the program was chosen as the third-best cop or legal show on "Best in TV: The Greatest TV Shows of Our Time." In 2013, *TV Guide* included it in its list of "The 60 Greatest Dramas of All Time" and ranked it at No. 33 on its list of "The 60 Best Series." More recently, a September 2016 issue of the iconic pop culture magazine *Rolling Stone* featured an article by the reputed journalist Rob Sheffield in which he rates *Columbo* as No. 44 out of 100 of the best shows. Even more recently, in June 2018, *Rolling Stone* declared Lieutenant Columbo the #1 television detective in their article "TV's Top Detectives: Small Screen's Masters of the Whodunit" (Sepinwall 267). While *Columbo*, technically, is not a whodunit but a suspense, inverted mystery, these rankings, tallied from consumer polls, television critics, and hack journalists alike, acknowledge and honor the quality of the show's production and its embeddedness in American popular culture.

Despite Columbo's fixed characterization by writers, producers, and his screen portrayer Peter Falk, the Lieutenant maintains popularity as the quirky detective of one of the most successful detective shows on television. Although some of Columbo's tactics behind each encounter of rhetorical inquiry are not suitable for application in our daily lives, this project studies his investigative style as manifest in his strategically "antipotent" persona (anti-authoritativeness, anti-threatening demeanor, credibility-shrouding), duplicitous communication, provocative behaviors, and subtle "knowing" expressions. In doing so, academicians join other professionals who have already found value in applying Columbo's investigative style in their workplace communications and relationships.

A Snapshot of Television and Film History: Pre-Columbo

Before the rise in crime rates in the later 1960s, television and film had already produced increasingly violent content despite the early internal regulating efforts of the Hays Commission of the Motion Picture Industry. In his book chapter "A History of Violence in the Media," Christopher Ferguson discusses prohibited content described in *The Hays Code*, established in 1930:

> Graphic depictions of violence, the techniques of murder or other crimes, smuggling and drug trafficking, the use of liquor (unless required by the plot), revenge, safecracking, train robberies, adultery (which was not to be presented as an attractive option), inter-racial relationships, sexually transmitted diseases, nudity, and even "lustful kissing" were all forbidden or strictly controlled under the Hays Commission.
>
> (Ferguson 23)

Hays's policies outline traditional but now outdated morality in an effort to clean up the world of gangster-ridden American cities and their professional, career criminals. Instead, the code advocates the primarily nonviolent and actionless, "armchair" or "drawing room mysteries" with detectives of singular murders that define the British "Golden Age Mystery" of the later nineteenth and early twentieth centuries. These whodunit crime stories set aristocrats in idyllic, wealthy mansions of the English countryside, where, generally, an especially intelligent individual takes on the role of amateur detective to solve a most unusual occurrence in their comfortable lives. The genre, also called "the cozy" for its use of cerebral investigation methods that lack life-threatening risk to the detective, was made famous during 1920–40 by Freeman Wills Crofts (1913–20s), Dorothy Sayers (1920s), Agatha Christie (1920–53), Ellery Queen (Frederic Dannay and Manfred Lee, 1929–45), and G.K. Chesterton (1908–35), to name a few (Haycraft). However, late twentieth-century television series cozies such as *Murder, She Wrote* (1984–96) portray Jessica Fletcher, the successful and prolific murder mystery writer, as coming across mysteries on a regular basis, though always as an "unusual occurrence." The traditional cozy operates in a place that cannot be located, in pleasantly isolated, small, charming British villages that are set apart from reality, allowing readers to get away from the close proximity of World War I and imaginatively indulge in the lifestyles of the wealthy aristocrats, while solving the whodunit with surprisingly capable amateur detectives.

Overseas in the United States, the urban centers experienced the violence and coercion from the illegal bootlegging businesses of organized crime groups during the Prohibition era, 1920–33, followed by the Great Depression (McGirr). In the early 1920s, Carroll John Daly and Dashiell Hammet pioneered the retooling of the detective genre for the American social context of the time, referred to as hard-boiled crime fiction. Typically published in the literary magazine *Black Mask*, short stories and installments of novel chapters reached audiences interested in stories that felt more relevant to their experience than the drawing room mysteries did (Ousby 89). In the late 1930s, James M. Cain and Raymond Chandler refined the genre (M. A. Collins 153–54). Then, in his 1944 *Atlantic Monthly* critical essay "The Simple Art of Murder," Raymond Chandler makes a strong argument against Dorothy Sayers's fantasy aspects of her golden age mysteries, lacking emotional and intellectual honesty and integrity. Countering the puzzle-solving approach to mysteries, Chandler advocates for the American crime experience story with its brutal street crimes of corruption, committed primarily by undereducated men from an ethnic minority. Crime in the U.S. responded to the atrocities of World War II: the technological progress of industrialized manufacturing; the fragmentation of production labor; the forced relocation of (lower-class) Americans from rural to urban; and suburban (middle-class) living for economic reasons.

In turn, the hard-boiled private investigators' tough attitudes and rough urban street language reflect a "distinctively American form of realism" (Knight, *Crime Fiction* 112). These villains are shown achieving the "American Dream" with the glorification of financial gain, but with no regard to the means by which that level of wealth, power, and control are attained and maintained by organizations of criminal terrorists at the expense of threatened working-class people. This context strays significantly from the high-class country estates with the Ivy-league educated suspects and amateur detectives who happen upon a bloodless murder.

By the mid-1940s, World War II was over, and soldiers were coming home after witnessing brutalities, losses, and the death camps. People were turning to television for entertainment. In 1949, the cost of a television went down, enabling middle-class families to afford them and regularly view programs. However, crime rates shot up, impacting television programming accordingly. In the agency's statistical reports, the U.S. Bureau of Justice portrays an American culture of increasing homicides, primarily due to firearm violence, particularly with handguns. By the end of the 1960s, the United States had experienced an increase of greater than two and a half times in homicides as well as other crimes such as assault, rape, muggings, vandalism, etc. over that decade.

Number of homicides, 1950–2005
Number of victims

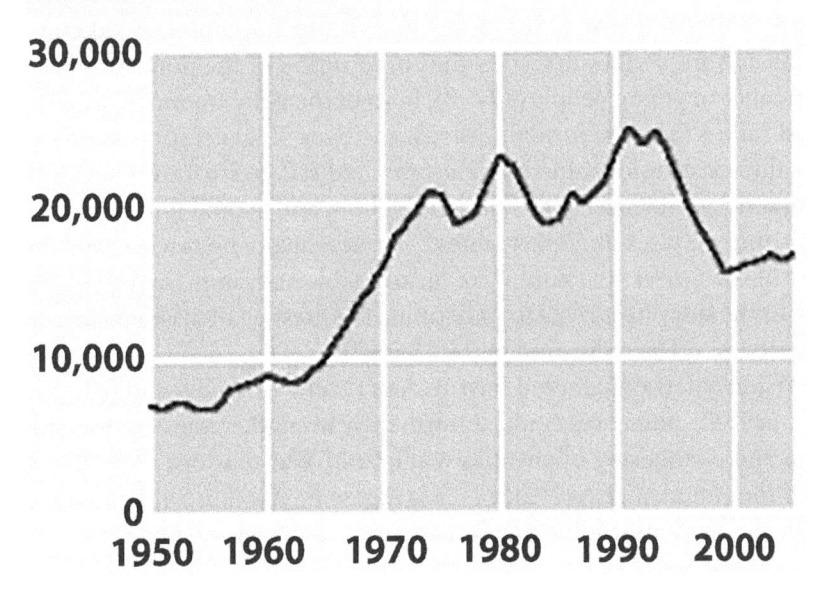

FIGURE 5: Homicide trends in the United States, 1950–2005. U.S. Bureau of Justice Statistics.

Homicide rates increased primarily due to gun violence by juveniles and young adult males. In Figure 5 above, the spike in homicides in the United States is clear and so was a discernible trend reflected in its fictional crime stories. In his 2013 essay "Decivilization in the 1960s," renowned psychological researcher Steven Pinker explains cultural symptoms of the sudden upsurge in homicides:

> The cities got particularly dangerous, especially New York, which became a symbol of the new criminality. [...]. The flood of violence from the 1960s through the 1980s reshaped American culture, the political scene, and everyday life [...]. New Yorkers imprisoned themselves in their apartments with batteries of latches and deadbolts. [...].Urbanites quit other American cities in droves, leaving burned-out cores surrounded by rings of suburbs, exurbs, and gated communities. Books, movies, and television series used intractable urban violence as their backdrop, including: *Little Murders; Taxi Driver; The Warriors; Escape from New York; Fort Apache, the Bronx; Hill Street Blues;* and *Bonfire of the Vanities*.

Pinker explores the presumed correlation between violence and a struggling economy but dismisses it, as the 1960s American economy was strong with low unemployment. Pinker's research draws upon economic theories and historical facts (Fukuyama), social scientific investigations, including criminology (Lierberson; Eisner; Skogan; Wilson; Wilkinson et al.), and the U.S. Bureau of Justice Statistics reports. Summarizing this multidisciplinary take on 1960s American culture, Pinker describes the composition of the population as having an abundance of young people (14–30), born of the Baby Boomers, who value the informal rather than the formal, distrust the over 30 generation and, especially distrust their institutions. Instead, they favored self-control over social control, and romanticize violence, lawlessness, rebellion, and mental illness in their music and literature. As a result, Pinker states, "The leveling of hierarchies and the harsh scrutiny of the power structure were unstoppable and, in many ways, desirable. But one of the side effects was to undermine the prestige of aristocratic and bourgeois lifestyles"("Decivilization in the 1960s").

Television entertainment fed into an American worldview and their post-war identity. In 1949, audiences could reaffirm their strength in the expanse of frontier thinking and conquering of enemies while Cold War tensions and race conflicts engulfed the American experience on a larger scale (Corkin 24; Lenihan 25–27). As Stephen Kiss, Senior Librarian in Language and Literature reports:

> On June 24, 1949, Hopalong Cassidy, played by William Boyd, and his horse Topper, rode across the small screen and into the homes of western film lovers. Soon other TV western series such as *Gunsmoke, Cheyenne, The Lone Ranger* and *The Rifleman* would follow. By 1959, westerns became so popular that they dominated other prime time TV series. From 1949 to the late '60s, there were over 100 western series that aired on the networks.

These Western television series depicted moral conflicts between good and evil, hero and villain, passing on an American code of ethics akin to fairytales. Action and violence-oriented Westerns taught moral lessons, violent Westerns such as *Gunsmoke* (1955–75), *Bonanza* (1959–73), and *Have Gun, Will Travel* (1957–63) featured criminal acts of violence, murder, and justifiable killing in self-defense.

In the late 1960s, there was a sudden drop in new Western television series due to declining audience ratings from the excess of television Westerns and the pressure from advocacy groups who claimed that Westerns had overly violent content for television family audiences (Slotkin 346). Straying from the nostalgic settings of the Old West, television viewers tuned into programs that were nonviolent, suburban, white, middle-class family shows with their own moralizing: *Father Knows Best* (1954–60), *Leave it to Beaver* (1957–63), *My Three Sons* (1960–72), and the like. In addition, action-seeking viewers gravitated to urban-centered programming, which

FIGURE 6: Screenshot: In the wildly popular television western *The Rifleman*, Chuck Connors plays Lucas McCain, a widowed fast-shooter and Civil War veteran with a Winchester rifle. He lives on a ranch outside the town of North Fork in the Mexican Territories and helps the marshal to bring justice and safety in the 1880s. Image from the show's opening credits. 1958–63, Four Star Productions, Four Star Television and Sussex Productions.

reflected current settings, characters, and problems to be solved by modern heroes. Replacing the dramatic Westerns were police procedurals, which is a subgenre of the detective genre with an emphasis on the realistic duties of professional urban police detectives conducting criminal investigations: forensics, inquiries, interrogations, crime scene analysis, background checks, and the like (Primasita and Ahimsa-Putra). Also called the police drama, police procedurals such as *Dragnet* (1951–59), *Peter Gunn* (1958–61), and *Naked City* (1958–62) were popular because of their focus on realism, morality, and good overcoming evil, just like the Westerns. A case in point is *Dragnet*: "The creator, writer, and lead actor, Jack Webb was obsessed with crafting an accurate and realistic depiction of the working life of police officers" (Dowler 5). The show's realism included urban street violence in an unemotional, impersonal investigation of realistic crimes, which had the feel of going on a "ride-along" with the detectives but from an assuredly safe distance (Dowler 5).

In this late 1960s American television culture of heightened violence depicted on television police dramas, the uncommonly gentle, comedic, and fanciful Columbo was born as an antithesis to realism-oriented mainstream programming. Within this television trend, the show's creators had to argue against much resistance by the network executives to maintain their concept of *Columbo* as the "American drawing room mystery" (Levinson and Link 88–89). They were successful in developing a cop show that steered away from the violent drama of the real and fictional worlds around them. As a result, the show indulges in stylized settings, colorful characterization, ingenious plots, and witty banter rather than realistic police procedures.

The Underestimated Detective (1910)

In addition to the nonviolent, armchair mystery influences from British detective fiction, elements can be gleaned from the tradition of underestimated detective made most famous by G.K. Chesterton's *Father Brown* series (1910–36). Instead of acting in the unlikely role of a parish priest as investigator, Columbo is a professional police Lieutenant, which comes with authority, respect, and the expectation of investigative efficacy. However, undermining that credibility is exactly what the Lieutenant strives to do. By engendering the ineffective lead investigator with his suspects, the Lieutenant can relax the suspect's circumspection while, at the same time, asking them questions that eventually implicate their culpability for the murder. John Skaggs explains the line of influence from Edgar Allan Poe's brilliant detective C. Auguste Dupin, to Emile Gaboriau's ingenious amateur detective Tabaret turned Inspector Lecoq, to Sir Arthur Conan Doyle's genius consulting detective Sherlock Holmes. More specific to this project, Gaboriau's amateur detective Tabaret appears in his first novel *L'Affair Lerouge* (1866), which

> features the unprepossessing hero who is the forerunner for such amateur detectives as Father Brown, the creation of G.K. Chesterton, an early twentieth-century historian and journalist and a political conservative and Catholic. Other similar characters include Agatha Christie's Hercule Poirot, and, much later, television's professional detective, Columbo, and it is characteristic of such detectives that they initially appear unimpressive or ineffectual.
> (Skaggs 22)

Manipulating the villains to see him as ill-suited for the challenge of figuring out their "perfect murder," the investigator manages to get answers to questions, discovering clues that reveal how the crime was committed as well as reasoned motives for the crime. Unlike other under-estimated detectives like Father Brown, Miss Jane Marple, and teen sleuth Nancy Drew, Columbo is a professional and decorated senior police detective who wouldn't otherwise be underestimated, except that he does all he can to create the misconception of inefficacy.

Scholarship and the Lieutenant

Although scholars such as Bowman, Turnbull, Knight, Meyers, Skaggs, and Gates reference *Columbo* in their histo-cultural academic commentaries and analyses of television crime shows, their discussions lack substantial examination of the show's content, character, style of investigation, or pop cultural influences. From a psychoanalytical critical perspective, *Resisting Arrest: Detective Fiction and Popular Culture* presents author Robert A. Rushing's examination of the history of the evolution of detective fiction in print, film, and television. Despite the prevalence of Columbo as an infamous detective of popular culture, Rushing neglects to mention the Lieutenant but discusses less prominent fictional crime investigators.

Over the five decades since the 1968 original broadcast of the first pilot "Prescription Murder," a few scholars have studied the detective with a bit of depth. In 1983, Ray Browne and Marshall Fishwick edited a collection of essays called *The Hero in Transition*, with an Introduction written by the latter editor. More specifically, the "Introduction" provides a historical documentation of how the central myth of the hero has changed with the governing politics, spiritual beliefs, communications and media revolution, sciences, economics, and cultural values of Western societies. He historicizes the death of the charismatic warrior, a "one dimensional hero or paragon" of Ancient Greece and the biologically focused Leadership kingdoms of Europe (10–12). In sum, Fishwick writes, "In what Westerners call classic times, their heroes were 'god-men'; in the Middle Ages, God's men; in the Renaissance, universal men; in the eighteenth century, gentlemen; in the nineteenth century, self-made men. Our century [twentieth] has seen the common man and the outsider become heroic" (10). The unrefined, humble, and relatively powerless individual, the anti-hero, has replaced the aggressive, self-seeking, ruthlessly ambitious hero of the past, transforming into our modern society's villain (8). Nonetheless, Fishwick references Ralph Waldo Emerson's wisdom from his essay "Heroism" to identify what Western cultures' hero types have in common: "The characteristic of a genuine heroism is its persistency." Relating Columbo and other such heroes to Northrop Frye's "Everyman hero," Fishwick may be suggesting that Columbo is one of those heroes that are "accidental, unlikely, befuddled, rhetorical" (13).

Within this collection, a focus on the modern antihero myth in psychoanalytic and structuralist terms is Gary L. Harmon's chapter titled "Tarzan and Columbo, Heroic Mediators." Identifying two twentieth-century everyman antiheroes, Harmon exemplifies how they rise to the level of myth in our collective unconscious minds. Citing the anthropologist Claude Levi-Straus's *Structural Anthropology* (197), Harmon illustrates how the Tarzan and Columbo character types and their stories become so deeply embedded in our thinking, cultural values, and expectations of heroism. As widely circulated via mass media, "transmogrified into numerous forms," and repeated over decades, these myths not only enculturate humans to think in myths but also to the extent that myths think in humans without their awareness (116). Harmon also applies the semiological theory that myth is a "speech type" as Roland Barthes explains in *Mythologies* (1972). Identifying myth as a "system of communication," Barthes argues that myth is a message that is socially assigned a "form, historical limits, conditions of use," and, then, is reintroduced into society in a variety of the recognizable message-laden forms (109).

As a mythic form, *Columbo* is, first, a police drama with unrealistic, comedic elements that transgress the genre's conventional form. Second, *Columbo* is an inverted mystery, which goes against the majority of police procedurals with the mystery structure. Third, *Columbo* has its own format, followed in each episode:

> The opening situation of setting, atmosphere, principal characters, and the commission of the crime revealed to viewers; the solving of the crime, accumulation of hard evidence and trapping the villain; and Columbo's solution of the case, culminating in the villain's arrest and the sense that the mythic quest of social transgressors being punished and the hero restoring order in favor of the "good" out of the "chaos" of crime.
>
> (Harmon 125)

As such, *Columbo* is its own subgenre of the police drama, formalized by the show's creators, reproduced by the various writers, and recognized and expected by viewers.

During the later twentieth century, what was formally known as conventional formulas of genre (drama, tragedy, comedy, the short story, and the like) was reconceived as "rhetorical genre" by theorists such as C. Bazerman (1988), C. Miller (1984), and L. Bitzer (1968). Agreeing on the social and rhetorical bases of communication and creative forms of writing, genres are shaped by contextualized historical audiences with specific social purposes, expectations from receivers within a defined community, and narrow interpretations and uses of the language for various functions like entertainment, understanding, disagreement, and persuasion (Dewitt 697). Within a clash of upper-class and working-class realms, word choices, style of communication, and social proprieties signal class distinctions. Through his educated vocabulary, cultural sophistication, and demonstrations of complex intellect, Columbo deliberately violates what the suspects would consider to be the social protocols of his professional status and its discourse. Harmon examines the system of binaries within *Columbo:* the content, self-sufficient, law-abiding, plain-clothed, working-class detective juxtaposed with the wealthy and powerful, consumer-oriented, industrial, machine-supported, and materialistic villain whose posh suburban homes portray the spoils of the capitalistic system for the successful competitor (126–28). By playing a bit of the fool, Columbo further differentiates himself from the suspects he investigates, playing far out of their league, a noncompetitor (Brunsdale 210).

Another aspect that is generic of *Columbo* is the episodes' previews of new technologies, which are key factors to solving the homicide cases. In more than just a reference, Amelie Hastie published a blog article about her current research on the technologies that are vital to the *Columbo* villains' means of committing murder. Examples of their tools of destruction include tape recorders, video recorders, digital cameras, photograph development, telephone manipulations, computers, and robotics, for starters. Through the curious and learning-oriented Lieutenant, viewers voyeuristically discover how these technologies work and were used in the commission of the murder presented at the beginning of the episode. Hastie illustrates the show's forecasting of the pioneering technological innovations that were just becoming available to the consumer in everyday American work and entertainment. In this way, the writers and the actor Peter Falk reflected American technological-social inventions while maintaining an air of nostalgia for the conventions of the Golden Age of mysteries: the grand estates, single murders committed by an opportunistic or accidental killer as opposed to a career criminal, in an otherwise genteel assembly of professional, wealthy, powerful, resourceful, and refined subculture.

One scholar performed a literary analysis of a particular episode of *Columbo*, comparing it with Shakespeare's *Macbeth*. In her essay "The Earnest Equivocator: *Columbo* Undoes *Macbeth*," Margaret Rose Jaster examines the *Columbo* episode "Dagger of the Mind." In a play within a play structure, "Dagger of the Mind" parallels the characters, theme, crime, and resolution of madness in Shakespeare's *Macbeth*. Uniquely based in London, the theatrical actors who play Lord and Lady Macbeth (vivaciously played by real actors Honor Blackman and Richard Basehart) are also the stereotypical arrogant British villains treating less refined American working-class detective of this *Columbo* episode. Of course, like other villains, they greatly underestimate the visiting Lieutenant's investigatory acumen. Columbo subjects the pseudo-concerned associates of the deceased to his usual repetitious intrusions with trivial questions and theories posed indirectly to the unsuspecting. In this episode, Levinson and Link's education and creativity shaped the development of the allegorical story, while Jackson Gillis completed the teleplay with intertextual attention to the Renaissance play.

Although several academics have discussed the investigative styles and approaches of famous fictional detectives such as Sherlock Holmes, none have included a detailed analysis of the Lieutenant's investigative methods (Brunsdale 210). In an anthology of critical essays about *Cop Shows,* Roger Sabin contributes a chapter historicizing *Columbo* in its context with other police dramas, both at its NBC beginnings and the ABC reboot (58–65). The chapter is an overview of the unique inverted mystery and detective's character aspects as a "cop show," and its place within the history of police dramas on television. In her work, Mareike Jenner provides notable contributions to the field's scholarly research on subgenres within detective fiction by way of investigative methods. More specifically, in *American TV Detective Dramas: Serial Investigations* (2016), Jenner illustrates how each "truth-finding" type (the whodunit, the irrational-subjective whodunit of action dramas, reverse whodunit such as *Columbo*) reflects the specific political, aesthetic, narrative, and industrial context of each work. Building from the work of these previous scholars, my work almost solely focuses on *Columbo*, expounding on its detective's unique style of investigation and offering the interpersonal value of adapting that style in everyday communications.

What Is to Come

This book is divided into three parts. Part 1 starts by definitively establishing the uniquely eclectic influences and components of the inverted mystery, its quirky and shrewd police investigator, and the erudite but deadly villains. To establish a rhetoric of inquiry that is informed by the example set by the fictional detective's investigative, collaborative, and communicative process, the following analytical methods are used:

- Psychological characterology of the detective, victims, and the suspects
- Rhetorical and detective genre criticism to dissect contexts of resistance in terms of suspects' cooperative façade, motive for killing, degree of harm and intention, and relationship with the detective
- Rhetorical and discourse analysis of the question-based detective-villain interactions, as related to purpose, outcome, and spectator relationships with these characters
- Theorizing of a rhetoric of inquiry with resistant responders that applies to everyday communications in the off-air world

"Chapter 2: *Columbo* and the Lieutenant: Literary Influences" examines *Columbo* and Lieutenant Columbo in context, providing brief, historical background to the show's subgenres and influences: particularly Edgar Allan Poe's *Murder in the Rue Morgues* (1841), Fyodor Dostoevsky's *Crime and Punishment* (1886), Arthur Conan Doyle's Sherlock Holmes series (1887–1927), the Golden Age British mysteries (1920–42), the underestimated detective and maladroit detective traditions ("The Purloined Letter" 1845), the American "hard-boiled" urban crime stories (mid 1920s–1950s), the television police procedurals (1945–present), as well as actual crime statistics surrounding *Columbo's* broadcast.

"Chapter 3: Characterology and Character-Based Detective TV Shows" defines the European approach to personality studies, characterology, as "the structural aspect of personality and the inner conditions of overt behavior that are, to a certain extent, constant" (Watson 519). His character is differentiated from other character-based detectives on crime dramas. Then, the Lieutenant's consistent character traits are discerned: the antipotent but brilliant and observant cop and his alter ego, the less resourceful, under-educated, annoyingly intrusive, and nonlinear-reasoning investigator. Finally, an overview of the unique mixture of character traits concludes this chapter before the next, which dissects the detective's duality of characters.

"Chapter 4: Columbo, the Suspect Charmer" delineates what we can discern as the "real" Lieutenant from his façade of unworldliness and average intelligence for the sake of the villains. Also, Plato's concept of *sophrosyne* is a term that relates to a Greek goddess of that name and translates to the application of temperance for gaining the audience's favor. *Sophrosyne* is germane for describing the detective's qualities of strategic reserve in expressing what he knows about the crime and what he suspects about the villain or the victim. In addition, I develop here a term I call "antipotency" to describe Columbo's patient, humble, unauthoritative, noncompetitive, and disarming façade which he puts on for the arrogant suspects of social and financial power.

"Chapter 5: The *Columbo* Killer" investigates influences from classical Greek rhetoric and mythology and how they characterize the excessive "hubris" embodied by the intelligent, clever, but self-assuming superiority of the murderers. Further, a brief study of early Christian devil mythology facilitates the characterization of the *Columbo* villain type: charming, intelligent, deceitful, rhetorically cunning, and manipulative. Such analysis yields what are the multiple layers of resistance that the detective must overcome: secrecy about the criminal act, an inflated ego of preeminence that denies Columbo's credibility, annoyance, and indignation with Columbo's persistent probing, use of powerful connections to maintain distance from the investigator, phony self-presentation and charm, and fake hospitality and cooperation.

In "Chapter 6: Columbo, Women of His Investigations, and the Equal Rights Movement," aspects of gender and villainy are related to Columbo's adjustments to investigating female killers of power, ambition, wealth, independence, and audacity who are disconnected with family. The show is compared with the cultural backdrop of American television trends and the Civil Rights Movement. Furthermore, the female killers have an additional resistance to the Lieutenant who strategically enacts male chauvinism to disturb their insincere presentations of feminine cooperation.

Part 2 examines the Lieutenant's method of investigation as a rhetoric of inquiry, discussed in four chapters. "Chapter 7: Crime Scene Investigation and Ratiocination" discusses Columbo's perspective on small details in reconstructing the crimes imaginatively, inconsistencies found and not found at the scenes, gaps in information, contradictory elements about motives and alibis, and his familiarity with human nature or typical behavior.

"Chapter 8: The Working Cop's Habit of Asking Questions: A Rhetoric of Inquiry" addresses Columbo's primary mode of investigation as conducting numerous, short interviews. Two classical Greek concepts are valuable in this discussion. Socrates' early philosophical dialogues generally ended a lesson in the state of *aporia*, which literally translates to "perplexity, impasse, puzzlement" rather than arriving at certitude or a clear sense of wisdom. The role of *aporia* in the Socratic pursuit of truth has clear parallels in Columbo's technique. In this chapter, the following aspects are analyzed: the specific types of questions the detective uses, the various functions of the questions, the effects on the Lieutenant's relationship with the suspects, and how his persona enables cooperation with the guilty suspects.

"Chapter 9: Killing Them Softly: Irritating the Suspects in Seven Modes" describes an advanced stage of his investigations when the Lieutenant progressively intensifies certain behaviors that originally projected innocence, simplicity, and nonthreatening demeanor, but now affect the guilty suspects' annoyance, stress, agitation, and hostility. The detective uses their irritated state to his advantage, leading them to self-incrimination with case-solving clues.

"Chapter 10: Columbo Closes the Case: Capture and Consequences" addresses the Lieutenant's means of closing cases and the ways that Columbo's methods of deceptive ignorance is akin to the villain's façade of innocent cooperation. The ethical implications of their personas as mutually disingenuous are related to spectatorship. In addition, the ways that the detective reveals his agency, authority, and potency is discussed in relation to the villain's plummet in power after having underestimated the detective-mastermind.

Part 3 explores ways in which the show and the character of Lieutenant Columbo are still alive in popular culture. "Chapter 11: Television Detectives Influenced by Lieutenant Columbo" argues for specific ways Columbo has influenced the police procedural and its detectives. Also, as mimicry is both an homage to and a critique of the subject being parodied, "Spoofing the Lieutenant" indulges in the smart humor of comics impersonating Columbo. "Chapter 12: Using Columbo's Method in Our Everyday Lives" identifies from Columbo's investigative methods a system of applicable communication strategies for enhancing collaboration with resistant responders. Finally, "Chapter 13: 'Just One More Thing': Columbo and Spectatorship" highlights the complications in viewer relationship that the show elicits because the Lieutenant's ratiocination and character are somewhat obscure while the villain, their M.O., motives, cover-up efforts, etc. are in plain sight.

This book seeks to integrate fans' familiarity, affection, and expertise about *Columbo* with scholarly attention to the theory and practice that is a unique rhetoric of inquiry, reminiscent of Socrates and other dialecticians pursuing knowledge. Further, this work strives to share practical ways to effectively implement Columbo's method of rhetorical inquiry within various personal, professional, and social communication situations with responders who resist disclosure, participation, discovery, identification, and persuasion for various reasons. I invite readers to enjoy the delights of *Columbo*'s quirky investigator, its creatively conceived investigation plots, its opulent settings, and its glamorous celebrity villains who verbally spar with the Lieutenant. Further, I hope you enjoy the rewards of an academic exploration of this highly celebrated but under-studied popular culture phenomenon.

2

Columbo and the Lieutenant: Literary Influences

Columbo's creators collaborated on producing the Columbo character from the contexts of literature and TV crime series; however, actor Peter Falk's contributions solidified the character in terms of wardrobe, cigar-smoking, a dog as the occasional and only sidekick, and other idiosyncrasies. Although East Coast Americans themselves, Richard Levinson and William Link created a New Yorker-style of working-class detective, who serves the West coast as a Lieutenant of the Los Angeles Police Department. In settings almost exclusively in Los Angeles contexts, the Lieutenant is an odd mix of influences, methods of investigation, and mindsets. As an "American Paradox," Columbo is a "happily married" man (though we never see his wife) with a seeming balance in his life, though he loses sleep at night over unresolved case puzzles. In contrast, the detective is not the typical loner, workaholic or alcoholic. He displays "non-toxic masculinity," avoiding any physical confrontation, as opposed to the stereotype of the aggressive, street-tough, American, hard-boiled detective who frequently finds himself in a scuffle such as Philip Marlowe and Sam Spade of Raymond Chandler and Dashiell Hammett fame respectively. The Lieutenant projects the "gentle detective" with a light-hearted sense of humor, trusting disposition, and simple needs, while most professional cops reveal characteristic cynicism and affectations of power. Columbo is a soberminded intellectual, fueled by "curiosity" that compels him to read and learn as a life philosophy instead of compulsively having casual sex or drinking to escape a broken and traumatic past (Skaggs).

Completely contrary to this, the Lieutenant fears guns, refusing to carry one, which is a deliberate, unrealistic fantasy in service to developing a unique character created by Levinson and Link (*Stay Tuned* 88–89). Columbo is in contrast to the uniquely American gun-toting pioneer with a collection of firearms (Jeremiah and Thad). What the *Fandomentals* popular culture blog writers achieve in their 2018 essay titled "The Top 5 Reasons Why Columbo Is an American Paradox" is to sort through American and non-American traits about the detective. In turn, the show is a creative reconstruction of the mystery detective genre with a quirky investigator who has earned the respect and loyalty of fans across the Western world. This chapter surveys the various literary crime and detective fiction texts that have influenced the unusual blend of nonviolent crime show, professional detective, and inverted mystery that developed from the creativity of Levinson and Link's college education and innovative vision.

The Firsts in Short and Long Detective Fiction in English (1841–62)

As the creator of the detective story before the word "detective" had been developed, Edgar Allan Poe wrote about the fictional French investigator C. Auguste Dupin for the first of three stories "The Murders in the Rue Morgue" (1841). Borrowed from the French, "ratiocination" is Poe's word to describe Dupin's cognitive investigative process for solving a case: conscious, rational inference from available information and reaching a conclusion. Dupin's ratiocination involves a retracing of events and statements in a causal connection, observations of people's behaviors and verbal and nonverbal communication, keen awareness of documents and rules, and identifying with the criminal to understand and anticipate actions. What is particularly remarkable is that Poe wrote "The Murders in the Rue Morgue" with its investigating amateur detective before Scotland Yard had organized a professional police force to investigate crimes (Moore). Poe not only forged the concept of the genius detective but also many of the standard conventions of the detective genre, greatly influencing, most notably, the development of the amateur detective Sherlock Holmes.

In addition to inventing the great detective that crime television academic John Skaggs describes as "a reasoning and observing machine," Poe also created what we call the sidekick or the "Watson" role (39), who often operates as the narrator of the story as well. The companion-narrator observes and comments on the great detective, which Skaggs argues is critical to the development of the genre and readership for three reasons:

- The narrator asks Dupin about his detection method, cementing the notion of the methodical detective in the genre;
- The narrator identifies two essential components of detection, which is observation and awareness of causality and the inference of clues to a rational conclusion; and
- The narrator provides a staple to the detective genre of the investigator demonstrating superior intellectual abilities, which is set apart from the less sophisticated narrator, corresponding to the average reader. (39)

In other words, readers discovering through the narrator who is in turn discovering through the great detective becomes a generic pattern.

While the writer of the first modern detective story is without dispute, the writer of the first detective novel in English is a controversy with updates based on scholars' archival research. For almost two centuries, critics and fellow mystery writers agreed that Wilkie Collins's novel *The Moonstone* (1868) was the first published, full-length fictional narrative focusing on a detective (Thomas 179). It was considered literary historical fact with a recognition of Collins's contributions to the Victorian detective novel:

- English country house robbery
- An "inside job"
- Red herrings
- A celebrated, skilled, professional investigator
- Bungling local constabulary
- Detective enquiries
- Large number of false suspects
- The "least likely suspect"
- A reconstruction of the crime
- A final twist in the plot. (Karl 9)

While Wilkie Collins certainly popularized the English detective novel, archival research by literary historians has solved the mystery, which is that Charles Felix's (pseudonym for Charles Warren Adams) lesser-known *Notting Hill Mystery* (1862–63) preceded *The Moonstone* by a number of years, using many of the techniques that came to define the genre (Symons 51; P. Collins 23). However, the novel still remains obscure to the readers and scholars of detective fiction in long form.

Fyodor Dostoevsky's Lieutenant Porfiry Petrovitch: Pretenses (1886)

Explicitly, Levinson and Link identify Fyodor Dostoevsky's *Crime and Punishment* (1886) as the most influential text on the development of the *Columbo* series (*Stay Tuned* 88–89). Having studied the novel together in college, the writers/producers adopted the story's plot structure as well as the character traits of the story's detective and villain (Brunsdale 210–03). The inverted mystery novel begins with an in-depth depiction of the killer's poverty-stricken life, desires, miseries, and overall emotional and mental states that precipitate his homicidal acts of moral retribution.

FIGURE 7: The book cover to *Crime and Punishment* by Fyodor Dostoevsky. Translated by Richard Pevear and Larissa Volokhonsky, London, Vintage Classics, Penguin Random House, 1993.

Crime and Punishment is a story about Rodion Romanovich, an impoverished ex-student, and murderer of the cruel pawnbroker, Alyona Ivanovna (Alyona). Disillusioned with his deprived destitution and vulnerability to exploitation at the hands of his fellow humans, Rodion is convinced that Alyona deserves to be killed. He faults her conscienceless practices of taking brutal and self-serving advantage of the poor, like himself, and of her enslaved, simple-minded sister, Lizaveta. Readers imaginatively accompany Rodion as he premeditates his arguably justified murder of the pawnbroker in her shop, executes it, and commits the inadvertent manslaughter of the innocent and screaming witness, Lizaveta. First-person narration reveals Rodion's psychological anxiety in covering up his illegal actions, getting investigated by the police and caught with enough evidence to be punished. In a suspense detective story such as *Crime and Punishment* as well as *Columbo*, readers are participant observers of the killer-investigator's dialogue about guilt and innocence, ethical and legal dimensions, and human psychology and human society.

In Part III, Chapter V, the first serious discussion about the murder case occurs between Inspector Porfiry Petrovitch (Porfiry), the suspect Rodion, and his college friend, Dmitri Prokofych Razumikhin (Dmitri). Realizing he must hedge off suspicion, Rodion suggests that he and the uninformed Dmitri take care of the investigator's call for a witness statement right away. Close reading of the dialogues between Rodion and Porfiry expose *Crime and Punishment*'s influence on Levinson and Link's *Columbo*: the inverted mystery format, the clever banter among suspect-investigator, the Magistrate's reserve with what he knows, and the inquiry-based style of investigation. During the first conversation, the seemingly low key and ignorant investigator Porfiry circuitously admits to coming across a philosophical academic article about social inequity that was authored by Rodion. As an obscure work out of the realm of the general public, Rodion probes skeptically, "How did you find out that the article was mine? It's only signed with an initial?" Here, Petrovitch back pedals to qualify the unlikely and fabricated coincidence: "I only learnt it by chance, the other day. Through the editor; I know him.... I was very much interested." Disingenuously projecting a vague recollection of his own essay, Rodion remarks, "I analyzed, if I remember, the psychology of a criminal before and after the crime." The killer diminishes the importance of his research scholarship to support an innocent and ignorant persona, deflecting associations with him and crime. Trying to explain how and why he found Rodion's critical writing purely out of philosophical curiosity, Porfiry backslides to affirm mutual interest and not his suspicion: "Read it with pleasure two months ago in the *Periodical Review*." Porfiry praises Rodion's work, diminishing his own accomplishments. Similarly, Columbo shows interest and admiration of the suspects by reading their books, seeing their work first-hand, or doing research on their accomplishments to learn more about the suspects. Thereby, the Magistrate and the Lieutenant focus their inquiries on the suspects, engaging them in details about their successful work, praising them for their ingenuity, and watching for some detail, accidentally revealed, that may prove significant.

In turn, Porfiry demonstrates substantial knowledge of the article's unique bias against applying public law to and punishing genius criminals:

> There is, if you recollect, a suggestion that there are certain persons who can... that is, not precisely are able to, but have a perfect right to commit breaches of morality and crimes, and that the law is not for them [...]. In his article all men are divided into "ordinary" and "extraordinary." Ordinary men have to live in submission, have no right to transgress the law, because, don't you see, they are ordinary. But extraordinary men have a right to commit any crime and to transgress the law in any way, just because they are extraordinary.
> (Dostoevsky pt. III, ch. V)

After asserting admiration of the suspect's intellectual prowess, Magistrate Porfiry subtly challenges the essay's systematic division of superior and inferior human beings and follows the logic to its conclusion: Rodion must consider himself extraordinary and superior by having contributed new thoughts in writing while the inferior members of society merely reproduce ideas, behaviors, and routines of current life. Therefore Rodion must consider himself immune to police punishment should he commit a crime. Nevertheless, the narrator illustrates the equally intelligent Magistrate as patient: "Porfiry Petrovich has no concrete evidence, but both his reason and his instinct tell him that Raskolnikov is the killer. Although his first attempt to provoke Raskolnikov into confession fails, he knows Raskolnikov will eventually slip and lie" (Brunsdale 202). Brilliant Rodion comprehends the inspector's implications and "smiled at the exaggerated and intentional distortion of his idea." Accepting the verbal challenge, Rodion audaciously defends his self-promoting ideas about law and justice in a hyperbolic, playful game of wits with the law-enforcing Magistrate.

As Temirra Pachmuss posits in her essay "Porfiry Petrovitch: A New Socrates," the Rodion-Porfiry model of dialogue shares much with Socrates' method of philosophical dialectic with his students who want to find clear, universal explanations to solve uncomfortable exceptions for each case. Pachmuss's reading of the detective-suspect dialectic in *Crime and Punishment* is as an exchange of ethical arguments about devaluing ordinary people who commit crimes and the valuation of the "exceptional cases" (Dostoevsky V). Porfiry projects kinship with the genius avenger, but his accolades are accompanied with Socratic counter questions. In doing so, Rodion must defend his position, being provoked to admit his unattractive truth: he is exceptional and superior to ordinary folks, i.e. he should be allowed to kill without punishment. As the inquiry progresses, the dialectic between Porfiry and

Rodion transforms into increasingly tense, exaggerated play, much to Dimitri's confusion and dismay at their "joking" and "making fun of one another" within the context of "those who have the right to murder" and the current murder investigation. In the following passage between Rodion and Porfiry, a few recognizable features of detective-suspect interaction can be noted as having been adapted by the Lieutenant: speaking hypothetically about the murder, soliciting the suspect's help in solving the case, praise of the suspect's ratiocination, and self-deprecating comments:

> Porfiry: "Thank you. But tell me this: how do you distinguish those extraordinary people from the ordinary ones? Are there signs at their birth? I feel there ought to be more exactitude, more external definition. Excuse the natural anxiety of a practical law-abiding citizen, but couldn't they adopt a special uniform, for instance, couldn't they wear something, be branded in some way? For you know if confusion arises and a member of one category imagines that he belongs to the other, begins to 'eliminate obstacles' as you so happily expressed it, then...."
>
> (Dostoevsky ch. V)

However, a distinction is that Porfiry and Rodion's playful banter is much darker than the Lieutenant's with his suspects, as shown in their jest about murder. While the dark humor in their intellectual exchange is generally good humored, the interview becomes more strategic and malicious in their duplicity. Significantly, the reader learns of each of their annoyance, hidden contempt, and communicative jousting through the narrator who reveals Rodion's reactions such as when questioned about his observations the day of the murder: "Rodion answered slowly, as though ransacking his memory, while at the same instant he was racking every nerve, almost swooning with anxiety to conjecture as quickly as possible where the trap lay and not to overlook anything. 'No, I didn't see them, and I don't think I noticed a flat like that open. ... But on the fourth story' (he had mastered the trap now and was triumphant)." Conversely, the narrator gives us insight into the investigator's thoughts such as when he contradicts the suspect's denial about identifying as a Napoleon-like superior individual, worthy of committing guilt-free murder: "Oh, come, don't we all think ourselves Napoleons now in Russia?" Porfiry Petrovitch says with alarming familiarity. Something peculiar betrayed itself in the very intonation of his voice. This insight into the Magistrate's self-doubts is intimate access to the inspector's character and strategies that *Columbo* fans are denied. Viewers can only surmise the Lieutenant's epiphanies from a repressed aside, micro expression of delighted discovery after the suspect has left the room, or private gesture with his back turned to the suspect. More specifically, he will show a knowing smile, eyes wide open while waiting for the suspect's reaction to the "bait" of information he just cast, throwing up his hands in frustration, or placing his fingers on his face to show internal deliberation about the new discovery. Since few scenes show Columbo alone or with non-suspects, viewers primarily see Columbo in his antipotent persona around suspects. For the most part, viewers experience Lieutenant Columbo as suspects experience him.

In *Crime and Punishment*, Magistrate Porfiry behaves like a gracious host with an anticipated guest for questioning. Since Columbo is rarely at the police station when he questions suspects, he doesn't play host, only enamored guest of their homes, a grateful new acquaintance, and fellow advocate of the deceased. So, the circumstances of Porfiry's inquiries position the Magistrate in his home turf and Rodion as the guest. Hospitality and graciousness aside, Rodion asserts his awareness of initial legal tactics between suspects and law enforcers:

> I believe it's a sort of legal rule, a sort of legal tradition—for all investigating lawyers—to begin their attack from afar, with a trivial, or at least an irrelevant subject, so as to encourage, or rather, to divert the man they are cross-examining, to disarm his caution and then all at once to give him an unexpected knock-down blow with some fatal question. Isn't that so? It's a sacred tradition, mentioned, I fancy, in all the manuals of the art?
>
> (Dostoevsky ch. V)

Unlike *Columbo* villains, Rodion establishes a "I know what you are doing to me" speech that stalls but does not derail Porfiry's inquiry. In making clear his cognizance of interrogation methods, he presents himself as a formidable opponent, revealing his reluctance to cooperate with such duplicity. In contrast, Columbo's suspects generally foster an impression of cooperation and concern for the victim and the investigation into catching the culprit.

Having resolutely triggered the suspect's irritation, Porfiry takes the effect further, acknowledging the discomfort and performing a rhetorical inquiry that resembles Columbo's "Just one more thing" or "Oh, I almost forgot" signature phrase. Along with the suspect's reluctant acquiescence to the additional disruption, Porfiry does a false exit:

> "Well, you may abuse me, be angry with me if you like," Porfiry Petrovitch began again, "but I can't resist. Allow me one little question (I know I am troubling you). There is just one little notion I want to express, simply that I may not forget it."
>
> "Very good, tell me your little notion," Raskolnikov stood waiting, pale and grave before him.
>
> (Dostoevsky ch. V)

The inspector's admission of knowingly taking up Rodion's time with an additional inquiry can be seen in *Columbo* as the suspect loses patience with the detective's intrusions. Just as the villain can relax and Columbo announces he is leaving, the investigator will say, "Oh, just one more thing…," "This won't take but a moment," and "Before I forget. …" These phrases are part of the Lieutenant's method of inquiring with significant information after the suspect thinks the conversation is over. With their guard down a bit and then further irritated by yet another question, the suspects are primed for giving honest reactions of shock, confusion, anger, or anxiety. In the passage above, Porfiry uses a qualifier "little" as in a "little question" to ingratiate the suspect into allowing the slight imposition. Like the suspects in Beverly Hills, Rodion is made anxious by the philosophical snare presented to him. Against his better instinct, Rodion (and the *Columbo* murderers alike) submits to entertaining the inspector's "little notion," as not doing so may appear incriminatingly uncooperative. Irritated, resentful, cornered, Rodion mocks Porfiry's obligating words but submits to his insistence.

Along the lines of the Lieutenant's underestimated detective skills, Porfiry performs self-disqualifying self-deprecation first before announcing his theory to Rodion: "Well, you see… I really don't know how to express it properly… It's a playful, psychological idea…. When you were writing your article, surely you couldn't have helped, he-he! fancying yourself… just a little, an 'extraordinary' man, uttering a *new word* in your sense …" Porfiry's use of self-aware silliness attempts to undermine the unflattering implications of the student's self-promoting argument to its conclusion. Hesitantly and vaguely, Rodion only confirms the possibility of it without admitting anything. The homicide investigator employs minor and common-sense principles to build toward a larger implication of ratiocination, though he will undo or camouflage his intentions to incriminate the student: "No, I was only interested on account of your article, from a literary point of view …"

Porfiry's denial that there was any rhetorical design behind his inquiry, only curiosity or directionless conversation, is a tactic Levinson and Link adapted for the Lieutenant. As one of many examples, the motivational researcher in "Double Exposure" (1973), Dr. Kepple (Robert Culp), calls out Columbo for asking questions that suggest his own culpability. In turn, Columbo dismisses the accusation: "I don't think it's proving anything Doc. As a matter of fact, I don't even know what it means. It's just one of those things that gets in my head and keeps rolling around in there like a marble." When killers confront Columbo for suspecting them, the detective characteristically uses the façade of cluelessness. This tactic seems to work more often than not, reaffirming the Lieutenant's crafted persona of antipotency (ineffectuality, under competence, disorganized nature, powerless position). However, in one episode, the suspect is not only aware of being manipulated by the detective's pretense but agrees to halting his own pretense. Television detective actor, Ward Fowler

(William Shatner), admits in "Fade in to Murder" (1976): "Listen Columbo, just for a minute, how about we stop pretending that I'm brilliant and you're simple!" Here, viewers get a "caught" sly smile and confirmation of Columbo's strategic con for eliciting incriminating information from suspects.

A final point of comparison between the Magistrate and the Lieutenant involves the overindulgence of social pleasantries, praise, and delight with suspects. Their similar investigative strategies manipulate their relationships with the suspects, ingratiating themselves, camouflaging their snares, and presenting themselves as a trusting friend who doesn't know to suspect the villains. Still, Columbo takes it to a greater intensity, perhaps, in part, because of the context of his murder investigation taking place on the villains' own properties, often being the scenes of the crime. The Lieutenant could easily ask for a warrant, but that would be a very direct and forcefully invasive rhetorical action, conveying his suspicions of the villains, which he works hard to hide from them. If serving a warrant is necessary, Columbo would do it only during the last act. At this time, he has a strong theory, a plan to trap the villain, and/or evidence. Further, the villains are anxious about remaining "innocent," irritated with Columbo's relentless intrusions and antipotent persona, and refuse to cooperate with his inquiries any longer.

Soliciting future visits as if they were new friends, Porfiry insincerely asks, "'Are you going already?' holding out his hand with excessive politeness, 'Very, very glad of your acquaintance.'" After offering to help Rodion with his unaffordable rent problem, Porfiry smoothly sneaks into the conversation what he knows about his guest: "'As one of the last to be *there* [at the crime scene], you might perhaps be able to tell us something,' he added with a most good-natured expression." Two things are going on here. On the one hand, Porfiry is positioning Rodion as a potentially valuable witness who may help him solve the crime. On the other hand, Rodion is still a person of interest in the case and who may "owe" him the favor of speaking to him further in gratitude for negotiating with his landlord about the rent. Subsequently, Rodion realizes that despite the polite exchanges or satisfying philosophical engagements between them, Porfiry is not letting go of him. Similarly, Columbo may admire, feel curiosity about, and enjoy the company of the killer, but those feelings do not interfere with his pursuit of the truth and the evidence to support it. In "Any Old Port in a Storm" (1973), Columbo shares a treasured bottle of wine with Adrian Carsini (Donald Pleasence) in a car that will take him to jail. Also, at the end of "Try and Catch Me" (1977), mystery writer Miss Abigail Mitchell (Ruth Gordon) admits, "I'm beginning to be very fond of you, Lieutenant. I think you're a very kind man." [To which Columbo responds,] "Don't count on that, Miss Mitchell. Don't count on it." Porfiry is not persuaded to let the arrogant Rodion free from punishment for his murders just as Columbo does not act on Mitchell's or any other suspect's flirtation, praise, deals, or pleas. There are rare exceptions to Columbo's "no mercy" arrest rule, such as when the arrest of the cognitively impaired murderer is delayed in "Forgotten Lady"(Janet Leigh 1975). In another episode, there is an accomplice who is not prosecuted along with her murderous mother in "It's All in the Game" (Faye Dunaway 1993).

Arthur Conan Doyle's Sherlock Holmes: Genius Detective (1887)

Related to Poe's detective-narrating sidekick model, Sherlock Holmes is exceptionally brilliant and very quickly notices clues and interprets them with sound reasoning. In turn, if the narrator were the Great Detective, as with the conventional first-person narrations in hard-boiled crime stories, readers would be given the solutions to the puzzles too soon. Therefore, it is important that the story *not* be told by these detectives to prevent readers from knowing everything the investigative genius is deducing. In turn, the mysteries have suspense rather than unsatisfyingly quick resolutions. However, the narrator has to remain very close to the detective or guessing at a solution or the mystery becomes too difficult (Danytė 8–9). To facilitate the right balance of clues, rationale, and mystery, some crime writers institute the "sidekick" or the team, which enable the exchange of known information. Such conversations throughout the investigations involve newly discovered clues and suspicions about culprits, motives, and *modus operandi*. Finally, the pair or the team participate in externalized and collaborative ratiocination to serve the plot and audiences' adherence to the pace of the story. More specifically, Doyle's stories use Dr. Watson as both the detective's investigative buddy and story narrator, though often leaving both Watson and the reader in the dark. When revealed, Holmes reasons that he holds the secret to maintain his sidekick's safety and genuine reactions of surprise or the like. By convention, the "Watson" role as narrator and sidekick "becomes the eyes and ears of the reader" (Skaggs 39). In turn, this narrative perspective maintains Holmes as mysterious, even with his closest associates as well as with the readers. Sir Arthur Conan Doyle wrote the Sherlock Holmes detective stories with a narrator that prevents readers from accessing the detective's tactics, theories, or suspicions in either an internal monologue and, often, external dialogue.

For example, in Sir Arthur Conan Doyle's *Hound of the Baskervilles*, Holmes sends Dr. Watson to stay at the Baskerville Estate on his own, until Holmes joins him a few days later. With a lame excuse of having city business, Holmes actually masquerades undercover as a nomadic Roma to observe the movements among the moorland's inhabitants. His disguises enable him to approach suspects in an unassuming way. In another story, Holmes performs an alter character, as Milda.

Danytė explains that this assumed identity facilitates Holmes's "attempts to stop the blackmailer in 'The Adventure of Charles Augustus Milverton.' [He] disguises himself as a workman and courts Milverton's housemaid to get the necessary details about the layout of the house" (Danytė 11). As evidenced by the multitudes of adaptations and reimaginings of the consulting private detective, the genius detective Sherlock Holmes continues to have an explicit and active presence in modern productions of film and television crime investigation narratives, as well as in the formative qualities of the good detective, Columbo. Not only can Sherlock Holmes be linked to the development of the Golden Age mysteries, but also to the American hard-boiled mode: "Indeed, it may be asserted that the intellectual side of his creation led to Golden Age crime fiction, while the image of Holmes as a young, vigorous man physically collecting evidence [sometimes incognito] affected the American hard-boiled detective genre" (Danytė 11). In *Columbo*, the Lieutenant plays a role in the guise of a lesser detective in order to discover or extract information from suspects or relations. His bumbling persona is his undercover character or alter identity.

British Golden Age, Drawing Room Mysteries, the Cozy (1920–40)

While Agatha Christie had a broader and more tolerant view of different kinds of people and their ways of life, her contemporary Golden Age mystery writers did not:

> Almost all of them were well-educated, middle-class people who tended, like Dorothy Sayers or Margery Allingham, to create detectives belonging to the aristocracy who have distinct class prejudices and rather irritatingly spend a good deal of time showing off their knowledge of fine wines and art, making references to works of literature not likely to be known by the masses, and classifying people by their accents and class origins.
>
> (Danytė 11)

While the Golden Age mystery writers portrayed their detectives as superior to or within the same socio-economic class as the suspects and victims, *Columbo* featured a working-class detective on murder cases involving rich, successful, and powerful villains and victims. Though, he doesn't fit into their worlds, the working cop invades every aspect of their lives, even their most personal quarters, uninvited and unexpected.

Still, parallels can be drawn between Agatha Christie's Hercule Poirot and the Lieutenant. For example, the "funny little man" detective of *Murder on the*

Orient Express has peculiar grooming habits and an uptight personality, which are flip sides of the same coin with Columbo's unrefined appearance, "like an unmade bed," as described by Suzanne Pleshette's character in *Columbo*: "Dead Weight" (1971). Tussled hair, random scratching of his head, hand to his brow, and trances in deep thought are a few of Columbo's odd behaviors that suggest lack of refinement and self-control over expressing emotions or cognitive states of mind that the wealthy villains exhibit as a matter of course. Regardless of whether the subject is the real detective Columbo or the unassuming pretense of detective Columbo, neither fit well in high society. Certainly, both Poirot and Columbo are respected as reliable and effective detectives, they remain outsiders to the elites in their domains, which means travels in Europe for the former and homicide investigations for the latter.

Another distinguishing aspect of the armchair detective story that influenced Levinson and Link's *Columbo* series as well as their subsequent series *Murder, She Wrote*, is the lack of depicted violence and realistic gore. *Columbo* offers stylized and mostly unseen murders, a cleaned-up crime scene, and bloodless victim corpse, which are typical of Golden Age mysteries. However, the lack of realistic gore and violence of the cozy enables the focus to be on the puzzle and mystery, while the absence of these realistic details also provides for comedic elements in *Columbo*. For example, the plagiarizing Scottish composer and conductor (Billy Connolly) of "Murder with Too Many Notes" (2001) throws his superior protégé off a roof top during a concert performance. There is comfort in this drawing room mystery, knowing that the victim was fatally poisoned before the giant drop. Without death screams, the unconscious victim of the fall is shown upon landing as an obviously fake dummy-corpse, donning an unrealistically small presentation of blood. In absurd timing, the fake corpse lands coincidentally right at the feet of a pair of rushing, tardy concert ticket holders, who become hysterical and run screaming into the concert. The scene is played comedically for viewers, shy of the realistic gore of a bloody, mangled corpse or dramatic trauma. While the grieving fiancé steers the narrative back into drama, the dramedy returns later in the film during the Antipotent Detective's interactions with the self-serving, conscienceless murderer.

In Agatha Christie's novel, *Murder on the Orient Express* (1934), the elitist English socialites refer to the distinguished investigator Poirot disparagingly. Using the term "frog," the arrogant and nationalistic Brits look down on the French for their oppositional history at war. Then, when they discover that he is, in fact, Belgian, they no longer despise him with competitive contempt, but they express their social, economic, and cultural sense of superiority. As a retired Belgian police officer and private detective, Poirot is middle class. Despite modest means, Poirot is given a first-class compartment on the luxurious Orient Express passenger train by courtesy of the train's executive in appreciation for his detection services. Like

Poirot, Columbo is a working-class detective investigating a murder among the wealthy classes. While Poirot's growing worldwide reputation for having successfully solved cases with his famous powers of detection, Columbo's intelligence is under the radar of the press and cultural knowledge, even after the cases are solved and his brilliance is evident. Similarly, Poirot and Columbo share an obsessive attention for small details and irregularities, quick, simple questions whose answers reveal much about the other's character and credibility of stated views. Importantly, they both possess an oddity of behavior that comprises of tenacious singular focus on an investigation, committing polite violations of social decorum, especially among murderers, and an incorruptibility of morals and fairness under the law.

3

Characterology and Character-Based Detective TV Shows

In making sense of the limited academic discussions of *Columbo*, the inter-generic conventions that comprise this unique television police story make the show and the character difficult to categorize. While the show has endured for a longer time span than any other detective series, literary and media scholars have given more critical attention to *Columbo*'s shorter broadcast but prolific contemporary television series: Captain Theo of *Kojak*, PIs of *Charlie's Angels*, PI from Barnaby Jones, the spies on *Mission Impossible*, PD detectives of *Miami Vice*, etc. (Meyers, Stark, Bowman). Perhaps the show's absence in scholarly discussions relates to its formula that stayed true over the years without compelling variations. *Columbo* is composed of what may appear to be irreconcilable components: working-class police investigations in wealthy estates; the Golden Age mystery traits of armchair ratiocination near a major city; and the comedic silliness that neutralizes intense emotional thrills from action or violence into intriguing and suspenseful anticipations of cleverness. Perhaps, scholars ignored the show because it ignored any social situatedness in current social conflicts about access and equal pay, racial crises and atrocities by law enforcement, assassinations of political and civil rights leaders, and the devastating and senseless manifestations of the cold war with the former Soviet Union. Conceivably, *Columbo* may be devalued as fluff or mindless entertainment, unworthy of academic analyses. Though, if this reasoning is accurate among scholars, it would be an argument for why the show should be examined critically. With the absence of clear rationale asserted in writing, the reasons for scholarly silence must be intuited.

Some scholars admit to the oversight but criticize *Columbo* and others in the dramedy genre for being "relatively unrealistic" with lead detectives that are "unlikely heroes" (Inciardi and Dee 29; Scharrer 2; Dill-Shackleford 8–9). Crime literature, film, and television shows in the hard-boiled mode have focused on realistically depicting the lives of detectives as working in "seedy environments" both in the office and on their investigations (Skaggs 55). On the contrary, Columbo investigates among high society in luxurious homes, offices, and recreational facilities. While forensic sciences have evolved and been integrated into crime stories, the Lieutenant's investigations rarely depend on analyzed forensic evidence, which is like the cozy. In addition, the legacy of action and violence from the American hard-boiled mode of crime fiction is secure in its hold on the police procedural. In direct reaction against this legacy, the Lieutenant does not run after suspects who do not run away from him. There are no fights, exchanges of gunfire, or other scene of danger for the detective. Unlike shows such as *Dragnet* and *The F.B.I.* that depict teams of law enforcement officers collaboratively solving crimes, in *Columbo* the detective largely works on his own, except for the Sergeants and beat cops who carry out arrests. Further, television shows increasingly rely on psychological theories, psychopathological behaviors, and employing psychiatrists and psychologists as experts on criminal aberrations (Panek 161–63). Conversely, Lieutenant Columbo is not extensively educated but successfully relies on understanding the practicalities of life, common behaviors in specific types of situations and relationships, as well as his detection of elements that are missing but would generally be present. Furthermore, Lieutenant is a rank that typically comprises a desk job, not a field job, but Columbo is rarely seen in the squad room. Unlike Lieutenants delegating tasks to detectives who report to him or her, Columbo, instead, investigates his homicide cases himself. In his chapter contribution to *The Cambridge Companion to American Crime Fiction*, Eddy Von Mueller explains how this great detective is a rare combination of traits:

> A partnerless mumbler who eschews tough talk and investigative routine, Lt. Columbo is also, tellingly, a virtual stranger to violence: he even has pals take his firearms tests for him. The denouement of his telefilm mysteries, like those of so many "drawing room" detectives, is usually a recitation to the killer of his or her actions, frequently astonishing his befuddled fellow officers. In other words, Columbo is a textbook great detective but a highly improbable cop.
> (98)

While the quirky detective has been primarily a staple of the amateur detective and the private investigator subgenres, the Lieutenant leads a strong follow-up of quirky police detectives such as intimidating and incongruous Captain Theodore Kojak (played by Telly Savalas), "the bald, Greek lollipop cop" of the NYPD known to say, "Who loves ya, baby?" in a deep voice, offering affection after being tough guy with the perps (*Kojak* 1973–78). There was also the mistakenly prosecuted ex-con with a soft touch, private investigator Jim Rockford (James Garner). While on cases, Jim tries to avoid confrontation and danger in

Los Angeles, lives in a trailer on Malibu Beach, takes primarily unsolved cold cases because of his compassion for his clients, and works with his sometimes sidekick, retired truck driver father (Noah Beery) endearingly called "Rocky" in *The Rockford Files* (1974–80). As a highly unorthodox NYPD plain clothes detective, street tough Tony Barretta navigates investigations with his sidekick on his shoulder, a cockatoo named Fred (*Baretta*, Robert Blake, 1975–78). Charles Townsend hires the most glamorous but under-utilized police officers from various Police Departments to work for him as private investigators. Charles is an employer they never see or meet in person. The undercover investigators of *Charlie's Angels* (1976–81) work in professional settings, wealthy estates, and occasionally on the street in illicit and illegal trades. While the previously discussed shows work on the streets of Los Angeles and New York City, Lieutenant Columbo is spared the grit and dirt, instead, snooping around grand mansions of the rich and famous in upscale Beverly Hills and Hollywood. The show's appeal derives from "good investigative plots, procedures, and comedic imperfections of its lead detective" (Berman 42). In addition, their settings are full of the charm and luxury germane to the Golden Age mysteries.

Unlike the team dynamics and delegations of work in the proper chain of command operating in police procedures, Columbo conducts his dialogue-based investigations largely on his own. This distinction of working independently is a convention of the amateur sleuth, the private investigator, and the government spy. Again, here is how Levinson and Link depart from the police procedural genre and integrate elements of "fantasy" to the character, settings, and investigative methods reminiscent of the classic mystery. As a Lieutenant of the Los Angeles Police Department, Columbo unrealistically works alone for most of the investigation beyond the initial crime scene analysis. With due attention, there are some episodes, such as "Murder with Too Many Notes" (2001), in which Sergeant DeGarmo (Richard Riehle) is a steady assistant to the Lieutenant. Operating as a liaison with the Coroner, in testing the purportedly nonfunctioning elevator, and in reconciling the incongruity of a completely silent, supposed suicide jumper or accidental fall victim, Sergeant DeGarmo facilitates the impractical, unreasonable, and implausible notion that a conscious person would likely be screaming all the way down from a high roof. However, an unconscious person may not scream, which was key for interpreting the death as murder. Also, in "The Greenhouse Jungle" (1972), Sergeant Wilson (Bob Dishy) is assigned to follow and assist Columbo to learn from his detection methods, which means that he appears in more scenes than Sergeants do in the typical episode.

In this inverted mystery, the greatest mystery is the detective-hero. Spectators are not privy to Columbo's personal life, thoughts, reactions, or rhetorical strategies: "Columbo's vague comments about his wife and his past. Gathered together, perhaps these could be used to unravel the mystery of the Lieutenant himself"

(Kaneko). Often unsure of what exactly Columbo knows or suspects, viewers rely on observations of his unsophisticated demeanor and communication style. Though not completely clueless, viewers recognize understated gestures such as a private smile of delight in discovering something incriminating about the suspects or when he stares off in thought, chewing his cigar and realizing a clue that reveals the suspect's dishonor. Further, regular viewers are familiar with the show's inverted mystery formula and the Lieutenant's penchant for noticing small inconsistencies, successfully reasoning the significance of the clue, and eliciting generative interviews, which are Columbo's primary investigative methods.

Mark Dawidziak's *The Columbo Phile* provides a fan-directed and useful sourcebook for scholars of the NBC original episodes from 1968 to 1978. In it he summarizes each episode's plots, characters, production information, and behind the scenes production insights. An extension of Dawidziak's work, Sheldon Catz's book *Columbo Under Glass* provides an inventory of all *Columbo*'s cases, clues, and lead detective character, making arguments that respond to many myths or confusions about the Lieutenant, his wife, his mental prowess, and relationships with the murderers. Since the Lieutenant works alone most of the time, except when gathering evidence from researched records and asking rhetorical questions of his hound, "Dog," he rarely verbalizes to the viewer his strategies, theories, or knowledge: "Columbo is the only regular character in the series. There is no grizzled police commissioner and no confidant with whom he can discuss the ratiocination of the cases. For Columbo, each guest villain becomes an ironic 'Watson'" (Bounds), a silent sidekick who knows what happened but cannot help him. Columbo and the 73 murderers spend most of the story playing off each other. In his façade of ineffectual detective, the Lieutenant discusses twists and turns of the case, the possible motives, and the implications of clues. Of course, the Lieutenant does not expect the prime suspects to confess immediately, but, over time, the conversations unnerve them slowly as they grasp the significant implications of his questions.

The Lieutenant with His Sergeants

While Columbo has no designated sidekick with whom he analyses clues on camera, there are a handful of episodes with Sergeants that facilitate the investigations. At the top of the list is Sergeant Kramer, explains blog founder Columbophile: "Aside from Columbo and 'Dog', the single-most recurring character was Bruce Kirby's Sergeant Kramer, who appears six times between 1974 and 1990."

However, there are a few others worth identifying, as their involvement in solving a particular aspect of the case is significantly more than the typical anonymous "Sergeant."

FIGURE 8: Screenshot: Sergeant Kramer (Bruce Kirby). Harvey Hart (dir.), "By Dawn's Early Light," *Columbo*, 1974. Universal Television. "The lovable but not-too-sharp Sergeant Kramer appears in six episodes." (Columbophile)

In "Publish or Perish" (1974), Columbo has a meeting at the police station in an interrogation room to think the crime details over after little sleep. Besides the brief scene at headquarters, the episode also includes discussions with a technical analyst of the tape recording by the victim, examination of a clue revealed by the technology with his Sergeant Young (Paul Shenar), and interviews with a locksmith, bomb specialist, and an audio transcriber. Clearly, this episode depicts more police procedure than the typical *Columbo* film formula. On the contrary, most episodes do not show much conversation among the police personnel, which deprives audiences of scenes that would illustrate the detective's collaborations and/or mentorship with other police officers and supervisors.

FIGURES 9–10: (top) Screenshot: Columbo reluctantly mentoring earnest Sergeant Wilson (Bob Dishy) who teaches Columbo a modern investigative technology that helps solve the case. Boris Sagal (dir.), "The Greenhouse Jungle," *Columbo*, 1972. Universal Television. (bottom) Screenshot: Arrogant, double-murdering photographer Paul Galesko (Dick Van Dyke) jabs Columbo, "Need any help with your spelling, Lieutenant?" Clearly, the devoted Sergeant Hoffman (Michael Strong) is not pleased with the disrespect shown to the Lieutenant. Alf Kjellin (dir.), "Negative Reaction," *Columbo*, 1974. Universal Television.

FIGURE 11: Screenshot: Sergeant Young (Paul Shenar) assists his Lieutenant with a perplexing puzzle and learns a few tricks from the master. Robert Butler (dir.), "Publish or Perish," *Columbo*, 1974. Universal Television.

Instead, the show prefers to portray Columbo less realistically as a lone detective hero. Since professional interactions are rare, audiences have few glimpses into the Lieutenant's intelligent, down to earth, and lifelong learning character as a respected Lieutenant among his fellow law enforcement officers. What we primarily witness is his dim-witted façade with suspects.

In "The Most Crucial Game," the true Columbo is featured talking to a criminal witness after baiting the surveillance expert back to the crime scene with empty threats of calling the forensics lab crew to scour Wagner's home for clues again. In the dark of Wagner's living room, the Lieutenant and a Sergeant wait for someone to arrive in an attempt to eliminate evidence against the greed-driven killer. To be sure, they caught Ralph Dobbs (Val Avery), the burglar/private investigator hired to take the audio surveillance devices out of the phones in the middle of the night. Despite being trapped with prosecutorial evidence against him, the man insists on keeping his client's name confidential as a matter of business policy.

However, detective Columbo has the advantage in negotiation for the name of the man who hired Dobbs because he is the police and Dobbs is related to a murder case. Uncharacteristically for the antipotent Columbo, the Lieutenant makes clear his superior authority and power in a calm, factual, and certain manner: "Well, I'm not worried since I can charge you as an accessory to murder. I know you're gonna help me out. You're gonna give me that information." Playfully slapping Dobbs's arm, Columbo gestures victory but without ill will. Conversely, Dobbs's downward head turn and frustrated stare signal his own defeat, though he holds out longer with information before the Lieutenant returns his P.I. license to him.

Pursuing Dobb's lead, the Lieutenant approaches the Wagner family lawyer, Walter Cullen (Dean Jagger), who admits to hiring Dobbs and, in turn, his subcontractor, Eve Babcock, because he suspects Hanlon's unethical maneuvers against the Wagner's best interest. Unsure why Eve is fired after just three days, Dobbs continues to be leveraged by the Lieutenant for help on interpreting the audio tapes of Hanlon's last call to the deceased, supposedly made from his stadium office. Doggedly, the Lieutenant replays and replays the recording with intense concentration. Reluctantly and half-wittingly, Dobbs coyly offers a suggestion to expedite Columbo's return of his audio equipment: "pay as close attention to sounds on the tape as to what sounds are not on the tape or should be on it." While reserving some contractual owner-client privilege agreement, Dobbs does provide useful insight for examining the tape for the right evidence. Respectful of the security professional's commitments to doing his job well, Columbo has got enough information for him to do his job well.

Furthermore, with actual witnesses who are innocent, the "real" or straight forward Columbo consistently adopts a calm, direct but sensitive approach to questioning. Despite implications of their relationship with the deceased being counter conventional at times, the Lieutenant reassures them of his nonjudgmental and case-oriented inquiry. Several episodes utilize scenes with cautious witnesses in sexually or sensually suggestive circumstances. Perhaps most profoundly in "The Most Crucial Game," Columbo interviews former office employee, Eve Babcock (Valerie Harper). Worried that the Lieutenant is there to arrest her, Babcock (perhaps a tongue in cheek name for a courtesan) starts to phone her lawyer, which Columbo interrupts by taking the handset of the rotary dial phone from her and replacing it on the base module: "Wait a minute. Instead of doing that, why don't you do yourself a favor. Take this appointment book someplace where I can't see it. Don't call your attorney because I'm not here to hurt ya." In this inquiry, the detective confirms the fact that Eve was paid off by the murdering team manager Paul Hanlon (Robert Culp) to stop doing surveillance of the team owner's phones, enabling his manipulation of the calls. Columbo also reveals his knowledge of her Hungarian accent, ancestry, and name, Ragozsi. While her background is insufficient to conclude whether her services are politically or just economically motivated, the most that can be gleaned from these fragmented details is that she tries to hide her Hungarian accent for whatever reason and has changed her name to further obscure her originating identity. (On a trivial note, the Hungarian element is perhaps a small homage to Peter Falk's grandmother's Hungarian ancestry.)

Another contrast to the lone investigating Columbo is the highly successful and ongoing CBS television series *Law and Order: Special Victims Unit* (1999–present, 18 seasons +), with the partner-focused detectives Olivia Benson (Mariska Hargitay) and Elliot Stabler (Christopher Meloni). Conventional staples of the police procedural genre involve conversations at the squad room or in their cars, exchanging information and theories, collaborating on research and interviews, and devising strategic plans for the investigation. In fact, the story is told through their investigation apart from the villains. Furthermore, audiences are privy to discussions about their personal emotional lives as well: Elliot's marital troubles and eventual divorce, Benson's own rape and trial as well as her birth being a product of her mother's rape, the relationship challenges between the partners, and so on. On the one hand, the stars of this police procedural portray multidimensional characters that evolve, get promoted within the ranks, and resign from the police force. On the other hand, the Lieutenant is a simple, static, self-effacing character in relentless pursuit of the killer's identity with rare scenes of a personal nature—him on the phone with his wife, at the squad room with colleagues though only discussing the case, or with other witnesses that reveal the "real Columbo" as opposed to the Columbo affect for the suspects (Catz 126). Perhaps, the Lieutenant's static character presents as not worthy of analysis by scholars or that the influence on popular culture is negligible. In any case, *Columbo* endures.

Columbo: *A Blend of Genres, Influences, and Deviations*

On the broadest level of genre, *Columbo* is a detective narrative with the four identifiable qualities that George N. Dove defines:

> First, the main character is a detective; this person may be male or female, professional or amateur, single or multiple, but there is an identifiable detection role; there may be love themes, ghost themes, social themes, or others, but the detection retains precedence. Second, the main plot of the story is the account of the investigation and resolution. Third, the mystery is no ordinary problem but a complex secret that appears impossible of solution. Finally, the mystery is solved; the solution may be unknown to the detective-protagonist, the official police, or anybody else in the story, but it must be known to the reader.
> (10)

Columbo is a show about a detective's investigative process, about a crime with a complex and secretive problem, which he manages to solve by the end of each episode. On Dove's fourth quality, the reader is immediately more aware of the crime and the criminal than the detective. Viewers know who murdered whom, why, where, when, and how. So, the murder case is not a mystery to viewers, which is why it has been termed the inverted mystery from the viewpoint of the viewer or reader.

While George N. Dove argues that the detective story genre relies on readers' intellectual participation of missing information to solve a mystery along with the detective: "The fact is that the blanks in the story are programmed in the genre" (22). In contrast, the blanks in *Columbo* are how the Lieutenant is going to figure out what we already know. The inverted mystery narrative focuses on creating suspense and intrigue about the Lieutenant's investigation process. More specifically, Columbo discovers facts about the events, inconsistencies in behaviors and statements and, minute cracks in alibis through carefully timed, worded, and directed questions of inquiry.

In some ways, *Columbo* is a police procedural, which "features the detailed investigation of a crime from the police point of view" (Dove 28–29), though without the characters and plots described by John Skaggs in his definition of "the hard-boiled mode" of realism, violence, aggression, or other action thriller feature (29–32). In the interest of being more realistic, most cop shows follow some authentic, basic behaviors and policies of policing as an aspect of the police procedural genre, which are character types, behaviors, and communications that audiences expect from a familiar genre. In spite of the hard-boiled broadcasting trends in police dramas, *Columbo* depicts few everyday police procedures.

Unlike the "cop show," Richard Levinson and William Link wanted to avoid portraying actual cop realities (the drug busts, the street murders, the prostitutes, and the back-alley shoot-outs). Instead, they wanted to create a program that paid homage to the classic mysteries: "the works of the Carrs, the Queens, and the Christies" (Levinson and Link 88–89). Along with this influence, Levinson and Link would not have any violence (except for barely seen murder), car chases, fights, foot chases, or gun battles (89). Other terms used to reference the "mysteries of the drawing room" include the "armchair mysteries," the dinner table of the "Golden Age British mysteries" of the grand, country estates, and "the Cozy." Named for being emotionally comfortable for audiences, cozies avoid "graphic violence, language, or sex" and instead "feature a series character that solves cases through intuition, gossip and knowledge of human nature rather than forensics" (Martha the Mobile Librarian). Similarly, the creators of *Columbo* created an "American equivalent of the English drawing room murder mystery, dependent almost entirely on dialogue and ingenuity" (90). Further, the classic mysteries commonly are set in mansions of the wealthy, which are adopted in the show as well, at the villain's estates, where the Lieutenant's homicide investigations take place for dramatic and comic effect: "Our rumpled cop would be much more amusing if he were always out of his element, playing his games of cat-and-mouse in the mansions and watering holes of the rich" (89).

Besides distinguishing itself among most police dramas as an inverted mystery, *Columbo* exhibits other peculiar traits that Sue Turnbull criticizes as unrealistic departures from the genre. The show is about a classic, puzzle-solving detective who appears only after the first 15 to 20 minutes, during which time a perpetrator is shown committing a murder. As the villain role is prominent in this inverted mystery, the acting part is characteristically played by celebrity guest stars such as Jack Cassidy, Robert Culp, Ruth Gordon, Janet Leigh, Patrick McGoohan, Johnny Cash, Faye Dunaway, and Robert Conrad, and the like. In fact, guest celebrity villain roles in *Columbo* became desirable acting work. Cited in Davidziak's *The Columbophile*, Robert Conrad, during a 1973 interview about his role in "Exercise in Fatality," admits, "I don't do a lot of guest-starring stuff. I'm usually the star of what I do. But I'd made an exception for *Columbo*. I really enjoyed working on a prestige show with quality people."

In this role, Conrad plays a morally corrupt "Jack LaLanne"–type health gym franchise owner, Milo Janus, who strangles his ethical but disagreeable business partner. In the second act, after preliminary crime scene observations, Detective Columbo meets the murderous Janus, appearing as the shambolic buffoon assigned to the case. As the investigation progresses toward incriminating clues, the suspense builds in the villain's rising tension from Columbo's badgering techniques. Because the audience knows that Janus is the murderer, how he strangled the victim, and how he tactically eliminated incriminating evidence against himself, the remaining suspense and pleasure is in following the depreciated detective as he "outsmarts" the arrogant, villainous mastermind. Columbo unravels their alibis, probes for motives, and manipulates them into making mistakes and misunderstandings about his competence and potential threat.

The procedure of the police when approaching a crime scene or witnesses is to announce who they are and their official police title as officers or detectives or, at least, their judicial department (e.g. NYPD). Often, this announcement is followed by the command to "open up!" if the door remains closed. If no one comes to the door and the detectives have a warrant, then they forcibly open it with a battering ram. The characteristic approach with suspected or alleged perpetrators is to establish their authority, demand compliance, use force if compliance does not materialize, and present weapons and restraining handcuffs that they are entitled to employ on the individuals.

FIGURE 12: Screenshot: Fitness guru and murderer Milo Janus (Robert Conrad) shows the Lieutenant how to drink a healthy breakfast. Bernard L. Kowalski (dir.), "Exercise in Fatality," *Columbo*, 1974. Universal Television.

Certainly, the circumstances present or promise danger to the lives of the police personnel involved, which necessitates caution and proactive self-preservation.

In contrast, Columbo and his police officers are rarely in any danger at all. Most of the villains are not generally violent characters, and none have harmed the police personnel. Though often investigating on his own, he does tell the department his itinerary and corresponding phone numbers, which are smart safety measures, and others can reach him with processed forensics reports as well. Columbo knocks and waits for the person to open the door, or, if the witnesses/suspects are at the crime scene, he will just begin with curious bystander-type questions. It is often only after they demand to know who he is that he humbly, apologetically, and absent-mindedly presents his identification as a police Lieutenant. If there is no answer at the door, he snoops and wanders around the property until he comes across someone, either the suspect or someone who will give him access to the person of interest. Although, legally, a police detective should state his authority, he delays doing so until his identity is demanded, and, when he does, he self-represents with a "Oh, I'm no one special. I'm from the police" type of self-diminishment. When he is new to a case and its players, narrowing likely suspects, and investigating with his suspect, he operates as an antipotent part of the investigation.

Undermining his professialism, Columbo mentions his family but viewers never see them, except for his police officer nephew getting married in "No Time to Die" (1992). Therefore, audiences only have vague notions about the mysterious detective's life. In many ways, *Columbo* deviates from dominant crime television crime dramas, which were operating in a movement of "New Realism" with an emphasis on procedural accuracy and legal codes to dictate right and wrong to stock characters operating within the machinery of the justice system (Arntfield 79). Contrastingly, *Columbo*'s investigator drives the plot and dialogue to carry the investigation. *Columbo* leads an approach to the crime show that includes an aspect of "play" through the "lightweight" humor in word play, visually obvious exaggerations, silliness, clever insults from the villains, and clever means of charming and ensnaring the villain.

4

Columbo, the Suspect Charmer

Suspects as Resistant Responders

As a way to refer to the dynamic nature of dialectic or conversation, the term "responder" designates the constantly shifting roles that participants or dialogists play as they listen, speak, react, and the like. Resistant responders include those who are closed-minded to information that contradicts their own set of assumptions, values, and life truths. For instance, voting for candidates solely according to political party affiliation maintains a sense of belonging and righteousness regardless of contrary facts or news. Blind, unwavering certitude protects the individual from seeing alternative viewpoints and conflicting information, which have the potential to disrupt their secure relationship with the group. Similarly, resistance in responders is summoned from pre-existing, intense dislikes or a vehement disdain for a persuader, organization, or subject. Even when presented with indisputable facts, such individuals desperately resist acknowledging the new information to avoid having to reconsider their position, which could beg for painful change. Such individuals are the least likely to change their minds, compromise, or admit fault. Their resistance is so adamant because change terrifies them or, in the case of the murderers, prison terrifies them (Berglas).

Resistance can also come in the form of shyness or introversion of one who is reserved and repressed about participating in a dialogue, whether as the persuader or the target of another's persuasion. With shyness, individuals may be simply unfamiliar with, uncomfortable with, or unaccustomed to establishing concert with others. Their social inhibitions prevent them from expressing agreement, disagreement, partial agreement, counterpoints, or the like. In some cases, the person may have a social anxiety or psychological disorder that is an inhibiting force in their communication. As a result, the individual's feelings of vulnerability, fear, paranoia, and threatened security can cause a psycho-intellectual shutdown. In turn, others are denied access to desired information, relationships, complicity, or resources from the resistant interlocutor. Furthermore, resistance is generally personal, exhibiting an individual's refusal to listen to, process, or validate a truth that may reflect unflattering implications. Therefore, their resistance is highly motivated by their need to feel potent, correct, or superior. As with the suspects in *Columbo* episodes, resistance involves an active form of secrecy to prevent others from finding the truth about them. Anticipating unpleasant consequences from others discovering this truth precipitates their resistance.

With only three exceptions among 69 films, the Lieutenant shows no anger, disdain, or vengeful attitudes toward the villains. Despite the villain committing murders, covering up crimes, or directing threats of physical harm or death, the detective is calm, remains intellectually grounded in ratiocination of the puzzle, imagination for the killer's motive and *modus operandi*, and in managing his antipotent façade. To do so, he asks an escalating set of questions from trivial and generic to challenging suspects about small details from their stated alibis, opportunity to commit the murder, and capability of committing the murder.

Maintaining a cool, relaxed demeanor, the Lieutenant is all brain in action, like a "reasoning and observing machine" (Skaggs 37). This chapter examines a variety of rhetorical theories (approaches to the presentation and exchange of messages, examining the timing, the situational features, the purposes, the character of the speakers, and the relationship among conversants) that analyzes the Lieutenant's investigating method of creating an unassuming persona with suspects to achieve an underestimated effect.

Charming the Stinging Villains

To manage his relationships with resistant suspects, Columbo operates figuratively like a bee charmer. To put it plainly, a bee charmer is "allegedly a person who can 'speak' to bees and, without any other special equipment or protective clothing, can talk them out of some honey without getting stung" (Walker). Certainly, the metaphor is not perfect. If honeybees sting a person, they themselves die, not the stung victim. As anaphylactic shock reactions to bee stings affect only about 5 to 7.5% of the population (Gill), most people only experience a mild irritation to the toxin. While most people do not want to be stung by a bee or several bees near a hive, beekeepers risk being stung, which is why aromatic smoke is implemented and protective gear is worn by many. However, it is a rare gift for a beekeeper to be able to lull bees into feeling calm, unthreatened, and unbothered by the human's presence and activity within their hives—both bee keeper and bee go about their business cooperatively. With a similar effect, the Lieutenant uses rhetorical inquiries to initially establish his antipotent persona: calm, nonthreatening, and in service to the suspects. In turn, the suspects react with dissonance to the unexpectedly friendly, unsuspecting, and nonthreatening treatment by the investigator, who often enlists their help, thereby lulling them into an affirmation of their own superiority and security. Maintaining an earnest focus on each case and on the villains' charmed lives, Columbo tames the suspects to allow him into their domestic, corporate, recreational, and artistic spaces, at least until they are irritated to desperation and eventually bested by him.

The killers violate the ancient gods' laws and human laws of classical democracy by showing excessive pride and wantonness, combined with murders, which are classical traits of "bad character." In contrast, the Lieutenant is humble, kind, patient, and generous with the suspects, acting as a counterreaction to their vices. Instead of debating and contesting with the villains, Columbo feeds their enormous egos with flattery, matches their grandiose arrogance with lowly self-effacement, displays calm and understanding in the face of their rising tempers, and offers himself in full service to the survivors of the murder victim, especially the guilty ones. Consequently, the Lieutenant shapes a persona that is difficult to criticize; he is a "good man," honorably doing a good job with integrity, and exhibiting earnest good will toward others, which Socrates and Aristotle define as virtuous.

Maintaining ambiguity about what exactly Columbo knows, thinks, and feels at crime scenes is, for the audience, the show's greatest mystery. Viewers see two distinct but not wholly opposite characters projected by the actor Peter Falk. There are the projections of the down-to-earth, dedicated, cunning, but practical policeman doing his job, in contrast with his persona in the presence of his suspects (which is most of the show), portraying disorganization, submissiveness, mumbling, simple-mindedness, and posing endless questions about trivial matters. Playing his persona with a comedic flair, the "real Columbo" gives the suspects mixed messages of mild absurdities by a high-ranking police Lieutenant conducting a murder investigation: "At first even the murderer is amused at the lieutenant's style and usually seems inclined to assume that if this is the best the Los Angeles police can offer, the murder[er] will never be found out" (Bounds). Much like with a bee colony, the charm or charmer "does not make them go away [...] but rather, calms them down" (Laity). In turn, the charmer benefits from the bounty provided by the calm bees. What results is a taming of the suspects, interrupting their defense responses, masking the threat behind the detective's invasion into their domiciles, and clandestinely procuring their assistance in solving the murder that they had committed. After Columbo's methodical barrage of seemingly benign questions and interruptions, his charm loses efficacy and is replaced by aggravation.

Glamour in *Columbo*

While the Lieutenant's intelligence is a central aspect of his excellence in detection, the harder to define social, communication, and personality elements are equally important both for the success of his inquiries with suspects and for maintaining an endearing persona with viewers over the extended lifespan of the series. The Lieutenant charms viewers by delighting and arousing admiration in audience members. The root of a "charming" affect ranges from ornamental, to shining with polish, to the careful crafting of words and nonverbal communication, to the magical in a traditional sense. Communications scholar and writer Virginia Postrel associates "being charmed" with the term "glamour," which she argues creates in audiences a longing for what appears to be ideal, with the qualification that the glamour obscures the hard work, time, cost, etc. that went into making something look easy, beautiful, flawless, and the like. One can charm others with their glamour, which suspends disbelief by creating a sense of enchantment, like magic. Some have a special, natural nobility about them (seemingly natural) that compels our gaze, attention, imitation, desire, and adherence, but idiosyncratically as opposed to universally. Postrel's theory of glamour is a rhetorical process of creating desire in others seeking, validating, and yearning for another installment of that desired glamour.

Examples include actor and activist Sidney Poitier, civil rights activist Martin Luther King, Jr., actress Marlena Dietrich, the shy Princess Diana, martial arts master Bruce Lee, entertainer Elvis Presley, actress and singer Marilyn Monroe, media and spiritual leader Oprah Winfrey, Catholic leader Pope Francis, political leader Nelson Mandela, U.S. President and entrepreneurial "savior" Donald Trump (Postrel), feminist activist Gloria Steinem, musician entertainer and quiet activist Tina Turner, former President Bill Clinton, spiritual leader Deepak Chopra, actress and model Lupita Nyong'o, Maestro Gustavo Dudamel, entertainment mogul and comedienne Lucille Ball, musician front man and reality television star Boy George, world entertainer and philanthropist Shakira, Mangalore actress and model Aishwarya Rai, dancer/actress and producer Michelle Yeoh, actress and civil rights crusader Selma Hayek, poet and visionary Maya Angelou, noble actress Dame Judi Dench, and the list goes on. Indeed, if brilliant and accomplished and beautiful people are not glamourized through media representations, the public would not fantasize about them and long for them.

Viewing one's particular preferences for glamour, audiences are mesmerized by their unusual beauty, understated confidence and pride, humility with achievement, unique creativity, and intensity of passion for their arts and sciences. Another way one can affect glamour is through their generosity and interest in others, courage in being publicly vulnerable, engagement on deeper emotional levels, grace in sharing their struggles without deterring others from doing the same, and brazen fortitude in the face of resistance. Some of the traits of charm can be learned and enacted while others seem to have the "Je ne sais quoi" element (Postrel, *The Power of Glamour*, "Trump Isn't Just Campaigning"; Haden). What is curious about glamour is that people can be enchanted by extraordinary abilities, unimagined diabolical actions, as well as by the grand façades of media magic. In fact, for viewers who have seen *Columbo* episodes multiple times, glamour is stated as one of the primary aspects of the show's appeal, second, of course, to the Lieutenant.

For these repeat viewers, particularly of the early NBC episodes, the dated décor of the sets, the single-camera filming, and celebrity actors from a time past may stir a nostalgic transport to what Pam Cook refers to as a "continuum of history and remembrance" (4). Imaging on this continuum, viewers respond to the artifacts of cultural history in the actors' hairstyles and clothing, car models, sunglasses, and such accouterments observed in the shows. Such recognition and, perhaps even, analyses can trigger recollections of previous spectatorship of the show or experiences of one's own experiences circa that episode's release. A. Holdsworth contends that viewing older shows is entirely different from viewing new shows set in a nostalgic past. In either form, nostalgia is by no means a simplistic or negative version of spectatorship, but, instead, nostalgia is more complicated than "being essentially inauthentic, ahistorical, sentimentalizing, regressive and exploitative" (Cook 103). On the many fan clubs' social media sites, members admit to having watched all of the 69 episodes two, three, or more times with great fondness, even addiction, to the show and its investigator. Longtime fans of the show certainly experience the full range of meanings, functions, and motivations of nostalgia in returning to episode after episode.

For first-time viewers and, in particular, young viewers, the historical nuances of the show's production may feel less familiar with an odd campiness to the styles and artifacts of 1970s Americana as well as the medium's (the film's) velvety texture, softer lighting, and obsolete coloration technology. Nonetheless, contemporary consumers desire to live vicariously in the past. A significant consumer television market share comprises of Americans watching cable networks devoted to nostalgic programming such as MeTV, Cozy, Grit, TCM, not to mention the major video streaming services, Amazon Prime, Netflix, and Hulu. Edited with contributions by Katharina Niemeyer, the anthology *Media and Nostalgia: Yearning for the Past, Present and Future*, offers interdisciplinary studies of a wide breadth of conceptions about nostalgia, how it is experienced, how it serves commercial aims, what it suggests about how Americans think about living in our present world, and the like. Moreover, these media scholars and others recognize the "nostalgic boom," which describes viewers' appetites for watching new programs set in the historical past, including major hits such as *Mad Men* (2007–15), *Game of Thrones* (2011–19), *Peaky Blinders* (2013–present), *The Alienist* (2018), *Doctor Who* (2005–present), *Sherlock* (2010–present), and others. While escapism from our current lives is one answer to the desire for nostalgia, another is desire for the effect of emergent sentiments from the flow of nostalgically mediated history and the narratives of characters within the nostalgic past (Kalinina). However, a serious treatment of ways that nostalgia functions in our complex, global world is outside of the scope of this work.

For viewers of *Columbo*, nostalgia is complicated, as the series continued to be broadcast with new episodes until 2003, which is not quite long enough to qualify for nostalgia in the traditional sense of yearning for a lost past and place. Indeed, consistency over the decades cements the largely ahistorical quality of the show. First, little variations can be noted in the Lieutenant's character in style, behavior, and appearance, save for Falk's natural aging process. Second, the villains are consistently wealthy, successful, and arrogant, though their lavish fashions and domiciles will reflect contemporary styles. Third, the generally single murders of passion, opportunity, or means to an end provide a stable intellectual suspense drama with comic relief that shared little with the outside world but the involvement of technologies in the murders and the previously noted stylistic elements. Levinson and Link have referenced *Columbo* and their detective as "irrelevant," meaning that the shows are not directly about social issues, political crises, or historical figures. *Columbo* is its own world, and viewers are invited in to observe the investigator match wits with clever suspects. It might be akin to watching a sporting event with the final result known by spectators and a guaranteed victory by the Lieutenant. While this formula appears quite banal, the writers, directors, and Peter Falk have taken care not to be too predictable in the details of the homicides or the glamour of the villains. Suspended in some disbelief, viewers know that, at the end of the day, the working detective drives his same Peugeot to his home, wherever that is, to his wife, whoever she is, and to Dog, with whom we are acquainted.

It is in the form of glamour, as Postrel defines it, haute couture fashions enrobing the successful characters, that the extravagances in a villain's arrogant demeanor rings part enviable and part deplorable. Moreover, the glamour of the celebrated actors, playing opposite to their typical "good boy/good girl" roles, bring to the villain characters a playful and majestically devious quality while basking in bravado and opulence on the sets of the Beverly Hills mansions. With these exceptions, the sets are in grand homes, making the murders particularly domestic: "Troubled Waters" (1975) set on a cruise ship, "A Matter of Honor" (1976) set in a mansion in Mexico, "Any Old Port in a Storm" (1973) set in wine country in California, and "Dagger of the Mind" (1972) set in London. Although the ostentatious houses and environments are so pristine, ornate, and elegant with a showroom quality, they lack the comfort of a home in which the average American lives, creating a glamourized fantasy of the rich and famous, no better illustrated than by Vera Miles in "Lovely but Lethal" (1973).

On the contrary, our humble detective is not a snappy dresser with the latest designer clothing. Humorously, the rich, dapper, and elegant murderers respond to the untailored Columbo, his lazy and droopy Basset Hound, and his shabby, barely operational antique Peugeot with judgment, dissidence, or disdain for being unsophisticated working class. And that is exactly how the Lieutenant wants them to react. Further, the show's writers have fun with the detective by writing cheeky moments when a suspect or support character confuses the Lieutenant with a homeless person or severely disadvantaged person such as by the generous and nurturing soup kitchen nun (Joyce Van Patten) in "Negative Reaction" (1974).

Likewise, the episode, "By Dawn's Early Light" (1974), portrays the commander of a military academy for boys and episode murderer Colonel Rumford (Patrick McGoohan) mistaking the Lieutenant for some bystander or intruder, commanding him, "Hey, you. Mister! You better hand that over to the police. This is a restricted area. You better leave." Immediately resuming his search for clues on the crime scene's grass field, he sluggishly but obediently answers, "I'm gonna do that, sir." Right after, the Colonel commands LAPD's Sergeant George Kramer (Bruce Kirby), "You better detain that man. [pointing to Columbo] He refuses to leave."

To clarify, Sergeant Kramer explains, "This man is Lieutenant Columbo, sir. He's in charge of the investigation." When the Sergeant introduces the Lieutenant to the surprised Colonel, Columbo barely shares a few words with him, avoiding eye contact with the Colonel, before resuming his search. His brevity displays a lack of proper etiquette and respect for the high-ranking officer, suggesting a lack of awareness and interest in the authoritative chain of command. While Columbo's advanced rank as Lieutenant reflects his credibility, experience, and authority, his Antipotent Detective persona veils those aspects of social and professional potency, power, and authority.

FIGURE 13: Screenshot: Gorgeous and glamorous Viveca Scott (Vera Miles) puts industry rival David Lang (Vincent Price) into his place by teasing him with odd sweetness about a secret new product. Jeannot Szwarc (dir.), "Lovely but Lethal," *Columbo*, 1973. Universal Television.

Viewers are privy to the occasional expression of sincere respect for and obedience to the Lieutenant shown by the Sergeants and police officers. They play along with the Lieutenant's façade of antipotency but show subdued befuddlement at times about his unconventional process or repressed thinking about a new bit of information. The other police personnel are impressed with his efficacy, surprised and amused by his antipotent presentation, and puzzled by his private ratiocination, just as viewers are. Again, during the first scene of investigation in "By Dawn's Early Light," Sergeant Kramer (Bruce Kirby) agrees with Captain Corso (Sidney Armus) that the old cannon blowing up was an obvious accident, requiring no further investigation of a homicide.

FIGURE 14: Screenshot: Columbo arrives underprepared Early Morning with Col. Lyle C. Rumford (Patrick McGoohan). Harvey Hart (dir.), "By Dawn's Early Light," *Columbo*, 1974. Universal Television.

Despite their certitude, the Lieutenant continues intently scanning the grass and scraping his shoe along its surface, with pointed toe, almost in a dance, perplexing and amusing all colleague-observers, and inviting underestimation by the murderous observer.

There is also charm in Columbo's interactions with "Dog," his unnamed, goofy, floppy-eared, slobbering, lackadaisical, and simple part-time sidekick. Dog brings to the Lieutenant a snapshot of a personal side—protective, sweet, good-natured but awkward, out of his element but comedically precious, treating him to ice cream in a messy nose-to-nose proximity. Dog and his car are as down to earth, silly, but dependable as the contently married Lieutenant doing his job. In contrast to this version of the Lieutenant with Dog, the Antipotent Detective is more dramatic as a dog lover. In "Ashes to Ashes" (1998), when investigating the home of the tabloid journalist and murder victim (Rue McClanahan), Columbo realizes that there is a puppy at the house who has been neglected since the night before. The detective's overreaction to get the pup water and other staples in a frenzy of life or death is hyperbolic, as the puppy wasn't dying of thirst or the like. Performing mental distraction and emotionality goes against the tough cop on the job persona of most police

FIGURE 15: Screenshot: Columbo with Dog. Harvey Hart (dir.), "Forgotten Lady," *Columbo*, 1975. Universal Television.

dramas. The Antipotent Detective's priority is puppy care, and the case can wait. While the Lieutenant does have affection for dogs and would be concerned about the puppy being taken care of, he pushes the behavior to firmly establish his antipotent persona immediately upon arriving at the crime scene.

Another glimpse of the "real" Lieutenant occurs in "Rest in Peace, Mrs. Columbo" (1990). The Lieutenant considers the case evidence over his favorite dish, chili at his favorite diner with Sergeant Brady (Tom Isbell). As stated, most episodes depict Columbo sharing little to nothing with the audience about his theories, suspicions, plans to capture a villain, or an assessment of the value of the evidence for prosecution. Atypically, the investigator discusses specifically these topics with the Sergeant. For instance, the scene at the diner shows Brady updating Columbo with the discovery of the murder weapon discarded on an empty lot in a neighborhood of disgruntled homeowners suing the deceased. After patiently listening to young Brady's report, the Lieutenant counterargues the incrimination of the homeowners: "Yeah, right, ah. Look, Brady, you're on the ball; I like that [...]. All terrific, but you're climbing the wrong ladder." Mentoring the earnest and diligent Sergeant, Columbo reviews evidence with him, leading him through an inquiry about the conflicting facts of the deceased having won $1,400 on basketball bets just hours earlier and an ATM withdrawal of $200 at the restaurant where Vivian was dining. In this rare moment, the Lieutenant demonstrates his ratiocination of the facts, generously sharing his interpretation of the incongruity of these two facts. Concluding, they would make sense only if a killer were trying to obscure the victim's time of death. Enacting a Socratic Inquiry in dialogue with his pupil/mentee, Columbo holds off making the case for Brady, allowing him to apply deductive reasoning to the evidence he is dissecting for the first time, guiding him in a process of analytical deliberation of the chain of events. When Brady is dumbfounded, the experienced Lieutenant explicates his theory of a "put up job." Recounting the series of events at the restaurant in relation to time of death, the Lieutenant identifies the condemning circumstantial evidence against Mrs. Dimitri and her suspicious alibi that "you can't break with a sledge hammer." Following the detective's presentation of clues, Columbo challenges Brady: "You figure it out."

Confirming the logical inference that the evidence leads to Vivian Dimitri, the Sergeant leaps to the conclusion, "Lieutenant, that's great; we've got her." While shaking his head in negation, the master detective questions his pupil, "Oh, yeah? How do you figure that?" As Brady listens to his explanation, Columbo pronounces the lack of sufficient evidence beyond his "theory and a set of circumstances" that could not lead to a conviction. In this rare conversation about his process of ratiocination, viewers vicariously learn Columbo's authority as a senior officer performing an inquiry-based teaching of the lessons in detection and case-building. Also, spectators are permitted to witness his astute cognitive process in action. Investigating with a temporary partner on the case enables such deliberations amongst police personnel that are generically absent from the *Columbo* format and, hence, limit spectators' access to the Lieutenant's real character. As emblematic of the show, audiences are privileged to hear the killer's private, internal monologue, commission of murder, construction of an alibi, and framing of the crime on innocents. However, few episodes provide parallel insight to the Lieutenant's analytical methods, rhetorical strategies behind his inquiries, or the degree to which the Antipotent Detective overlaps with the Lieutenant.

With that said, there are some recognizable consistencies between the two characters. Whether interacting on the phone with his wife, at the crime scene with police officers, with witnesses, or with suspects, Columbo is consistently even-tempered, patient, and respectful to all. Reporting for *The Daily Mail*, a journalist identifies a key element of the detective's appeal: "The really likeable aspect of Falk's performance was the fact that he made his hero humble, he never gloated about bagging a condescending killer [...]. He always addressed villains, no matter how evil, with 'ma'am,' or 'sir' as the deceptively bumbling detective distracted their smooth patter midway by plucking a boiled egg from his pocket, or delivering that famous line after exiting a room" (*Daily Mail* Reporter). Such unflappable polite manners, regardless of direct insults from suspects, is a quality of British aristocratic "gentleman/lady" amateur detectives of the Golden Age of mystery. Drawing from England's socio-economic barriers, Richard Levinson and William Link explain the basis of their story and character that share much with the cozy: "the crime scenes at the estates and other properties of the wealthy, the wealthy villains (rarely the Butlers!), and careful, polite investigator" (*Stay Tuned* 90). However, Columbo has an unusual blend of traits: earnest, good-natured, polite working-class man who lacks some of the finishing, refinement of the well-bred, old-moneyed suspects he investigates and arrests. As an outsider to the various worlds of the rich and famous, the Lieutenant observes carefully how the elite criminals operate, coming and going with them in every aspect of their lives. Strategically, Columbo emphasizes his inadequacy in their territories, intentionally exaggerating clumsiness, flawed memory, absent-mindedness, disorganization, lack of knowledge, basic literacy, awkward social etiquette; in turn he widens the social status gap between him and the suspects. For Levinson and Link, their deliberate "contrast and juxtaposition" created a playfully "cerebral battle of wits between two characters," for an engaging detective-suspect dynamic (90). With Columbo "always out of his element" for humor's sake, not realism's sake, he exchanges with his "superior" suspects clever inquiries, evasions, and retorts. Manipulating the villains to see him as ill-suited for the challenge of figuring out their "perfect murder," the investigator manages to get answers to questions that reveal how the crime was committed as well as reasoned motives for the crime, resulting in a solid case. In the next section, the Lieutenant and the Antipotent Detective will be illustrated and discerned.

Two Sides of Columbo Presented on a Case-by-Case Basis

Columbo Talks to "Dog," "Étude in Black" (1972)

About the time that maestro orchestra conductor Alex Benedict (John Cassavetes) committed the murder of his lover and piano ingénue Jenifer Welles (Anjamette Comer) by blunt force trauma, the Lieutenant is at the veterinarian's office to get vaccinations for an old basset hound, whom he just saved from getting euthanized at the "pound." While he seems out of his comfort zone with the new dog and the doctor's hypodermic needles, he is confident about having done the right thing and wanting to do his best for the pooch. Having rescued the dog from death shows serious compassion for animals without presenting a haughty sense of himself as the hero. He seems to be as-a-matter-of-fact about having done the only thing one can do. Columbo has his back to "Dog" because he is about to get vaccinated by injections, which upsets the Lieutenant. Unfortunately for the detective, when the phone rings, the veterinarian asks Columbo to hold the hypodermic needle, a request he honors but with distress over the long, sharp object. The veterinarian says the call is for the detective, who gladly exchanges the phone for the needle. Answering the call with polite expediency, Columbo assumes the call is from the precinct.

Without reservation, he identifies himself and his location as being "at the doctor." Assuming he was referring to a human doctor, there is an inquiry about his well-being on the other end of the call. Reassuring them, though not clarifying the type of doctor, he says, "No. It's not serious," and explains that he will be there as soon as possible. He is not confused, scratching his head, looking for a pencil, smoking a cigar intrusively, looking down, over talking, muttering, telling inane stories, or any of the discrediting behaviors his character is known for when he inquires with the suspects. He is straightforward, curt but not dismissive, prioritizes his family's/dog's health and makes time for it, balances personal with the professional and does not inject too much personal detail. On top of this, he respects the physician's time, thanking him for staying extra late to accommodate the Lieutenant's "peculiar hours." Switching on the television, the two shared the genuine enjoyment of classical music previously recorded, featuring Alex Benedict conducting an orchestra. As the homicide detective is called to duty this evening, he graciously and caringly picks up his dog off of the examination table and carries him out, revealing his soft spot for animals and substantial sense of responsibility for their care.

This next scene shows his interaction with a neighbor girl who is definitely not a suspect but is suspicious and challenging toward the detective. Having locked his car with "Dog" in it, Columbo returns to the vehicle after investigating the crime scene at Jenifer Welles's apartment, finding the young girl looking into his car. He offers a quick, "Hi" with some curiosity at what the girl is looking at in his car. Greeting him with pursed lips, arms crossed, and a disapproving tone, middle-school aged Audrey (Dawn Frame) whips around to confront the Lieutenant, "Is this your dog?!" Keeping his cool against the obnoxious girl, "Well, I guess it is." [As a note, it was evening with cool temperatures, meaning "Dog" was not in danger of overheating.] In a rhetorical question, Audrey asks haughtily, "How would you like it if somebody locked you up with the windows closed and everything?" Defending himself against his formidable and self-righteous inquisitor, Columbo responds with the simple answer, "Well, I didn't want him to get out." Still scowling, the precocious Audrey corrects the Lieutenant with further instructions: "Ok then, leave the windows open a crack." In quick agreement, Columbo says, "Ok, good idea." Then, he explains to her about having just adopted the dog, "You see, this happens to be my first dog, and I just haven't gotten onto the ropes yet. But I appreciate you telling me that Miss ... [waits for her to respond with her name] not gonna tell me." Hands on her hips, donning a floral bath robe, lips pushed forward from her buck teeth, Audrey reluctantly tells him after the detective nonchalantly gives his name first. Showing off in a childish, know-it-all way, Audrey reveals her knowledge about the legal limitations when cops conduct interviews with suspects that require stating the Miranda rights before beginning. Willing to correct her so that she knows the law, Columbo explains firmly, "That's not right. I only have to read you your rights if you are a suspect, and you're not a suspect." Columbo addresses Audrey as a resistant responder but not a suspect. He shows his authority as a police officer more than he does with the suspects. Reacting to her fears and suspicions about authority figures, the detective provides a firm but civil reaction. Establishing a boundary of civility, Columbo does not dismiss her as a neighbor and potential witness to the murder or relevant details. In fact, he proceeds to ask questions of her to discover her relationship to the deceased pianist, her knowledge of the woman, and if she has seen anyone enter or exit Jenifer's apartment. While still on her guard, Audrey cooperates. To further reify her authority as a valued person, he asks her what she thinks about the dog name "Fido." In her usual superior demeanor, Audrey, rolling her eyes, has the last word, sarcastically criticizing him for being uncreative about naming his dog. To this, Columbo shakes his head and lets the unkind implications go, characteristically choosing not to be bothered by or engage with petty ego-oriented reproaches.

Columbo and a Resistant Responder, "Double Shock" (1973)

"Double Shock" (1973) features Martin Landau in the dual roles as the villainous twin nephews, Dexter and Norman Paris, who murdered their wealthy uncle before he could officially change his Last Will, which would leave his estate to his new, young wife, whimsically played by Julie Newmar. This episode emphasizes Columbo's nature as a type of unclean and unrefined "bull in the china shop," which is in contrast with the obsessively clean and neat nature of the housekeeper Mrs. Peck (Jeanett Nolan). The conflict between them carries throughout the episode, with her reprimanding the Lieutenant for his boorish affectation, ill-mannered cigar-smoking habits, and off-putting, plain spoken communication style. In particular, the outraged, persnickety housekeeper/family nanny, Mrs. Peck repeatedly takes her stress, defensiveness, and temper over the murder out on the detective. In fact, the maternal-like, fierce protector of the Paris twins has personally denigrated the Lieutenant with references to him "belonging in a pig sty" and being a "bum," with angry commands to "Get him out of here!" as if he were an intruder who does not belong in the house. He announces that there has been an autopsy of the Uncle's body, reclassifying his death as a homicide by electrical shock rather than a death by seemingly natural causes. Drawing the arrogant, guilty, greedy twin nephews closer allows Columbo to see their characters. Allowing them to question the Lieutenant's projected weak credibility, the Lieutenant observes their inflated self-importance and delight in degrading their perceived inferiors without conscience. Maintaining an affable smile, the detective says nothing when Dexter Paris refers to him as "your everyday, average, typical, downtrodden American Husband." This is an excellent example of the kind of bullying the Lieutenant endures gladly while empowering the villains to believe they have the upper hand.

On the other hand, Mrs. Peck is so emotionally overwhelmed by the news of her employer/friend's heart attack and death that hearing the possibility of her wards bearing responsibility is too much stress on her life views, security, and sense of truth. In turn, she misplaces personal indignation toward the Lieutenant, who is doing his job respectfully, though with annoying violations of her pristine house. At one point, the upset Mrs. Peck demands to see the police officer in charge of the investigation, assuming it could not be the unpolished Lieutenant. In clarification, the detective politely reminds the housekeeper of his authority and jurisdiction: "Now, Ma'am, I am THE police officer." When Dexter accuses Columbo of "really trying to make it seem like there's foul play," he counterargues deductively, scrutinizing the meaning of each clue individually as well as how they fit into a sequential narrative. While making no accusations, only considering the clues before him, Columbo presents no affront, threat, or argument of their guilt. Instead, the Lieutenant expresses confused dissatisfaction: "It doesn't make sense to me. Does it make sense to you?" Without directly answering Columbo's rhetorical question, the suspects defend their cover-up efforts by insisting that their uncle died of a naturally occurring heart attack and that murder is just a fabrication of the homicide detective's obsessive imagination. Refusing to react emotionally, Columbo ignores the Paris brothers' use of culpability-deflecting rhetorical tactics.

After respecting her sensitive emotions of grief and indignation, Columbo reaches his abuse limit during a subsequent visit to the Paris mansion while an estate sale is underway. Ashing his cigar in a newly polished silver platter, which he thought was an ash tray, once again triggers Mrs. Peck to loudly berate the detective. Unlike his usual practice of projecting a simple, fumbling, and directionless persona, he appropriately initiates clarifying his position and intentions, defending himself against the "resistant" Peck, who challenges his right to do his job in her house. He has to set a boundary with Peck because she is getting in his way of conducting the investigation. Unlike with suspects who do not generally bother him when they are pejorative, Columbo shows genuine frustration and ill-ease at Mrs. Peck's pecking at him repeatedly with unrestrained criticisms and degrading remarks. However, he handles it with restraint and respect.

While she cleans the antique silver dish of his cigar ashes in the kitchen, Columbo goes to confront her directly by acknowledging his lifelong "untidy" nature as a fault and his "unpleasant" purposes as the murder investigator in her house that she loves. He then addresses their relationship and communication dynamic: "I have feelings, too, Mrs. Peck. ... But I've never been rude to you, Mrs. Peck, and if you keep on treating me like the enemy just because I'm here to find out who killed the man you worked for, for 33 years, well then, I think you're a very unfair person." Instead of heavy-handedly projecting his socially sanctioned authority as the lead law enforcer on the case, Columbo personalizes his response, expressing awareness of the sanctity of her home, connecting as a human being with the reactionary and uncooperative witness as a resistant responder. Further, he reminds her of their shared concern for the truth behind the murder of Clifford Paris. The scene ends with Peck surrendering her resistance to the detective, acknowledging his being a "very hard-working police officer" and making a peace offering, "a plate of Mr. Paris's favourite health cookies and a glass of milk." He graciously accepts her gesture of truce. Here, Columbo confronts two different types of resistant responders: the murderous twins and the loyal-to-a-fault housekeeper. Without malice, Columbo invasively investigates the homes, workplaces, and personal lives of the victims' familiars with the goal of finding motive, opportunity, and capability from suspected killers. Mrs. Peck finally realizes this fact and checks her temper toward the dutiful policeman, which shows how Columbo can defuse resistant responders' anxiety with his knowledge of human beings and his ability to communicate noncompetitively.

Dual Personae, "An Exercise in Fatality" (1974)

Perhaps the clearest example of the two characters of Columbo is in "An Exercise in Fatality," starring Robert Conrad as Milo Janus, the villainous gym franchise owner. In this episode, there is an unusually long period of time between Columbo's arrival at the crime scene, the gym, and the appearance of the villain on site. Here, viewers are able to watch the real Columbo investigating as opposed to the underwhelming Columbo with the suspects. When the Lieutenant arrives at the crime scene, he is immediately acknowledged by his rank and title by a Sergeant, "Good morning, Lieutenant." With his patrolmen, investigating the crime scene, he expresses sleepiness and a need for coffee to wake up his mind. Barely past dawn, the detective is notified about a phone call to be taken in the victim's office. Surprised and protective, Columbo immediately recognizes the caller and exasperates, "What are you doing up this early? Do you know what time it is?" After a pause while the speaker on the other end of the phone call explains, Columbo telegraphs to the audience who the caller is and what the concern is: "Who's coming?

Wait a minute. Harry and Ethel, Norman, Uncle Gene, and the twins. (pause) Well, how would I know what to feed them? What did you feed them last time? [pause] You want to give them spaghetti, give them spaghetti." While goofing on their guests' "ridiculous" diets, the detective is constantly scanning the murdered partner's office for inconsistencies or clues about his last few hours. Multitasking, Columbo engages in a mundane problem-solving discussion with his wife with humor and tension-deflation, while rummaging through the victim's things on and around the desk. In the trashcan, he finds an empty box of Chinese food, which sparks another suggestion and some jest: "Wait a minute. Would you be quiet for two seconds? [pause] I got an idea. I'll bring something back. [pause] Chinese, ok?" In a kind and reassuring manner to ease his wife's stress and indecision, Columbo gives her the liberty of choosing the meal and ordering it so that he would pick it up on his drive home. Not waiting to be asked to run the errand, Columbo offers to help her, making the dinner a shared task. Amicably, he jokes with her, smiling and chuckling as he says, "Look, I gotta go back to work. I'm gonna hang up. [pause] You can keep talking but I'm gonna hang up." Amused, he shakes his head at the silliness that he clearly enjoys. Rifling through the victim's Chinese food remains, Columbo is left wondering and searching further but without ratiocination. This scene of him being on the phone with his wife in front of the viewer's gaze differs from the countless references Columbo makes about his wife to suspects. In these conversations, the Lieutenant describes her as homey, simple, overweight, a television-viewing housewife who dotes on celebrities, can't cook a recipe by a television chef, treasures autographs from socially celebrated villains to give her humdrum life meaning. To be fair, he implicates himself in that simple, average, married relationship.

Following up with the custodian about suspicious brown shoe scuff marks on the clean floor, he asks all of the policemen to check to see if their shoes are brown. In obedient response to their commanding officer, all dozen or so policemen check their shoes and confirm that they are wearing the required uniform black shoes. Columbo plainly but respectfully asks the janitor about the maintenance of the floors and the location of the deceased man's locker. Here, he finds brown-soled shoes. Upon first meeting Milo Janus, the Lieutenant compliments him on his healthful and youthful physical shape and attributes Janus's television show to saving his marriage. He goes into some detail about depression over feeling fat that lead to comfort eating, which Janus chimes in on, "And the more she ate, the fatter she got." Now, the detective has Janus's full attention on his story about how his health and fitness television show saved his marriage: "Now, a couple of months ago, she started watching your television show [...] the one with the exercise. She got involved, every day, on her back, kicking her legs. You know, from the waist, down, up, down up [...]." With awkward hand gestures to accompany his poor descriptions of his wife's exercises, Columbo projects an unsophisticated, unpolished, unimpressive but content married man. In fact, he contrasts the fitness guru's ideals of thinness, health, and longevity with his own preference for his wife to have extra curves (as suggested by other hand gestures) rather than be too thin. However, his story continues with his wife no longer being depressed, forgetting to eat, exercising, and eating healthy, which he presents as an unfortunate development that affects his own preferred diet of chili, steak, and Italian specialties. Taking the story too long without a satisfying conclusion of commitment to proper eating, the detective loses Janus's interest and attention. Yet, in doing so, Columbo's alter has been firmly established with the villain.

Columbo characteristically mentions her as a well-known suspect's admirer or, even, fan, asking for his or her autograph or the like on his wife's behalf. In addition, he often offers his own gesture of esteem and veneration, which is designed to endear himself to the villain. Conversely, Columbo's deference is also designed to reduce his credibility as detective. Juxtaposed to his simple folk descriptions of his wife, their real conversations are as respectful and playful, as two well-suited spouses.

Columbo and the Ancient Greek Virtue of Sophrosyne

Sophrosyne is the ancient Greek virtue relating to the mythological figure, Sophrosyne, "the personified spirit of moderation, self-control, temperance, restraint, and discretion" (North). In Plato's dialogue, *Charmides*, the narrator Socrates is shown to have a conversation with Plato's uncle, Charmides, and with first cousin to Charmides, Critias. Their discussion centers on the meaning of *Sophrosyne*, which John M. Cooper admits is only roughly translated to mean "temperance." Cooper goes on to define the term as used in this dialogue:

> Sophrosyne is a well-developed consciousness of oneself and one's legitimate duties in relation to others (where it will involve self-restraint and showing due respect) and in relation to one's own ambitions, social standing, and the relevant expectations as regards one's own behavior.
>
> (639)

While Socrates claims that *sophrosyne* is a type of "self-mastery," Plato uses the dialogue to argue that it is more than the mere abstention from certain forms of physical pleasure: it is a form of *phronêsis*, practical wisdom (Santas). In other words, it's not just about what you don't do, but what you do and why that is central to being a wise person who is living a virtuous life, not just for him or herself. More importantly, the wisdom informs optimal participation in a hierarchical society that is navigated through purposeful and audience-related communication. Through dialectical argumentation, Socrates collaboratively attempts to discover a universally meaningful definition of *sophrosyne* as the right condition and disposition of a citizen in all situations of the mind, body, and soul. Through dialectic they agree that moderation is not always the best mindset or practice, such as in athletics. In reading and writing, quietness and reserve may not always best serve those making and doing something; but it does sometimes. In war, restraint doesn't benefit a soldier being attacked. While charm or being charmed through words is a part of *sophrosyne* as it relates to interpersonal relationships, charm can be used as dark magic, facilitating another's demise. In *Charmides*, Socrates sets out to create a fixed definition of *Sophrosyne*/temperance as an ideal of a good man; his inability to do so, inadvertently perhaps, infers that the concept may generalize about one's character and actions but may also depend on the situation for its full value.

In *Sophrosyne and the Rhetoric of Self-Restraint: Polysemy and Persuasive Use of an Ancient Greek Value Term*, Adriaan Rademaker illustrates how the Ancient Greeks apply the virtues of *sophrosyne* in terms of behavior: "[It] invariably acts as a kind of restraint; it inhibits behavior that either harms oneself (fighting with a God, giving away the plot of revenge) or infringes on social decorum" (Rademaker 50). As a guide to successful relationships with those in superior social positions, the term is used to advocate how effective citizens ought to present their positions by embodying soundness of mind and prudence, obedience, or subordination to social power structures. To do so enables the superiors to feel confidence in their authority, which is being respected and honored rather than challenged by those of lower status. Aristotle incorporated *sophrosyne* into his theory of rhetoric when accommodating audiences of superior social authority (Rademaker). As a rhetorical performance of deference, underclass citizens adopt the socially appropriate role of self-deprecating subordinate as a tactic for enabling advantageous rhetoric with those who assume to hold the power in a society. In turn, the superiors not only let their guards down, feeling safe in the proper relationship with their subordinates, but may develop an open and positive disposition toward those asking for favors, permission, assistance, forgiveness, leniency, promotion, or the like.

Like the demagogues of Ancient Greece, Columbo's villains possess social privilege from their financial clout, childhood expectations of achievement, education from the best-rated institutions, access to networks of highly successful people, broad vocabularies, and eloquent elocution. Further, this rhetorical tactic reassures the privileged class members that there is acknowledgment of and respect for their higher authority. As members of the high society elite, the self-important suspects display officious, impatient manners toward those inferior to themselves, especially the downplayed public servants of the Los Angeles Police Department. Expectantly, the villains await accommodation, accolades, and expediency from the ordinary citizen who should exist in "quiet, moderate social modesty" (*sophrosyne*—its antonym, hubris) (Rademaker 224–25).

Possessing sophrosynic humility is not only the investigator's basic character trait, it is what enables more effective working relationships with the condescending upper-class villains. When asked about his alter ego, Peter Falk explains, "[Columbo] is content with himself, he's good at his job, he loves his work and he's not preoccupied with some of the shallow material things and ideas the rest of the world is preoccupied with" (Anderson C11). In turn, the working detective is missing two qualities the suspects expect of him and others without their fiscal means: envy and corruptibility.

Sophrosyne in "Prescription Murder" (1968)

As demonstrated in the first film, *Columbo*: "Prescription Murder" (1968), the wealthy psychiatrist, Dr. Ray Flemming (Gene Barry) has wealthy lawyer friends who have social connections with high-ranking government authorities. In turn, the lawyer's social leverage holds sway for the doctor's benefit after "a few calls." By showing no suspicion toward the suspect, Columbo nurtures Dr. Flemming's inflated ego about his intellectual superiority and advantageous social connections, further intensifying his confidence about having a "perfect alibi." Instead of emphasizing his credentials as the top-ranking officer on the scene, specializing in homicide, Columbo employs a counterintuitive rhetorical strategy of poor ethos, just a man doing a job for modest pay.

Only when provoked by the lawyer's calls to his government officers, requesting to have Columbo removed from the case, does the detective reveal his secure position on the case. Despite manipulation of the justice system from the well-connected lawyer and Dr. Flemming, the Lieutenant's connections to his department's chief as a reliable and successful police detective proves to trump the nervous doctor's. In an uncommon moment, Columbo flexes his authority in order to continue on the Flemming case, which is granted due to his credible ethos. Uninhibited by Flemming's threats of professional censure or ruin, Columbo doesn't push back at the lawyer's insults or threats; the Lieutenant maintains momentum in his investigation toward the villain's self-incrimination. While briefly departing from his usual embodiment of lower status temperance, humility, and measured reserve, Columbo is forced to reveal a hint of his power with the murderous psychiatrist: "I think I'm too suspicious. I don't trust people.

FIGURE 16: Screenshot: Wife-murdering psychiatrist Dr. Flemming (Gene Barry) smugly suggests a toast as he thinks he has defeated the Lieutenant, but is about to hear otherwise. Richard Irving (dir.), "Prescription Murder," *Columbo*, 1968. Universal Television.

That's my trouble. For instance, when I get taken off a case, right away I figure somebody put the pressure on. Right away I ask myself, 'why?' " His response triggers the impressively perceptive Dr. Flemming to demand that the detective leave immediately, threatening to talk to his superiors. Rather than engage in an argument with the suspect, Columbo merely comments on his astute observation, implying the inconsistent action of trying to stop an investigator as a supposedly innocent man in the murder of his wife: "You've been talking to a lot of people these days, Doctor." The Lieutenant's acknowledgment of the doctor's unusual behavior is direct but without explicit accusation, though Dr. Flemming knows better.

    He's an expert at reading people, nuances of language, implications, and deduction. Uncharacteristically, "Prescription Murder" lays out before the viewer the investigation methods and evasion tactics of the case between the Lieutenant and the villain. Dr. Ray of this first *Columbo* film recognizes and conveys his awareness of Columbo's contrived persona as deliberately fraudulent. Initially, the psychiatrist labels Columbo's behavior in psychological terms as if unintentionally a symptom of low self-esteem; then, his diagnosis evolves to intentional rhetorical purpose:

DR. FLEMMING: I'm going to tell you something about yourself. You think you need a psychologist. Maybe you do, maybe you don't, but you are a textbook example of compensation.
LT. COLUMBO: Oh, what, Doc?
DR. FLEMMING: Compensation. Adaptability. You're an intelligent man, Columbo, but you hide it. You pretend you're something you're not. Why, because of your appearance you think you can't get by on looks or polish, so you turn a defect into a virtue. You take people by surprise. They underestimate you. And that's where you trip them up.

The astute psychiatrist calls Columbo out for who he is and what game he's playing and why, which is unusual among the villains, though it happens again in the second *Columbo* film.

Sophrosyne in "Ransom for a Dead Man" (1971)

In "Ransom for a Dead Man," the powerful tort attorney Leslie Williams (Lee Grant) literally describes his fabricated persona as phony:

LESLIE: You know Columbo, you're almost likeable in a shabby sort of way. Maybe it's the way you come slouching in here with your shopworn bag of tricks.
LT. COLUMBO: Me? Tricks?
LESLIE: The humility, the seeming absentmindedness, the homey anecdotes about the family, the wife, you know.
LT. COLUMBO: Really?
LESLIE: Yeah, Lt. Columbo fumbling and stumbling along, but it's always the jugular that he's after. And I imagine that more often than not he's successful.

The lawyer uses words such as "seeming" and juxtaposes nonthreatening down-to-earth traits with aggressive and scheming qualities. In doing so, Ms. Williams dichotomizes Columbo's fake persona and tactics with his true authority, intentions, and abilities as a homicide detective. As an especially sharp and remarkable villain, Ms. Williams is also narcissistic and "lacking a conscience," making the prospect of self-censorship undesirable. Certainly, avoiding self-incrimination, the husband murderer is infallible in reading Columbo's inauthentic false modesty and worshipful deportment.

Sophrosyne in "Fade In to Murder" (1976)

In a comedic and self-parodying meta television detective case, "Fade in to Murder" (1976), William Shatner plays the actor, blackmail victim, and murderer Ward Fowler, who plays a television detective, Lieutenant Lucerne. Surprising to Columbo, Fowler sees through the veil and explicitly points out the inconsistency of the detective's low-key demeanor in what is not a routine investigation. The fact that the high-ranking detective, a Lieutenant, is on the scene is evidence that the death is viewed as a homicide investigation of the actor's deceased, blackmailing producer, Claire Daley (Lola Albright). Prompted to explain further, Fowler cites the detective's vague and meandering inquiry regarding the whereabouts of the victim's husband and seemingly directionless while soliciting someone's assistance in finding him; this ambling does not correspond with the title Lieutenant, unless it is feigned. However, the Lieutenant Columbo and the fictional Lieutenant Lucerne cooperate in the investigation in hypotheticals until Fowler acknowledges that the only suspect remaining is himself, though a self-proclaimed "sympathetic murderer."

While these three realized early on that his behaviors are contrivances to affect underestimation by the suspects, other villains do not catch on until later in the episodes. Perhaps this is a new direction that writers of the show took in order to avoid the repetition of this dialogue. If the villains are oblivious to his façade as a rouse, there are more opportunities to gain the villains' trust or their vulnerability. Regardless, a delay in villains' awareness of Columbo's tactical rhetorical inquiries and false affect becomes part of the successful *Columbo* formula.

Looking for the Right Word: Antipotency

Rather than presenting a potency of abilities and experience or impotency in the same regard, this project needed the development of a new term to connote a persona that isn't totally ineffectual but hides any expression of power (as in being undercover, for example) that would intimidate or push villains to be wary of the police detective. The term needed to convey how the investigator resists, undermines, and diminishes presentations of power and authority over his villainous interlocutors. Shrouding his high rank as Lieutenant, Columbo's behavior and communication style manipulate his suspects' perceptions of him. To them he appears unsophisticated, not astute at finding clues, intellectually subpar in the ratiocination of details discovered into a plausible elucidation of what happened and who was responsible. As the investigation progresses, the villains slowly recognize the Lieutenant's talents and purposeful rhetorical actions. Accordingly, the murderers terminate their cooperation, attempting to ban the detective from their premises. The investigator is "potent," in that he is successful, engineers desired outcomes, and is advanced in the Police ranks of responsibility. To qualify these truths, Columbo's potency is deliberately under cover, not obvious, shrouded by a persona that portrays lower skills and abilities than he actually possesses. The merging of the "anti" prefix brings meanings of "opposition," what is opposite of, what counteracts or is used instead of the word it precedes. The blended connotations of "anti" and "potent" faithfully describe the investigator's identity construct:

- Egoless in inviting cooperation and assistance while not being an egotistical narcissist
- Asks questions of experts and familiars that serve the case regardless of appearing inept
- Determined and curious with theories and tactics while enabling a misstep by villains
- Uncompetitive and unchallenging until necessary, when his authority is required

By playing the fool, the detective elicits trustworthiness and partnership in the investigation. Put more simply, the investigator lulls a villain into a sense of calm security in the company of a doting, less intelligent, and unsuspecting admirer. Columbo projects his identity as disorganized, unprepared, and unprofessional by portraying, from the first impression onward, some confusion and cloudy thinking, sleepiness, head-scratching uncleanliness, and the desperate search for coffee and pencils so that he can do his job minimally. His discourse reinforces his antipotency when expressing incomplete utterances and the most basic questions. When he does admit to finding a clue, the detective seems unable to put meaning, cause, effect, motive, or *modus operandi* to the crime scene details he has. Rather than portraying the experienced, capable, and brilliant detective that he is, the Lieutenant conveys dislocation at the crime scene, as if new to the job and lacking authority. The villains are shown a barely capable man with a badge who needs not to be feared, though the police officers on the scene know exactly who he is: the one in charge of the investigation.

The Underestimated Detective with the Intelligent Villains: Socrates and Columbo

One only has to type "Columbo and Socrates" into a search engine to find multiple results that make claims about their similarities in the pursuit of truths, albeit not critically or substantially. Both characters engage in a construction of conversation in which they methodically ask a lot of questions and different kinds of questions to test concepts and meanings in universal application. As philosopher and teacher Tim Madigan writes, "Both were polite but persistent interviewers, and while people with nothing to hide usually enjoyed their company, those who did not wish to have their alibis or ignorance probed would react in exasperation or with violent threats. Suddenly Socrates would no longer seem such an off-putting character." To develop this analysis further, a comparison and contrast between the two figures reveals more differences than similarities. While Socrates's partners in dialogue are his students participating with their teacher in a quest for understanding, Socrates's endgame is the ongoing business of learning in a dialectical model of teaching through the practice of argumentation. Socrates is the more learned person mentoring his students, the interns. His method relies in part on that teacher-learner type dynamic that instructs in a challenging way, refusing to give the answers to students but instead facilitating their learning through questions. He undermines his students' assumptions with questions about the verity of minor premises or the application of a claim into generalizations that cannot hold up to universally held truths. Socrates's students never forget who is their honorable, great teacher and who is the humble, ignorant pupil.

Columbo's fellow conversant is a suspect who holds the truth of his or her culpability in secrecy. Columbo's endgame is a decisive action of arrest, based on the construction of argument regarding the guilt of the murderer, which will hold up to scrutiny in the court system for the prosecution. Columbo's relationship with suspects is complex with a consistently crafted persona of antipotency, amplifying the suspect's authority, positioning himself as the intern with the maestro. His questions reinforce a socially inferior status as working class with the rich, educated, and powerful. However, the suspect's superiority is a presumption made and constructed by the arrogant villain. To propagate the villain's superiority, Columbo uses rhetorical or strategic acts of deference, self-deprecation, unreciprocated expressions of admiration and praise, requests for assistance in performing routine tasks for his job, and repetitive pseudo apologies for missteps, hastily drawn conclusions, and being bothersome about qualified important or irrelevant "loose ends." The suspects are lulled into forgetting that Columbo is a high-ranking police officer with years of detective experience and the authority to arrest them and contribute to their demise in a court of law. Columbo's submissive, simple-minded, and devotional affect promotes the villains' underestimation of his abilities, claustrophobic irritation with his tireless inquiries, and their own emotional fatigue from keeping up their appearances with the perpetually present investigator. These and other aspects of his investigative method wear down the villains' energy reserves and patience, having to keep up the appearance of feigning innocence of the homicide and interest in cooperating with the police investigation.

Antipotency with Dick Van Dyke's Villain in "Negative Reaction" (1974)

Columbo's use of feigned ignorance is a rhetorical projection of a persona that is designed to enhance the villain's false sense of superiority:

> In most cases, class comes into play with the murderer always assuming he or she is smarter and better than that rumpled lieutenant, but no one plays dumb on purpose better than this detective. So when he makes the case on the cultured killer, they inevitably are surprised that this little man in the tattered raincoat, always seeming to be forgetful and driving that Peugeot 403 convertible that looks as if it could crumble into a million pieces at any moment beat them.
> (Copeland)

All of these characteristics help Lieutenant Columbo project informality and lack of professional polish as a ruse to keep the villains from realizing that his investigation is building evidence against them. Columbo holds consistent with his façade of underqualified and calm tempered, even when villains demean the detective openly. Remaining unbothered and secure in the face of mockery, Columbo waits for the villains to make a mistake in their false sense of impenetrability.

For example, in "Negative Reaction," Dick Van Dyke plays Paul Galesko, a henpecked professional photographer with a demoralizing and miserly wife. Finally, at his wit's end, he pretends to kidnap her for ransom but, instead, kills her. In order to cover up his culpability, Galesko hires the assistance of a sincerely rehabilitated ex-con who is grateful for the employment. Self-servingly and without remorse, Galesko makes the trusting ex-con his second murder victim and frames him for his wife's murder. Highly agitated for being called to speak with the detective once again after days of being stalked by the Lieutenant with his endless questions, the villain uses rhetorical questions to explicitly mock Columbo. At a table strewn with newspaper fragments of cut out letters, Columbo is recreating the ransom note that Galesko himself originally wrote. Unnerved by the dramatic re-enactment of his cover-up story, Galesko jeers, "Need help with your spelling, Lieutenant?" As if he didn't just hear the pejorative slam against his intelligence and lack of education, Columbo continues with his efforts to piece together the note without leaving a mess, which is a critical concern in framing the ex-con, Alvin Deschler (Don Gordon). Via abductive reasoning, Columbo challenges a contradiction in the frame story with Deschler supposedly creating the mess-making ransom note in the motel room that hadn't been cleaned but is missing the necessary bits of paper resulting from the process. High strung in counter explanations and rapid-fire predictions of Columbo's failure to close the case, Galesko basks in the detective's lack of prosecutorial evidence that would prove him guilty: "But if I killed my wife—and I did say 'if'—you're never going to be able to *prove* it."

Moreover, the effectively empowered villain dares to offer obnoxious and inappropriate threats to the homicide detective as demonstrated by "I warned you." As if his power is greater than the Lieutenant's, the villain laughs at the detective and criticizes him in front of his subordinate officers, saying "You're crazy," and giving a compliment undermined by an insult: "Lieutenant, you're priceless. You're a gem. You're a little flawed and you're not too bright, but you're one of a kind." In response to this cajoling and bravado, Columbo keeps on his course of antipotency and does not disclose the progress of prideful Galesko's certain arrest. Encouraging the villain to correct his own deliberately performed mistake, the Lieutenant lets the "master" (Galesko) instruct the "pupil" (Columbo). Regardless of the insults, Columbo respectfully defers to the apathetic and condescending two-time killer, addressing him with the undeserving politeness, "Sir."

After performing the placating, inexperienced detective, the villains invariably think they are smarter than Columbo. Not only does he let the villains think he is intellectually inferior to them, but he proves it with his consistent character-defining behavior: he always looks for things he has misplaced; he seems out of place at the decadent events or residences; he enacts proletariat awe and enchantment with the exorbitant lifestyles of the wealthy suspects; he states agreement with misleading comments made by the antagonists; he orders a root beer at a restaurant when the villain has a sherry; he drives an old beat-up car while the suspects drive new high-end, high-gloss waxed models; he wears understated, generic clothing in comparison with the socialite's expensive and tailor-made fashion; he dons a modest barber shop style while killers sport ostentatious coifs, and the like. These contrasts in a workingman's lifestyle, income, and persona of naïve delight not only reify simple taste and lack of sophistication, but also highlight his lower socio-economic class status, a formulaic tension on which the show's writers have capitalized (Levinson and Link 89). While numerous critics have mentioned the socio-economic class conflict between the honest working-class, "Everyman" hero–detective and his consistently arrogant old-moneyed, privileged villains, the show's creators insist that they did not set out to make a social critique against the upper class. Instead, they wanted to invent character relationships of contrast so that the Lieutenant is, by formula, out of his element among the excesses absent from his own life (Levinson and Link 80). Equally true is the position of the villains—each performing the strained façade of friendliness and genuine desire to help the detective solve their own crime. In doing so, the villains are drawn into the police investigator's world to not only participate in the rhetorical process of the murder investigation but to develop a substantial level of intimate familiarity with Columbo. As he references family members, past experiences, and personal preferences throughout the inquiry, the Lieutenant gains the knowledge needed to shape his duplicitous persona of under-effectuality, which, ironically, does effectively lure the cautious killer out of defensiveness and anxiety into false confidence and trust in the detective's inferiority.

The temperate and restrained (sophron) Lieutenant continues his highly strategic rhetorical ruse until he has identified enough condemning evidence to close the investigation.

5

The *Columbo* Killer

If there is one human experience that is ruled by myth, it is certainly that of evil [...] maleficent powers [...] that seduce the human heart and persuade it to do evil.

(Ricoeur 280)

Ricoeur's statement above certainly explains the expression, "The devil made me do it," as reasoning for the emergence of bad behavior, rejecting personal responsibility, and ascribing self-victimhood under the influence of evil. This chapter examines the nature of the consistent figure of the *Columbo* villain, the narrative perspective of the inverted mystery, how varying degrees of sympathy and ambipathy are part of *Columbo* spectatorship, and the pretense villains play in response to the Lieutenant's antipotency and method of detection.

The social role of villains in folklore, fairy tales, crime stories, and horror has been a role for promoting societal norms and warning readers of the consequences of transgressing the bounds of appropriate behavior and values. However, the narratives also invite audiences to role-play fantasies of power or dare to face fear in a safe context, of course. To take this a step further, in his book titled *I Wear the Black Hat: Grappling with Villains (Real and Imagined)*, Chuck Klosterman deliberately complicates the false binaries of good vs. evil and hero vs. villain because neither type of character is presented as pure goodness or pure badness, particularly in gang- and drug-related narratives. Both hero and villain have contradictory qualities that enable audiences to identify with them, to be attracted to them, and to reject them for their violations as well as their attainments. Focusing on the villains here, Klosterman examines the lead heroes and villains of two successful television series about the illegal drug industry: AMC's *Breaking Bad* (2008–13) and HBO's *The Wire* (2002–08). With narrative points of view that construct the drug makers and dealers as businessmen doing their jobs, murder is at times "unavoidable." Because their characters are intriguing, rational, charismatic, smart, violent, greedy, and the like, they draw viewers into complex spectator relationships: "We feel for them when they kill, and we understand why it had to happen. We actively want them to get away with murder because we are on their side" (48). Further, Klosterman argues that audience sympathies shift to moral condemnation when the villains act on a "dispassionate application of [their] intelligence. It's the calculation. It's someone who views life as a game where the rules are poorly written and designed for abuse" (19). By disrupting our learned dichotomous thinking, contemporary villains call viewers to a state of ambivalence or to experience ambipathy with them, the latter being a mixture of sympathy and antipathy, or conflicting feelings. Certainly, the Lieutenant knew this about his killers:

> And I'll tell you something else. Even with some of the murderers that I meet, I even like them, too. Sometimes like them and even respect them. Not for what they did, certainly not for that. But for that part of them which is intelligent or funny or just nice. Because there's niceness in everyone. A little bit anyhow. You can take a cop's word for it.
>
> ("Try and Catch Me")

While his overplayed speech given to a lady's luncheon, featuring the mystery writer Abigail Mitchell (Ruth Gordon), is teeming with "good cop" sentiments, the Lieutenant meets highly successful and celebrated men and women who warrant esteem, aside from their homicidal deeds.

At the farthest end of the spectrum, some villains, who are generally decent people with good intentions but emotionally demanding circumstances, inspire propathy in their viewers. Having a propathetic affection for another is one of six primary emotions described by Dr. Gordon Coates in his work *Wanterfall: A Practical Approach to the Understanding and Healing of Everyday Emotions of Everyday Life*. More specifically, propathy involves general feelings of warmth and friendliness, good will toward, support of, admiration for, and desire for another's well-being, success, and/or evasion from capture (Coates Section 2). For example, many fans agree that Abigail Mitchell of "Try and Catch Me" is sweet, charming and warm-hearted towards most people, except for her former nephew-in-law who killed her beloved niece. Her amiable character, exhibiting relatable indignation toward the injustice of his going unpunished, establishes with viewers an almost universally propathetic relationship. However, for some viewers, ambivalence toward Abigail remains: the murderous nephew-in-law, having suffocated over days in the vault-safe, instead serves as the emotional locus, his death commanding pity despite his greed. Hence, ambivalence in the audience remains.

More so than most mystery villains, viewers are intimately familiar with the *Columbo* killer through the narrative structure of the first act of each episode: watching the relationship with the victim, the motive for murder, and the setup, commission, and cover-up of the crime through the perspective of an intriguing, contextualized, single murderer. Viewers see what our crime solver does not know. Audiences are like voyeurs peeping through a hole in the wall (*Psycho* reference intended), vicariously experiencing the villain's travail and transgression. Spectators are, of course, implicated with the burden and gift of the knowledge that the Lieutenant must discover and substantiate with evidentiary proof. Simultaneously, the intimacy of being at the scene of the crime during the lethal act offers viewers exhilaration and the privileged position as an insider to the detective story's mystery rather than as an outsider to the mystery, discovering the story as it unfolds. Arguably, viewers have a greater understanding of the villain than of Columbo, regardless of how sympathetic or evil he or she is. Moreover, the exceedingly curious and larger-than-life villains have a jarring effect on the viewers, awakening them from the passivity of being guided by the brilliant detective. The narrative point of view begs the question: are viewers imaginatively accomplices to the murderers, possessing his or her secrets, or to the eccentric, mysterious detective on the right side of the law? While police procedurals portray the legal justice system at work, upholding laws, crime dramas show how complicated human actions and relationships can be, defying reductive classification into right or wrong. Given the relatability of some of *Columbo*'s villains, the narrative point of view is split between the detective and the suspects.

Classical Greek and Christian Villainy in Columbo

Regardless of viewers' successful identification with the detective or the villain, the show must project an imaginable realness or sense of authenticity through its narrative, characters, crime, setting, and the like. The Greek term "phantasia," according to Christopher Shields, was used by Aristotle to describe a vivid imagining in the minds of the audience that is important for understanding both a subject and arguments presented:

> In a brief discussion dedicated to imagination (*De Anima* iii 3), Aristotle identifies it as "that in virtue of which an image occurs in us" (*De Anima* iii 3, 428aa1–2), where this is evidently given a broad range of application to the activities involved in thoughts, dreams, and memories. Because he tends to treat imagination pictographically (*De Anima* iii 3, 429a2–4; cf. *De Sensu* 1, 437a3–17; 3, 439b6), Aristotle seems to regard the images used in cognitive processes as representations best thought of on the model of copies or likenesses of external objects.

A storyteller's ability to produce *phantasia* in their audience is critical to achieving a desired rhetorical effect, whether it is pure pathos (emotion), understanding through a combination of persuasive appeals to logic (or the audience's accepted particular construction of knowledge and common sense), or speaker's ethos (storyteller integrity). In fact, the accepted authenticity of the story (willing suspension of disbelief by the audience) is the rhetorical outcome of the storyteller's credibility, the charisma and dynamism of the telling, and the audience's belief that the story is worth reading, hearing, or viewing. While our imaginations naturally produce images in our minds with words or sense experiences, television viewers are given images, which might suggest that *phantasia* is not relevant to watching moving pictures. However, spectatorship involves a constant reverberation between the images that are on the screen versus the images that come to viewers' imaginations. Similarities between what is seen and what is imagined create a state of consonance or emotional security, safety, predictability, consistency among attitudes and beliefs, and comfort. Contradictions or ambivalence between artistic imagery and individual *phantasia* can produce surprise, amazement, disturbance, incongruity, and unpredictability associated with the vigilance and insecurity of dissonant experience. However, audiences' agreeable and disagreeable reactions shape and enhance their spectator relationships with all characters—villain, hero, victim, support—despite the production of disparate emotional states. In this chapter, the focus is on the male villains in terms of spectatorship being a function of narrative perspective.

While the Lieutenant clearly embodies features of the Greek goddess Sophrosyne, evidenced by his careful, deliberate, and temperate communications with the suspects, the villains are the embodiment of Hybris, the ancient Greek goddess of pride, arrogance, and insolence. Professor Emeritus of Ancient History Nick R. E. Fisher critiques the scholarly tradition of oversimplifying the term "hubris" as behaviors of excessive pride. Calling on Aristotle's *Rhetoric*, Fisher appropriately complicates our understanding of hubris as serious moral condemnation, central to the Greek's concern with shame and honor brought on the individual:

> *Hubris* is "doing and saying things at which the victim incurs shame [...] simply to get pleasure from it. The cause of the pleasure for those committing *hubris* is that by harming people, they think themselves superior; that is why the young and the rich are *hubristic,* as they think they are superior when they commit *hubris*" (*Rhetorica* 1378^{b}23–30). *Hubris* is most often the insulting infliction of physical force or violence [...] gloat[ing] over the body of their battered victim in the manner of a triumphant fighting-cock [...].
>
> (Fisher)

Correspondingly, Fisher expands the denotations of hubris as the root of criminal behaviors: the villains share an inflated sense of self about their intellectual abilities, monetary power, influence over others, biological breeding, cultural education and experience, and the certitude of getting away with murder in the midst of inferior police officers. With cavalier confidence, they ostentatiously display their wealth, education, and achievements, just as Aristotle qualified. Notably, the majority of *Columbo*'s murderers behave expecting to impose their wills on lesser individuals, the working class, which includes the Lieutenant. The hubris seems to escalate in accordance with the decline in inefficacy. More specifically, when he demonstrates mild forms of ineptitude, inefficiency, and absent-mindedness, the detective is reassuringly harmless to the villains, who adopt the pretense of "innocence" of the crime. However, by repeatedly stalling and interrupting the important worlds of the rich, famous, and licentious, the pesky, working-class Columbo fuels the grandiose suspects' intensifying frustration and indignation with having to feign cooperation with the nuisance investigation. Certainly, this is the Lieutenant's process by design, interacting with the resistant responders, which will be discussed more specifically in the chapter "Columbo's Method of Rhetorical Inquiry."

Rhetoric and Villainy

Villains are wrongdoers. The last denotation of villainy concerns its social impact, highlighting a villain's social or rhetorical aims with victims. Villainy is not something one embodies or acts upon in isolation. Villainy is defined by its negative imposition on others, who suffer from the behavior used against them by the agent of villainous deeds. Villainy is more than antisocial words, deeds, and relationships. By definition, villains commit shameful acts that they may not consider to be shameful if they feel no guilt or remorse. However, the condition of shame must involve an audience of judges, a law agreed upon by a community, or receivers of those heinous acts. Therefore, criminals hide their behaviors to avoid judgment and punishment from a society, who determines what behaviors are reprehensible and worthy of shame. A central element of assessing the degree of heinousness or depravity of villainous acts is the agent's motivations, their relationships with, and consequences for, the victims.

As Anna Fahraeus and Kikmen Yakali-Camoglu argue, some villains act on motivations of pleasing their self-interest as a means to an end, or as a strategy for acquiring their desires. In these cases, the victims are necessarily eliminated from being the obstacles to or inhibitors of the murderer's best interests or desired outcomes. There may be no animosity toward the victim, the kill may be void of personal feelings toward the killed, and the killer may even feel some degree of remorse or at least regret for having to take such drastic measures for what they want. It would be a kill of opportunity and strategy rather than passion. They can also act on ill-will, spitefulness, and antipathy, making others' misery the end in itself (Keen et al. 129). Certainly, the more passive examples are of the former class as the miscreants show no malice or regard for others, who are by circumstance vulnerable and victimized as a result of the agent's apathy or total lack of connection. Acts inspired by the ego or self-interest include greed, pride, arrogance and avarice, while sins motivated by spitefulness are envy, anger, revenge, and cruelty (Keen et al. 129).

The *Columbo* villain generally kills out of ego, self-interest, self-preservation, and, occasionally, revenge. The show evades crimes of sexuality, torturous cruelty, or diabolical destruction for its own sake, which would alter a crime drama to thriller or horror and intensify the viewers' emotional response. Instead *Columbo* inspires puzzle solving or curiosity in the viewer, which are considered light-suspense cognitive activities. Acknowledging that *Columbo* is a lighter dramedy, Sheldon Catz categorizes the types of motives that the villains exhibit in their homicides:

> The majority of *Columbo* episodes (27) "feature a villain out for "money or power" and the next group (18) have the murderer acting "to silence someone" who would reveal something unsavory [fraud, affair, cowardice] that the murderer wants kept quiet [...] The next group, what I have called 'hold onto something dear' often (but not always) appear in an episode in which there is a sympathetic relationship Columbo and the murderer (8). [...] The "revenge category" is an interesting mixture of sympathetic murderer episodes (7). [...] The "past murder cover-up" motive (3) [is designed] to eliminate a witness, accomplice, or blackmailer (13), [...] Episodes with the "complete frame-up" motive (6) [is a premeditated kill as originally planned] [...]. The "accidental/self-defense" motives [catalyze murders in (7) episodes].
>
> (Catz 227–33)

To further Catz's point, contemporary, psychological profiling shows ascribe various forms of mental instability as a driving motive behind homicides and serial murders. However, psychological pathologies are not a notable factor in *Columbo*'s villains, whether they are male or female, though there are some episodes that display less extreme forms of pathologies. In "Forgotten Lady" (1975) Grace Wheeler Willis (Janet Leigh) actually has mental disease that manifests as impulsive and compartmentalized behavior, amnesia, and a demented existence in the past as her current reality. While her mental state offers an explanation for her killing her husband and framing his poisoning as suicide, she presents as sympathetic with an unprosecutable case. In "Bird in the Hand" (1991), the villain Delores McCain (Tyne Daly) presents mental instability and deterioration in a similar way to Nicholas Frame (Richard Basehart) in "Dagger of the Mind" (1972). When caught by the Lieutenant, their psyches degrade to an alternate sphere, rejecting the reality of being arrested because it is too unbearable to face.

There are several episodes with villains displaying an infuriating pathology of apathy and narcissism, particularly toward their victims. In "Prescription Murder," Dr. Flemming exhibits resourceful and extreme survival instincts, going as far as murdering his own wife, in order to maintain his circumstances in high life, which are provided by his wife's money. Leslie Williams is the lawyer whose pathological boredom, emotional disconnection from even her husband, and greed in "Ransom for a Dead Man" inspires Columbo to say, "You just don't have a conscience." In "Stitch in Crime," "Exercise in Fatality," and "A Deadly State of Mind," the villains have cold, calculating personalities, narcissistic and antisocial sentiments, and obsessively pursue ambitions of celebrity and achievement. While they lead a double life based on lies, they generally are neither cruel nor displaying signs of *Schadenfreude* (the malicious pleasure at another's pain, loss, or humiliation). Instead, a majority of the villains use murder as a means to an end with a regard for their victims as obstacles to be overcome.

Villainy Embodied, Villainy Experienced

Villains captivate audiences who crave a vicarious experience of transgressions, taboos, and the abject in our culture. In *Comic Book Crime: Truth, Justice, and the American Way*, Nickie Phillips and Stacy Stroble draw upon criminologist Mike Presdee to adapt his theories about the audience's pleasures in identifying with criminals to his analysis of comic book readership: "There is pleasure in both engaging in transgressive acts such as crime and violence and merely consuming transgressive acts as entertainment. Similarly, there is pleasure in meting out punishment to those perceived as deserving" (83–84). Moreover, viewers' pleasure in identifying with villains and their antisocial behaviors is a form of transgression that can result in an individual's guilt or discomfort for enjoying it so much. Such narratives compel audiences into fantasies of villainous power and control, challenging crises to overcome, purgative fright, curiosity, and imaginings of superior esteem against inferior moral deviants. Within a narrative of villainy, the text calls for the restoration of a semblance of order when justice is served, whether by the courts or by vigilante, hero, or heroine outlaw ethics when the impotent legal system fails to enable satisfying moral resolve and/or appropriate punishment. In fact, Phillips and Stroble distinguish important deviations in fictional and criminal justice responses to villainous behavior: "[In fiction], psychopathological causes of crime are explicitly depicted, yet calls for retributive forms of justice usually follow. Conversely, in criminological theory, the policy response to pathological crime often relates to rehabilitation or incapacitation—not retribution" (84). With the fictional detective's closing the case and eliminating the threat posed by the villain, viewers can relax after the suspense and tension. In contrast, the justice system often cannot offer swift justice; particularly as court cases are drawn out, media coverage is sensationalist, and evidentiary technicalities are inhibitive of prosecution. In a given episode of *Columbo*, the fantasy is that even minute details or inconsistencies are enough to prosecute a murderer.

Much of Western society's basis of the villain can be traced back to the Judeo-Christian *Bible*'s devil figures. In 1589, German Jesuit Priest, Bishop, theologian, demonologist, and witch hunter Peter Binsfeld wrote *Treatise on Confessions of Evildoers and Witches* in which he paired demons according to the seven deadly sins. Adopted as an inquisitor's guide across Europe—as it was translated into several European languages—Peter Binsfeld gave procedure to the witch hunts of the sixteenth century, which encouraged denouncements of witches and sanctions for the repetition of torture (Guiley 28–29). In her reference work, *The Encyclopedia of Demons and Demonology*, Rosemary Ellen Guiley explains Binsfeld's taxonomy, but only a selection is provided here, starting with Lucifer:

> He [is the] demon associated with Pride. His rebellion against God with the sin of pride caused him and his followers to be cast from heaven. (154). Satan means adversary and is the personification of anger (222–23). Binsfeld associates the archdemon Mammon (meaning "riches" in Aramaic) with avarice, greed, covetousness, and temptation, personifying the "desire for material wealth or gain, ignoring the realm of the spiritual."
>
> (167)

I did not reference all seven of Binsfeld's devil categories related to the deadly sins because not all were directly applicable to the *Columbo* villain. Citing Biblical references that describe the qualities of the Devil/Satan, J. B. Phillips identifies the following passages: Lying Rhetor, Tempter, Trickster, soul-taker, business opportunist without ethics (4:1–11, Luke 4:13), Murderer (John 8:44b), skillful manipulator, tactician, masquerader of righteousness (2 Corinthians 11:14–15a), deviser of falsehood, armed with all powers to deceive, (Thessalonians 2:9–10a), enemy, predator (Peter 5:8–9). Certainly, these descriptions veer from some portrayals of the dark angel as monster, demon, hideous beast, and horned fiend. They describe the brilliant, rhetorically sophisticated, and duplicitously charming masterminds of *Columbo*'s villain: the devils in disguise. Though donning glamorous shells to adorn their exaggerated smiles, viewers are not fooled because we know what they did.

Explaining the modern popularity of villains exuding insatiable greed, Adam Shannon contextualizes mainstream American society's values and expectations:

> You live in possibly the most pampered, consumerist society since the Roman Empire. People have always been immoral, shiftless, and self-gratifying. For ages, humankind struggled to find a conceptual system to operationalize their spiritual shortcomings. [...].The Seven Deadly Sins are those transgressions which are fatal to spiritual progress [lead you to Hell].

Despite the threat of eternal damnation within a Judeo-Christian mythology, the seven sins make solid sources of evil in fiction because of the embeddedness of those values in Western culture. Until the end, audiences enjoy the transgressions via their imaginations before they are awakened from the transportation into a fantasy with a moral message:

> Villainy is integral in narratives that reflect the innermost fears of the human psyche, and is often a significant part of the construction of loss, whether it is loss of innocence, loss of loved ones, loss of power, or loss of self and/or identity.
> (Fahraeus and Yakali-Camoglu vii)

Serving as a deterrent, fictional villains are the embodiment of the seven mortal sins when they are caught and punished by the agents of moral righteousness—the law, religious virtue and doctrine, ethics, and society.

Much of what we understand about villains is informed by various theories of psychology that help us to analyze and construct our Jungian "shadow" characters. In fiction, the darker side of human nature, often hidden from the public, is negotiated with public personae by the character. Viewing or reading fiction, the audience witnesses the process of choosing what to reveal, how much to reveal, in what manner to reveal it, what to omit in discussion, what to deny or deflect, and what to lie about and explain away. Villains are formed by popular cultural contexts of what frightens people at the socio-historical time. In binary terms, they are dependent on each other for signification—hero and villain are counterparts, or are each other's "yin and yang" (Phillips). In application, a satisfying villain is the dark side of the hero, "personified by those opposite qualities and behaviors that infuriate and sicken the hero to obsessive action" (Kaufman). Determined to nullify the villain's malevolent acts and/or exterminate the source of the malevolence, the hero/ine must understand the villain to effectively formulate these terminating plans. If the villain's psycho-criminal disposition is situational, the hero may simply need to change the circumstances or follow through with a just, corrective, and punitive response. If the villain's psycho-criminal nature has a fixed pathological determinism, then the hero/ine would have to neutralize the criminally insane individual or organization to avoid the likely risk of encountering similar future crises—though this is also the precise basis for a sequel.

In truth, the most memorable and serialized villains demonstrate an intriguing combination of characteristics: "powerful, intelligent, immoral, wounded, and determined" (Del Drago), as well as "some redeeming or admirable qualities such as intelligence or a wounded past or tremendous skill or the like. This combo of negative and positive qualities makes for a complex character" (Phillips). While the use of "weak" and "strong" to differentiate types of villains is a bit misleading, Enrique Camara Arenas provides constructive contributions to understanding audiences' interpersonal relationships with anthropomorphic villains. On the one hand, monsters and other threatening entities are destructive by nature, making them poor subjects of psychological or moral analysis. On the other hand, human villains express understandable motivation, the exercise of will, adaptive intelligence to follow through with threatening schemes, and self-awareness that makes mere physical movement into intended social behavior—all of which allow for psychological analysis of the character (6–7). Furthermore, these villains are subject to ethical and moral analyses because their behavior, words, and choices can be "measured in terms of social responsibility and are easily perceived as negative figures against the background of expected humane behavior" (7). After such context-based analyses, audiences assess a villain's degree of humane behavior and social responsibility, further defining their spectator relationship with that character.

Tom Hurka's categorization of the range of vices includes "the *pure* ones (e.g., malice, *Schadenfreude*, sadism) at one end of the spectrum, through those of *indifference* (e.g., callousness, sloth, smugness), to the mildest forms at the other end, which he calls vices of *disproportion* (e.g., foolhardiness, avarice, intemperance)." His taxonomy is a reminder of the richness of our moral vocabulary and of the basic symmetry to be found when comparing virtue and vice. They both come in various forms and degrees and can be similarly codified by intensity and the relative value of their respective objects and fields.

Demographics of *Columbo*'s Villains

Among *Columbo*'s 73 villains, 59 are Caucasian males (including Hispanic), except for fourteen female killers and seven female willing accomplices. (Gender factors are the focus of discussion in Chapter 6.) This is not to suggest that race, national identity, spiritual affiliation, or socio-economic status is irrelevant in projecting fictional characters or villains, specifically. However, *Columbo*'s villains are all wealthy, privileged, and, if not powerful and influential, certainly resourceful. It is not unusual to see British or foreign actors in American film-and-television villain roles. Their accented speech, unique facial expressions, and unfamiliar names, to name a few character traits, add to the otherness and transgressive nature of villainy and plays to American xenophobia. While Caucasian is the only race represented among the villain actors, 27 of the villains (Patrick McGoohan played four and William Shatner two) represent diversity in ethnic and national origin:

- Polish-born Ross Martin in "Suitable for Framing" (1971);
- Three Canadian actors: Susan Clark in "Lady in Waiting" (1971), Helen Shaver in "Rest in Peace, Mrs. Columbo" (1990), and William Shatner in "Fade in to Murder" (1976) and "Butterfly in Shades of Grey" (1994);
- Lithuanian-born South African-reared English actor Laurence Harvey in "The Most Dangerous Match" (1973);
- Puerto Rican-born Jose Ferrer in "Mind Over Mayhem" (1974);
- American-born Hector Elizondo of Basque and Puerto Rican descent in "A Case of Immunity" (1975);
- Austrian actor Oskar Werner in "Playback" (1975);
- Mexican-born Ricardo Montalban in "A Matter of Honor" (1976);
- Austrian-American Jewish actor Theodore Bikel in "The Bye-Bye Sky High IQ Murder Case" (1977);
- French film-and-television actor Louis Jourdan in "Murder Under Glass" (1978);
- New Zealand singer and actor Clive Revill in "The Conspirators" (1978);
- Belgian-born actor Patrick Bauchau in "Murder: A Self-Portrait" (1989);
- Three Scottish-born actors: Nicol Williamson in "How to Dial a Murder" (1978), Billy Connolly in "Murder With Too Many Notes" (1998), and Ian Buchanan in "Columbo Cries Wolf" (1990);
- Two Welsh actors: Ray Milland in "The Greenhouse Jungle" (1972), and Matthew Rhys in "Columbo Likes the Nightlife" (2003); and
- Five English actors: Roddy McDowall in "Short Fuse" (1972), Donald Pleasance in "Any Old Port in a Storm" (1973), Anthony Andrews in "Columbo Goes to the Guillotine" (1989), Honor Blackman in "Dagger of the Mind" (1972), and the American-born but reared in England and Ireland actor Patrick McGoohan in "By Dawn's Early Light" (1974), "Identity Crisis" (1975), "Agenda for Murder" (1990), and "Ashes to Ashes" (1998).

Co-creator William Link acknowledges the studio and network executives preferred to have big-name stars play the villains; they worried that the international actors would not have enough "name recognition" with American audiences. However, this concern has likely served the show's success by enhancing international appeal with audiences, broadening spectatorship globally.

Another variable among the villains is their ages, which also distinguishes them from other police procedurals. When these accomplished actors starred in *Columbo*, a third of the celebrity guest villains fell between age 35 and 45, half a dozen were as young as 26, but the majority were above 45 years of age. Ruth Gordon was the oldest during her appearance on the show at age 79, followed by Patrick McGoohan at 70 in "Ashes to Ashes." Apparently, homicide on *Columbo* is not for the young.

As with the female murderers, domesticity rarely appears in any significant way in these single murder cases (with few exceptions). Perhaps, the notion of killing a spouse transforms into an act far more monstrous when there are young children involved. More specifically, six of the seventy-four villains have an adult child, five are daughters and one is a son. The percentage of male villains who have children is 7% (4/60) and of the female villains is 14% (2/14), though Leslie Williams is the pathologically indifferent and, perhaps even, agonistic stepmother-murderess-widow to Margaret (Patricia Mattick) in "Ransom for a Dead Man." It can be argued that whether or not a villain has a child differs little between genders among *Columbo*'s scoundrels. However, their progenies represent a below-average rate of parenthood (6.7%) in the United States at that time (about 70%): Marshall Cahill's son Neil (Robert Walker) in "Mind Over Mayhem"; Luis Montoya's daughter Nina (Maria Grimm) in "A Matter of Honor"; The Great Santini's daughter and magician's assistant Della (Cynthia Sikes) in "Now You See Him"; Lauren Staton's daughter Lisa (Claudia Christian) in "It's All in the Game"; and Fielding Chase's daughter Victoria (Molly Hagen) in "Butterfly in Shades of Grey." Young children and home family life are not of interest to *Columbo*'s ambitious professionals. As an adult son of the celebrated scientist Dr. Cahill from "Mind Over Mayhem," Neil begins his career in his father's shadow with a discovered act of plagiarism that Dr. Cahill Sr. covers up with murder. Contrastively, the murder victim Commodore Otis Swanson's daughter Joanna Clay (Diane Baker) plays prominently in "Last Salute to a Commodore," though she is not the killer. In a unique case, the murderers are the college-aged children (Justin Rowe played by Stephen Gafferty and Cooper Redman played by Gary Hershberger) with their parents defending them in "Columbo Goes to College." While episodes feature adult uncles, aunts, nieces, nephews, and siblings, the domestic life of the heterosexual married couple with young children has no place in this police drama among the white, rich, and famous. In fact, expressions of disinterest in parenthood are detectable.

These examples illustrate suspects' ennui regarding mundane matters of offspring, budgets, and general domesticity. As Columbo mentions his wife's likely displeasure with the cost of the dinner to Adrian Carsini and his somber assistant

(Julie Andrews) in "Any Old Port in the Storm," they ask about Mrs. Columbo. The Lieutenant explains that there was trouble getting a babysitter, which is why his wife could not attend the dinner engagement. Even at dinner with Carsini, Columbo is at work on a homicide case with a murderer, which is no place for his wife and children. Using a rhetorical tag, "You know how it is when you have kids," the Lieutenant insists on Carsini's agreement. Noticeably, Carsini ignores the comment altogether, changing the subject to that evening's luxurious dinner and wine arrangements. Clearly, Adrian doesn't know how kids are, nor does he care to, which is exactly why the clever Columbo manipulates the vintner into foreign territory: parenting. His focus, life's work, and source of pride is singularly about excellence in winemaking and, of course, getting away with his brother's murder. A second example: Leon Lamarr (Rip Torn) has no children, only a nephew, Freddie. In order to keep the lottery winnings among themselves, not wanting to share it with his soon to be ex-wife, Nancy (Jamie Rose), Freddie asks for his uncle's help. However, family ties are terribly loose for this villain who has been having an affair with Freddie's wife, Nancy, for some time. Apparently, blood does not trump sex. For the financial reward, Uncle Leon and Nancy kill Freddie for his lottery winnings. Family loyalty, love, and moral values are a rarity among the murderers of *Columbo*, qualities that serve to construct their villainy.

Audience–Villain Relationships: Antipathy, Ambipathy, and Sympathy

Are the relationships between detective and suspect distinct from audience–villain relationships? The answer depends on whether audiences have a spectator response to *Columbo* that is different from the subject position of identification with the Lieutenant elicited by the dramatic texts. In other words, certain audience members deviate from genre-prescribed identification with the hero–detective, his challenge, and his victory. Instead, some spectators, like me, for instance, become especially familiar with, sympathetic to, and intrigued by the brilliant or relatable villain of select episodes, even more so than with the mysterious investigator. Classifying Columbo's relationships with murderers, Sheldon Catz distinguishes three types of detective–villain relationships related to the murderers' motives and *modus operandi*, victims' innocence or deserved punishment, and the verbal interplay between investigator and suspect.

Perhaps the most common villain type is one that starts with a spectatorship of antipathy for the villain, which is sustained throughout the narrative. Examples of the classic *Columbo* villain include Jack Cassidy's three roles on *Columbo*, Robert Culp's three roles, Patrick McGoohan's three roles (his fourth role in "Dawn's Early Light" arguably elicits sympathy or, at least, ambipathy), Robert

Conrad's gym facility corporation and workout equipment line owner in "Exercise in Fatality," Rip Torn's duplicitous and disloyal uncle role in "Murder Hits the Jackpot," and so on. The first one is described as the "standard antagonistic relationship" (261) that is based on "agonism" between detective and villain (Berzsenyi, "Teaching Interlocutor Relationships"). More specifically, Columbo pursues evidence from a villain who resists his inquiries, cooperative cues, interruptions, and implications of guilt throughout the investigation. The second type describes the "sympathetic murderer relationship" (261), shaped by the circumstances and motives surrounding the murder, such as accidental death during a dispute, self-defense, self-preservation from a malicious blackmailer, or revenge. In these cases, the deceased occupies a villain–victim role in the crime narrative. Catz refers to the third type as "the 'all-in-the-game' paradigm", which is typified by clever exchanges between the detective–hunter and the killer–prey. As exemplified in *Crime and Punishment* between the criminal and the Magistrate, this type of relationship has the murderers trying to allude capture by appearing to enjoy Columbo's company, "but [are] in fact faking it" (261).

Perceptions of villainy depend on the killer's motives: desperation to keep something dear; care for someone else; damage from disloyalty or rejection; retribution for an unfair dismissal or wrongdoing; self-serving usage of another's life to cover up one's homicide and frame the second victim for it. Furthermore, the degree of villainy is also measured by the extent of harm or cruelty involved in the specific *modus operandi* (quick, less violent, or slowly and callously injurious). Certainly, whether someone kills by accident or from intended action affects the character's villainous profile.

For this project, spectator relationships with villains are not *Columbo*-based. Instead, spectatorship of sympathy, ambipathy, and antipathy describe villain characterology in relation to their victims as a dynamic model with the narrative. In several episodes, the killer is more sympathetic than the victim who is murdered (Galbraith). Such examples include Ruth Gordon's avenging mystery writer in "Try and Catch Me," Faye Dunaway's mother avenging her mistreated daughter in "It's All in the Game," and the paternal Jose Ferrer's regretful Dr. Marshall Cahill in "Mind over Mayhem." In other episodes, the murderer may be peculiarly vulnerable or compliant as an underdog until they snap or until they descend into a madness that can warrant audience's sympathy: Janet Leigh's terminally ill actress in "Forgotten Lady," Patricia Van Patten's spinster museum curator in "Old Fashioned Murder," Johnny Cash's dominated husband and gospel singer in "Swan Song," and Donald Pleasence's vintner, desperate to keep his treasured way of life in "Any Old Port in a Storm." What results is an ambivalent spectator–villain relationship with conflicting feelings about the villain's fate: conjuring leniency toward the suspect, wishing to spare him or her from punishment in prison or even from the due process under the law. With these villains of general harmless nature, audiences may "root for the villain" to "get away with the crime" (Philippa). Early in the investigation, the narrative draws the audience into familiarity with and compassion for the killer's situation and recourse. As the episode progresses, certain villainous actions dilute the original sympathetic response into an ambivalent relationship to the murder. In some cases, sympathy for the villain can transform to antipathy once they cross a moral line of self-interest at the expense of their innocent appearance. For example, Dick Van Dyke plays an abused husband, which garners sympathy. However, this sympathy disappears when he apathetically murders and frames the eager-to-please and reformed ex-con in "Negative Reaction." In "Lovely but Lethal" the narrative elicits viewers' sympathy towards Vera Miles in her role as a blackmailed and falling beauty mogul because she accidentally kills her blackmailer (Martin Sheen). But when she deliberately kills her doting assistant, albeit a blackmailer as well, she loses some of this sympathy. Susan Clark's role as an understated, oppressed sibling who cannot take her brother's tyranny any longer (Richard Anderson) merits compassion, until she transforms into a materialistic oppressor just like her brother in "Lady in Waiting." In "Bird in Hand," Tyne Daly plays an ignored and irrelevant wife who runs down her abandoning husband, which may be understandable to viewers. However, when she premeditates the murder of her disloyal, gold-digging lover (Greg Evigan), she is no longer viewed sympathetically, especially as she descends into volatile mental instability. Villains who kill a second time become accustomed to homicide to support their self-centered world view, self-justified in victimhood and deserving of all advantages previously denied to them. What disrupts their sympathetic status is their villainous aftermath.

From the active weblog *The Columbophile*, several members discussed sympathy for villains and their fates with the justice system. This sentiment speaks less about their loyalty and identification with the Lieutenant than how they feel about the intriguing and brilliant villain characters, the relatability of many of their motives, and the sense that the punishment of incarceration is a penalty too heavy for the circumstances. For example, in the blog article entitled "Top 10 Most Sympathetic *Columbo* Killers," Columbophile (the mysterious blog writer) lists those killers based on a spectrum of the audience's sympathy with the villain. The trailers present villains while positioning audiences into one of the spectator roles defining a type of identification with the villain. In his critique of Quinn Martin Productions' *Barnaby Jones*, Jonathan Etter distinguishes the mostly accidental, average-person killers of *Barnaby Jones* from the financially elite and socially powerful murderers of *Columbo*:

> As a result, the viewer felt pity for [*Barnaby Jones*'s killer] characters. He could easily imagine himself in that situation. That wasn't the case on *Columbo*. Not being in the same social or economic strata as the *Columbo* villains, TV viewers

couldn't be sympathetic towards them because they couldn't identify with them. The show wasn't structured that way anyway.

(147)

Although *Columbo*'s murderers are largely premeditated, self-serving, egocentric, opportunistic killers, who do not warrant sympathy from the audience, there are a few points to counterargue here. One is that the murders on *Columbo* were not all identical in being premeditated kills; some were accidental ("Dagger of the Mind," "Last Port in the Storm," "Columbo Likes the Nightlife," to list a few). Further, even among those that were premeditated homicides, motives varied, including desperate acts against blackmailers, making the victim villainous as well. Some of the deliberate murderers were sympathetic and relatable, despite their wealth and success ("Try and Catch Me," "Swan Song," "It's All in the Game," to name a few). Such episodes elicit sympathy to the point of spectators' hoping for their escape from police arrest, prosecution, and incarceration. Finally, the suspects' fame, luxurious lifestyles, and status may also be a source of viewer fascination and intrigue with how the upper-class might live differently with the options that money and connections afford. Certainly, viewer jealousy, resentment, or the like may play a role in spectatorship. However, the fantasy-like homes and lifestyles of these villains draw viewer interest, attention, and cinematic desire.

What I suggest is that it is the very format and structure of the inverted mystery that enables viewers' identification with the villains. The first scene shows the commission of the crime, motives, and strategies, establishing a clear sense of what, why, who, where, when, and how the villain kills the victim. Gathering together this knowledge of the villain, viewers experience the mystery of the Lieutenant's theories, hunches, research results, and feelings about the cases. In fact, the show's structure enables the viewers to be more familiar with the villains and less familiar with the detective. We are behind the scenes with the "real" villain characters and in their heads and secrets, while Columbo is portrayed on screen primarily in his underestimated detective façade, enacted for the suspects—and, in turn, viewers. Unlike with the single appearance of each villain character, after viewing several episodes, the audience's familiarity with the professional sleuth grows, as does their sense of loyalty to the recurring, lead hero–detective.

Villain Types and Audience–Villain Relationships Examined

Without question, spectatorship cannot be overgeneralized, arguing for certain or universal reactions to behaviors and circumstances associated with the villain. Still, the narrative point of view creates a lens through which to view the recorded performance, as guided by the film's direction and editing, the actor's interpretation of the character, and the composition of dialogue and plot by the writer. The following is a five-type classification of audience–villain relationships in *Columbo* that analyzes how the narrative points of view in the episodes suggest shifts in those relationships and responses to the murderers:

1. Antipathy to Dissociation
2. Ambipathy to Antipathy to Dissociation
3. Sympathy to Antipathy to Dissociation
4. Ambipathy to Sympathy
5. Sympathy.

Antipathy for the Villain

As noted, qualities that signal particularly high levels of villainy include a character's licentious, self-serving motives and excessive hubris, the presence of *Schadenfreude* during the kill, and undeserving victims. This combination of factors elicits strong judgments about their villainy and desires for the villain's disempowerment in capture, humiliation, and loss in the battle of brilliant minds with the reputed detective. As the denouement approaches, the killer's desperation, wretchedness, exhaustion, or dishonorable deeds garner a response that defies compassion for them; instead, the pathetic criminal on the run calls upon viewers' dissociation from the disgraceful and no longer intriguing murderer. The murderer's fall from grace happens after the previously experienced pleasure of antipathy (imaginative reproach of the killer and identification with the hero–detective) or ambipathy (mixed feelings about the culpability of the villain and the righteousness of capture by the Lieutenant).

The quintessential *Columbo* celebrity villains who appeared multiple times on the show include Jack Cassidy, Robert Culp, Patrick McGoohan, and Robert Vaughn, according to consensus on fan sites. The villains' seething sense of superiority to the police Lieutenant, smug certitude about committing the perfect murder and getting away with it, use of connections to inhibit Columbo's investigations, and nauseating self-aggrandizement are the usual ingredients of the show's villains. Indeed, while only appearing once in the series, several actors follow suit. Gene Barry, Robert Conrad, Ross Martin, Eddie Albert, and Leonard Nimoy offer the most astute of regular viewers a satisfying experience of smart, ruthless, egotistical, privileged, and perfectly despicable villains. However, the most despicable of the villains are arguably those who threaten, plan, or execute murderous schemes to kill the Lieutenant. These deplorable schemes can be seen in the characters of the desperate Beth Chadwick in "Lady in Waiting," the revenge-obsessed Vivian Dimitri in "Rest in Peace, Mrs. Columbo," the poisoner Paul Gerard in "Murder under Glass," behavioral psychologist and deadly attack-dog trainer Dr. Eric Mason in "How to Dial a Murder," phony psychic and vengeful executioner Eliot Blake in "Columbo Goes to the Guillotine," and the fatally possessive father and gossip radio show host Fielding Chase in "Butterfly in Shades of Grey." Typically, these villains' threats or attempts at killing the detective implement the same weapons or means of murder as they deployed in their first murders. While they plan an attack, "[i]t is Columbo orchestrating these events, finessing the villain into this act and then using it to prove he knew how the original crime was committed" (Catz 184).

In addition, when Columbo excitedly shows condemnation of the villain's reproachful behavior as opposed to his usual calm, methodical investigative demeanor, he decreases the villain's sympathetic nature. More specifically, in "Exercise in Fatality" (as well as in "A Stitch in Crime"), Brian Fairbanks writes a review of the episode for IMDb.com, showing exceptionally intense reactions from the investigator: "Columbo drops the pretense and loses his temper with his suspect. Its rarity makes it all the more delicious." Fairbanks goes on to explain the malevolence of Robert Conrad's Milo Janus:

> Excellent *Columbo* [italics provided] finds the perceptive detective matching wits with health guru Robert Conrad who bumped off a business partner and made it look like murder. The contrast between the self-effacing but brilliant detective and the vain, arrogant icon of physical fitness is highlighted throughout. Conrad never dares Falk to knock a battery off his shoulder, but his sense of superiority makes him less sympathetic than most of Columbo's adversaries, and it's very satisfying when the usually mild-mannered detective displays a rare flash of temper during a conversation with his prey.

As the narrative presents the amoral or immoral motivations, self-serving cunning, the repeated lying and arrogance, *and* the hero's impassioned condemnation of the health club evildoer, the audience has no alternative but to side with the Lieutenant rather than the despicable murderer.

Ambipathy to Antipathy for the Villain

While this is a category that is the most underrepresented in *Columbo*, there are some villains whose situations and motives call upon viewers' understanding of the villain's reasons for choosing to kill another. While they may not seem to be a murderer by nature, they are by circumstance. Either the villain kills inadvertently in an unpremeditated altercation with the victim, or they fight for what they feel is theirs, perceiving a lack of alternatives to killing an unsympathetic victim. However, there are other qualities of villainy that resist an audience's purely sympathetic response, and instead inspire ambiguity toward the arrogant, dark, weird, overly self-protecting killer. As the episode progresses, the villain may behave with indecency or may harm an innocent person for self-protection against being discovered as the guilty party to the murder. When villains are only out for themselves at all costs to those around them, their original, seemingly reasonable action is no longer engendering sympathy from audiences. In other words, the narrative steers spectatorship to antipathy for the selfish, narcissistic, and arrogant fiend. After a pathetic display that is unbecoming of a brilliant, sure, and powerful offender, the narrative coaxes the audience to rethink their identification or fascination with the killer, and, instead, reproach the weak culprit with contemptuous pity, disesteem, and/or disappointment. What follows is a reading of the episode "Étude in Black," illustrating a perspective of the villain at various plot and character shifts in the narrative and, therefore, affecting spectatorship.

FIGURE 17: Screenshot: Alex Benedict (John Cassavetes) in the act of murdering his demanding mistress Jenifer Welles (Anjanette Comer). Nicholas Colasanto (dir.), "Étude in Black," *Columbo*, 1972. Universal Television.

During the opening, an orchestra conductor maestro, Alex Benedict (John Cassavetes) slips away from the performing hall, clad in dark sunglasses (as if that would disguise the distinct face of the actor), a double-breasted, tan trench coat (a deliberate choice to play on Columbo's trench coat?), and his formal performance tuxedo with a special carnation boutonniere given to him by his wife, Janice (Blithe Danner). Putting a planned kill and alibi into action, Alex, undetected, silently enters his mistress's home, that of the young and talented concert pianist Jenifer Welles (Anjanette Comer), while she vigorously plays a light-hearted composition on the piano. Gradually settling into his murderous plot, the deadpan Alex creeps up behind Jenifer, studying the back of his prey's head and neck before advancing in a sudden and decisive move to her.

Looming over her from behind, Alex holds a briefcase with one hand and, with the other, reaches around and seizes her throat, as if to choke her or break her neck. Jerked back, Jenifer gasps, frightfully startled by this stalking stealth, made unfamiliar by his masking shades and aggressive as well as unexpected intrusion. Covering up his practice kill, Alex pulls Jenifer's head to his cheek. Realizing it is her lover, she smiles in relief and surprise. Uneasy and falling into a patronizing, satisfied grin at his power over the naturally startled young woman, Alex observes the obvious effect on her and poses the rhetorical question: "What's the matter? Did I scare you? You're shaking." The desperate villain knowingly scares her and, then, taunts her for her instinctively startled response, as if he did not intentionally shock her. His prank projects the maestro's angst over losing his station in life to start over without his wife's money. Sneaking up on her tests his prowling prowess and operates, for the moment, as passive aggressive with his young, idealistic, but demanding lover.

As a last effort, Alex tries to talk her out of acting on her ultimatum, which would force him to divorce his wife—so that they could have a romantically exclusive relationship that is no longer a secret—or else she will make a scandal of their love affair. Jenifer requires Alex to make a decision by providing no option than to do as she demands. Though she is murdered, her victimhood elicits less sympathy both for her selfish desire to ruin his marriage and for her use of coercion rather than argumentation. Realizing her conviction is unmovable about his having to leave his wife and her mother's financial backing (Myrna Loy), Alex cannot bear the thought of damaging his career because of his, now, demanding and controlling mistress. Certainly, Alex is childishly wanton and infuriatingly entitled to assume he can have it all without consequences. He has a doting wife who thinks he feels the same about her. He has a dependable financial support system through her mother, who is a patron solely because of her loyalty to her daughter and seemingly faithful husband. He enjoys a successful career, building notoriety and respect, making records and touring with audience approval. He benefits from the sexual excitement and doting of a lover in the shadows, who is cooperatively incognito, protecting his secret of infidelity, so that he can have all of the other perks while she lives with the taboo of being the illegitimate other woman.

Removing his coat and setting his briefcase down, the maestro parades across the room toward the sexy, seated pianist in the plunging neckline. He sports a wide, showy grin of smugness, self-satisfaction, and gallows humor. With penetrating eye contact, Alex removes his sunglasses, places them on the piano, and takes Jenifer by the neck and head again. With a dominant grip, he kisses her lips, a force to which she yields with desire. Recovering from the passion, Jenifer informs him, "I thought you weren't coming." In response, Alex corrects her with a fake question that reinforces what he wants her to know: "I said I would, didn't I?" Further discrediting her, the conductor immediately adds, "Just don't rely on your woman's intuition. It's never correct." Disregarding his sexist insult to her intelligence and gender, Jenifer coyly but daringly confronts Alex with the likelihood of his resenting her for the outcome of their last discussion, "Well, I thought you might be a little angry." With the use of "little," Jenifer euphemizes her certain knowledge of Alex's serious anger, as is seen during one of the many blistering disagreements about the subject. Reactively, the maestro plays the romantic to deflect her focus on his repressed rage, asking a hypothetical question rather than answering her inquiry: "How could I be angry when looking at you?"

She stares into his face with certitude and confidence while he looks down, like a saddened school boy being reprimanded by his female teacher. Oddly, the embodiment of imposing hubris, now, shyly states a fact, "I just don't like ultimatums, that's all." In two ways, Alex minimizes his true indignation toward her, when he uses the justifier "just" and the tag "that's all" in order to avoid an emotional argument, again. Furthermore, stating that one does not like ultimatums is like asserting one does not care to be in pain. An ultimatum is a universal aversion, denying one's ability to make a choice with viable, competing options. Jenifer is exercising power over her lover, making him do what he does not want to do, coercing the course of his life against his will. Based on the dialogue between the two, this same heated argument has happened numerous times along with her expressing displeasure with "being a secret mistress," as it is not her "style." Confirming that Jenifer is truly the dominant one in the relationship, she reductively presents the situation and limits his permitted action to fulfill her needs: "It's very simple. I have to be open and free."

Giving up hope of changing her mind, the conductor puts his arm around her, looks her directly in the face, and agrees, "So do I, love." With a relaxed face, knowing eyes, and smile of resolve, Alex realizes what he feels he must do to continue the support of his wife and her mother. In fact, the piano virtuoso sees something alter in his expression and inquisitively states, "You look a little funny." Addressing her dismissively, Alex sarcastically reiterates that she has given him a "marvelous choice" (ultimatum), acknowledging her intentions to scandalize his life and family if he does not comply with her demands. To which she insists, "Alexander, I'm right, and you know it." Surrendering to her demands to end the futile argument, the maestro acquiesces: "I know that. You told me." In an unusual combination of dedication to the relationship and to the other's well-being with pronouncements of imperatives and retaliation, Jenifer forecasts her ideal life together with her lover, if he adheres to her terms. Perhaps the moment that Jenifer seals her fate is when she eliminates any delusions that he worries about his wife's feelings and states the truth: "You're just reluctant to lose her mother's backing. And all that money." While first cutting him down, she bolsters his ego by reassuring him, like a mother might to her boy, that he will be fine without it, being a "genius." Telling him that he should not worry, the pianist fortifies Alex while acknowledging his fears: "You'll always have everything. You're just a little weak, deep inside." With each layer of benevolent dictatorship, Jenifer reassures Alex of his only option to get rid of his wife and keep her, as "all you really need is me, and I need you." This is her justification for forcing him into a decision to leave his wife. Alex is a control-hungry manipulator who lies to orchestrate his life and the people within it for his sole benefit via deceits and role-play. He has what he needs, wants to keep "the bird in hand," over the risky "two birds in the bush." However, maintaining the affair with Jenifer is no longer an option. Having anyone, especially an emotional, intuition-driven woman, exert power over him strikes the fight in him to protect what he has.

Satisfied with herself, she thinks she has provided a sound argument and convinced the conductor of her claim, but Alex only allays her determination by nominally giving up, agreeing he will speak with Janice, exclaiming, "What choice do I have?" Feeling victorious that the matter is settled, she grabs his face to push a kiss on him, but he declines, "No. Let's not do that now. Play something for me." Telegraphing, the maestro declares he will make them a drink to celebrate their last night in secrecy. Selecting a lively and expressive Chopin composition in triple time, Jenifer plays the piano joyfully while Alex puts on gloves, uses a cloth to cover a glass ashtray, and joins Jenifer with a glare of dark purpose, striking her in a sideways swing to the head (see Figure 17). While it is not Jenifer's fault that Alex decides to kill her or that he goes through with it, there is a chain of communicative events, combined with his desperate need for financial security and even greed for it all that ends in murder. In an attempt to cover up the murder as an act of suicide by stove gas asphyxiation, he moves the body to the kitchen. He then puts on his sunglasses again, as if disguising himself from himself, and begins to clean up the house—trying to eliminate evidence of his presence and hide the murder he has just committed. With a spoiler alert, audiences know that his carnation boutonniere gets rubbed off and left behind on the carpet when he carries her body to the kitchen, creating a key piece of evidence contradicting his alibi's timeline of events.

Sympathy to Antipathy for the Villain

A limited number of episodes begin with a sympathetic villain who kills for understandable reasons but then degrades in charm and integrity while becoming more desperate about self-preservation at the cost of others' lives; by the end, the narrative point of view primes spectators to feel ready to punish the scoundrel. A great example of this spectatorship is "A Deadly State of Mind," with Nadia Donner (Leslie Ann Warren) as a patient and lover of her psychiatrist-hypnotherapist, Marcus Collier (George Hamilton). Having discovered that his wife is involved in yet another extramarital affair, the indignant Karl Donner (Stephen Elliott) confronts Nadia and her latest male companion at their beach house. Pushed over the edge, Karl assaults both of them in a frenzy of strikes and shoves, but focuses his energy on the offending Nadia, a waif being tossed about, receiving Karl's intensifying blows. While Karl continues his violent retribution against his unfaithful wife, Marcus grabs the nearest weapon, a fireplace poker, and fatally knocks out Karl to stop his battering of Nadia. Although Karl's feelings are justified, his actions are over the top. At this point, Marcus is a type of hero for saving Nadia from further blows by her irate husband. At least, he is a sympathetic killer. The situation could have ended with the not-so-innocent Nadia murdered—though guilt for infidelity does not warrant homicide.

While the homicide was not premeditated, in the heat of the battle, Marcus decides that a robbery cover story should be conjured rather than going to the police about the manslaughter of his patient-lover's husband. Significantly, Marcus knows he has crossed an ethical line by having a sexual relationship with his patient; having this fact made public would likely disrupt his book project, position at the institute, and career overall. Against her own judgment, the new widow is complicit in backing her lover's alibi, though her unstable nervous condition makes her unreliable. Simultaneously, Nadia is eager to please Marcus, cooperating with his wishes and plans, and she is teetering on the edge of a full nervous breakdown. Through hypnotic suggestion, Marcus influences her to jump off of a balcony and kill herself. These decisions for self-preservation add layers of vilification, creating a blindly ambitious, under-achieving, and desperate researcher-psychiatrist, particularly in juxtaposition to the weak-willed, physically powerless, attention-dependent, impressionable, and personality-shifting Nadia. With his performative confidence, haughty attitude, and rhetoric of certitude, the manipulative doctor cares only for himself and destroys anyone in his way, without regret or remorse. Consequently, the narrative directs audiences into antipathy, making the fiendish Marcus Collier a terrifically unsympathetic or antagonistic villain.

Ambipathy for the Villain

As I have already defined, ambipathy describes an audience's state of mixed and conflicting responses to a character, measuring traits of goodness against those of badness. Ambipathy remains only as long as a behavior or event has not pushed the viewer to judge the character as more sympathetic or more antipathetic. In this category of spectatorship, the audience expresses both conflicting attitudes about the villain; as the story progresses, more decency is shown than moral turpitude. In "Any Old Port in the Storm," Adrian Carsini (Donald Pleasence) is generally regarded by fans, who vote in surveys and blogs, to be a sympathetic killer (Columbophile). His singular devotion to his family's vineyards and wine-making evinces an admirable and enviable passion for award-winning wines and certitude that he has found his life's calling. Characterized as a smug connoisseur and prideful vintner, Adrian Carsini disrespects his estranged, beach-bum younger half-brother, Ric Carsini, who cares not for the family business, only for the money to continue his adventurous, carefree lifestyle. The half-brothers are polar opposites: Adrian enjoys life as a celibate but celebrated wine maker, while Ric values business profits, travel, and multiple marriages. When Ric announces that he will sell his inheritance, meaning the land on which Adrian's wine business depends, Adrian's disappointment, indignation, and desperation are palpable. After failing to convince Ric to reconsider his decision, Adrian cannot bear the loss of the vineyard, around which his life revolves. Therefore, when Adrian acts out in a murderous rage, knocking Ric unconscious with a heavy object, the narrative reveals his dual nature, the Dr. Jekyll and the Mr. Hyde. As there is strong evidence that Adrian is not purely a sympathetic villain, he does elicit ambipathy through his obsession with the art and science of fine wines and his rash bout of violence. More importantly than his crime of passion is Adrian's callous, calculating treatment of his brother's unconscious and bound body, locked in the overheated wine cellar to suffocate. With the certainty that Ric will suffer greatly until dying, Adrian's degree of villainy is substantial, though his motivation for knocking Ric out is relatable.

As the investigation progresses and Adrian Carsini and Columbo become well acquainted, the ambipathy of his character remains. On the one hand, Adrian is honorable, passionate, generous, disciplined, and unmaterialistic, treating the Lieutenant well as a simpatico teacher and host. On the other hand, he is extremely arrogant and self-righteous, imbalanced, and unrealistic; an insensitive and hierarchical boss, an asexual tease, a callous murderer, and a cunning cover-up schemer. With such a contradictory character profile, Adrian Carsini proves to be not so much a sympathetic villain as an ambipathetic villain. With that settled, what is to be made of the hundreds of blog member posts, tweets, or other social media messages that consider Carsini to be unambiguously sympathetic?

Sympathy for the Villain

For a majority of *Columbo* villains, audiences maintain identification with the Lieutenant and the deserved justice he brings unto them with substantiated arrest. However, a minority of *Columbo* villains earn audiences' admiration, kinship, and sympathy. A key factor is how the audience perceives the villain to be a victim of terrible circumstances, which would correspond to the judgment that they had little to no choice but to perform the criminal act. Therefore, they deserve some clemency at the least, to be enabled to escape, and/or released with impunity. Several *Columbophile* blog members comment on the "Top 10 Most Sympathetic Columbo Killers" article posted by Columbophile on August 16, 2016:

> "Wade Anders, from *Murder Can Be Hazardous to Your Health*. Ok the man is a touch arrogant and, in all honesty, he makes so many silly mistakes with his murder you can't really sympathize but I just feel he was put in a dreadful position. After rising up from nowhere and becoming a major television star, he faces complete ruin just for a mistake he made when he was younger" (HARRYSBOY 17 August 2015); "It's rare where a villain can upstage Columbo but I though [sic] Trish Van Devere did ('Make Me a Perfect Murder'). The angst she gave while performing the murder, and the anxiety of finding the gun in the elevator and her desperateness at retrieving it were palpable" (Itsspideyman 24, Sept. 2016); and "I actually think they went a little overboard on Grace Wheeler ('Forgotten Lady'). She's so sympathetic that the episode becomes depressing instead of entertaining. Watching Columbo apply his tricks of the trade to a suspect with dementia is like watching Mike Tyson go a few rounds with Stephen Hawking" (Craverguy 21 Jan 2017).

After considering so many of the alternative sympathetic villains posited by the members, the *Columbophile* list has almost doubled in size to include, as of present, nineteen nominations. Besides Alex Benedict, who embodied, at least, a convolution of sympathetic and antipathetic behaviors and motives (encouraging ambipathy from audiences) during the opening scene in "Étude in Black," Hayden Danziger (Robert Vaughn) in "Troubled Waters" is the only character who encourages ambipathy from audiences, playing a philandering, happily married husband being blackmailed by his lover. Danziger's extra-marital dalliance is with a wickedly opportunistic and obstinate vocalist Rosanna Welles (Poupée Bocar), who threatens to expose their affair to Danziger's older, rich wife, and to destroy his business reputation for financial gain. In turn, Hayden is provoked to shoot her to death to protect his marriage, reputation, and his economically elite status and lifestyle. Similarly, the two male villains are not murderous by nature, nor do they gain pleasure from homicide; killing their blackmailers is the means by which to escape from the impossible situation constructed by their mistresses. These opportunistic blackmailers are villainous before they switch victim roles with the killer.

In the following chapter, "Columbo, Women of His Investigations, and the Equal Rights Movement," conflicting cross-cultural attitudes toward women's roles in society are examined in terms of how the show ignores and responds to the cultural revolution of the Equal Rights Movement.

6

Columbo, Women of His Investigations, and the Equal Rights Movement

"[Flying is] a great release for me, Lieutenant," Leslie Williams admits. "Being up here, all alone, totally free."
(Lee Grant, *Columbo*: "Ransom for a Dead Man" 1971)

Taken from the *Columbo* pilot, "Ransom for a Dead Man," Lee Grant's portrayal of the ambitious, brilliant, beautiful, and voraciously independent femme fatale sets a counter-cultural tone early in the show's rendering of murder investigations in fictionalized Los Angeles high society. This chapter examines character constructions of the female villains, identifying several aspects that deviate from the construction of the typical male villain. Like their male counterparts, the female murderer is generally middle-aged, attractive, intelligent, successful, privileged, and entitled. They lead their companies with their creativity, intellectual abilities, years of knowledge and experience, unconventional attitudes, confidence, and arrogance. These overlaps with male villains, on the one hand, empower the women killers by sharing the combination of cultural virtues and vices. On the other hand, such transgressions of the cultural norms of "woman" highlight the unusual or "unnatural" role of women as murderers, violating the social paradigm of supportive wife or employee, nurturing mother, and self-sacrificing entity who serves others' needs. Such violations of social norms provoke dislocated spectator relationships characterized by dissonance. Even though the female killer is attractive and feminine in appearance, her womanliness is combined with a perversion signified by leadership, working in the public sphere, making self-serving decisions, earning a good living, navigating the direction of her life as an independent person, and being direct about her needs, expectations of others, and desires (Creed).

Through the medium of television, normative representations of women appear: thin, glamorous, ultrafeminine, and sexually inviting. In his textual analysis of films about early Hollywood as well as his historical insights about the business of early Hollywood, Christopher Ames reveals the unfair fate of aging actresses:

> Indeed, aging has always been tougher on women than on men in the movies, in part because of the very factors that once made actresses the center of the screen world: the mixture of innocence and youthful sex appeal, that "fresh, dewy quality." [Molly] Haskell points out that actors like Fred Astaire and Cary Grant played romantic leads for generations "while their partners were forced to play mothers or character parts or go wilting into retirement" (16).
>
> (43)

Going against Hollywood's practice of putting middle-aged and older women into the background of stories, *Columbo* features appropriately aged women in the roles of successful business entrepreneurs and professionals, highlighting mature beauty. Unlike the less visible acting parts of domestic women such as mothers, grandmothers, aunts, neighbors, and the like, *Columbo's* seasoned actresses are featured in these prominent villain roles as celebrated actresses.

Contrary to popular depictions of victimized or negligible women in television and film, *Columbo's* female villains threaten equal power, control, and change in men's lives and patriarchal structures. As author and journal staff writer Paul Hughes notes, "For in conventional terms, these were reflections of American life as women asserted their own bad selves, entered the workforce, and began to do many things previously reserved for men—including kill people [...]. They don't want to be married, married at all, or marriage" (11–13). While Hughes warns against interpreting the show and its writers as feminist crusaders, he recognizes *Columbo's* relationship to the wider cultural context of the women's movement toward greater equality, participation, and independent agency in public and economic spheres of influence: "In the infancy of the new show, the makers and presenters show exponential expansion in a particular view of woman" (13). Portraying credible women, corporate executives, academically educated professionals, lawyers, and celebrated performers as killers certainly responds to the country's cultural shifts or pressures to shift toward the empowerment of women and away from their being "put in their place."

In A. L. Kellermann and J. A. Mercy's study of 215,273 homicides during 1976–1987 (as reported by the Federal Bureau of Investigation), social scientists showed that women in the United States were responsible for 14.7% of murders, a statistic closely mirrored by *Columbo*, of which fourteen of the 74 murderers, or 18.9%, are female. Among the 14.7% of homicides by women, 60% of them involved victims who were spouses, intimate partners, or acquaintances; only

20% of kills by men observed these victim characteristics. In comparison, out of the fourteen of *Columbo*'s lethal female villains, ten of them murdered spouses and intimate partners or acquaintances, which is 71% (though it is not a statistically significant number of participants in the small sample). In short, *Columbo*'s female murderers are portrayed in traditional relationships where power and control by men over women become emotional factors leading to murderous motives and deeds.

When audiences, particularly women, root for the fictional female renegade who operates outside of the law but for the purpose of doing good, spectators celebrate women's autonomy, virility, and power to enact violence that protects, remedies, and rescues victims, including themselves. Seminal American feminist cultural critics, such as Gloria Steinem (1963–present), Betty Friedman (1963), Ti-Grace Atkinson (1967), and Susan Brownmiller (1970), to name just a few, understand the importance of women working for financial and personal independence and to question the lifelong expectations of self-sacrifice and self-denial in traditional gender roles of marriage and motherhood. In the 1960s, 38% of adult women were employed, and, in 1970, 43% of women worked, though the jobs largely involved support or subordinate staff positions to white male professionals (US Labor Statistics). In 1970, women employees filed a sexual discrimination lawsuit against their employer *Newsweek Magazine*, which they won, putting pressure on television networks to hire and promote women fairly at all levels. Also targeted by women's equal rights coalitions were television shows' limited and negative portrayals of women as sex objects or in unremarkable domestic roles supporting husbands and children (Davis). Furthermore, the stereotypical damsel in distress, an image that permeates television and film, is a disservice to social equality. Viewers long for more diverse, accurate, and valuing portrayals of real women: strong, hardworking, and courageous human beings and survivors. The wealthy, villainous women of *Columbo* are brilliant, self-serving, cunning, and capable of committing mortal trouble, though typically in feminine high society style.

Columbo's *Female Villains: Ladylike but Lethal*

Despite the women's movement enacting these and other professional demands, heroic action by women is conventionally characterized as aberrant and rare in television. An even greater gender role transgression is when females act out in villainy, which directly opposes the social expectations of women as mothers: protecting, nourishing, peace-keeping, and nurturing (Berzsenyi, "'Evil, Beautiful, Deadly'"; Creed). In turn, women, possessing the potent, destructive, determined, and criminal traits characteristic of villains, present conflicts for more traditionally minded mass audiences. These perspectives expect characters that embody sex roles of female femininity and male masculinity to be linked through prescribed narrative roles of victim, hero, and villain (Clover 12–13). While much of the research about gendered reactions to gendered characterizations in narrative never make it to mass consciousness, they are observable in the popular media texts and testable by social, cultural, and cognitive scientists (Berenstein, among others).

When asked about the comparatively low number of female killers and absence of diversity among all of the murderers, one of the show's creators, William Link, justifies the decisions as inadvertent rather than made by design, which unfortunately matches the common uncritical attitudes about diversity at the time. Certainly, the film and television industry could further expand the multicultural profile of actors hired to work in productions. However, the women do represent diversity in age, which counters Hollywood trends that have generally favored young women over middle-aged or golden-aged. Further, the beauty aspect of the female villains demonstrates a range of loveliness. Rather than solely relying on young beauty queens/models for the purpose of attracting mainstream heterosexual male audiences, *Columbo* exhibits smart writing, genius masterminds with ambition and confidence, and less conventional projections of female allure with the power of professional success; the women villains are intriguing beyond just good looks and sexy flirtations.

Of course, other exceptions to the portrayal of impotent women as submissive or damsels in distress can be found in the horror genre. Female villainy is often "founded upon her transgressive and somewhat ambiguous sexual identity, which is constituted as markedly 'male' in several ways" (Springer 158): rejecting marriage, motherhood, and the traditional home life for the professional, public, social, performative, and talent-challenging spheres outside of the home. In a character analysis of the unnamed Woman who is both "victim and villain" in the 1956 psychological thriller, *Daughter of Horror* (Adrienne Barrett), John Springer exemplifies the "mad" woman's vilification via rejection of a child holding out a toy for her:

> The Woman does not take it and moves away. Is this a refusal of "parental" love on the part of the Woman? Or perhaps (an even more subversive possibility) there is a critique of the family in that lonely gesture towards play and companionship that the child makes and the Woman refuses. At the very least, the Woman's indifference to the child suggests an unwillingness to occupy the role of 'mother' and nurturer that our culture imposes on women generally.
> (159)

Certainly, a departure from conventional domestic life is shared by almost all of *Columbo*'s female villains and accomplices. Even an involvement in an extramarital affair rejects the traditional vows of fidelity. Those vows and other social and legal constraints are deselected by the female criminals, opting, instead, for the less conventional life. They make choices that empower themselves in careers for independence from the male-centered authority of their worlds/our worlds, undermining patriarchy as the established power structure that has long favored men. Particularly in the workplace, where men thrive, earn their incomes, and establish dominant social status, women executives contradict expected gender roles: instead of supporting male CEOs, they are the ones being supported and competing for power, resources, profits, and the like.

To avoid triggering patriarchal backlashes against their authority from male coworkers, some women portray deference. More specifically, Joan Riviere explains that female workers and professionals

> may put on a mask of womanliness to avert anxiety and the retribution feared from men [...] to affect womanliness in order to ensure that men will not feel threatened by their success and assertiveness. In doing so, men are reassured that she is not competing with them on their terms, like a man, but rather in an unthreatening, womanly way that is charming, feminine, accommodating, and attractive.
>
> (210)

In no episode is this tactic more obviously played than in "Lovely but Lethal" with the murderous cosmetics empire founder and top executive Viveca Scott, who placates the patronizing, sexist Lieutenant in his guise. While the actress Vera Miles's beauty is unquestionable, audiences may feel ambivalence toward her, a combination of desire and enchantment, as well as compassion and repulsion owing to her desperation and multiple murderous deeds (Berzsenyi, "'Evil, Beautiful, Deadly'" 182–83). Women's decisions to pioneer into new territories comprise courageous acts of creativity, intelligence, persistence, and the usurping of men's social territories. However, their triumphs of agency, even in these fictional crime narratives, do not excuse the violence, excesses of hubris and greed, or calculated actions to satisfy dark fantasies of how they think their world should operate around them. The female villains are no less culpable than their male counterparts.

Within the context of the women's equal rights movement in the late 1960s and 1970s, as well as other civil rights movements, backlashes to women seeking work outside of the home appeared in many morality-laden narratives. For example: police procedurals featured working women victims. Women's employment and independent living were seen as a threat to traditional family values and, more specifically, to the male role as patriarch, sole bread-winner, and the one in control of the family's finances, expenditures, rewards, and so forth. With some variation, women in *Columbo* episodes certainly play victim roles, but they also play villain and accomplice roles, which are both representative of physical and mental power and action as well as control. The leadership capacities of these successful, talented and wealthy female villains are muted by the establishment when they are caught and confined. While it is true that these female killers require being captured in detective narratives, other strong women characters in the show are killed. In contrast, most female support characters are subdued, uninformed, and powerless, while the same is not true of male support characters.

To take "Prescription Murder" as an example, the female character of Carol Flemming is a powerful, albeit angry and scorned, woman who is killed by her husband. His mistress and accomplice, Joan Hudson, is not only compliant and lovesick, she is a martyr for Ray's sake, acting on his best interest as she assumes his equal devotion to her. Mrs. Flemming's female friends at the wedding anniversary party are forgettable props, as is Dr. Flemming's secretary. This configuration of support female characters is consistently banal.

On the contrary, the female villains are memorable but unconventional. Among the fourteen lethal women, the marital status breakdown goes as follows:

- **One is divorced but dating happily** (Vanessa Farrow in "Columbo Likes the Nightlife")
- **One is a sad widow** avenging her late husband's murder (Vivian Dimitri in "Rest in Peace, Mrs. Columbo")
- **One is happily married** and murdering partners (Lilian Stanhope in "Dagger of the Mind")
- **Three are unhappily married** (Leslie Williams in "Ransom for a Dead Man," Grace Wheeler Willis in "Forgotten Lady," and Delores McCain in "A Bird in the Hand")
- **Two never married but have tyrannical brothers** they need to free themselves of (Ruth Lytton in "Old-Fashioned Murder" and Beth Chadwick in "Lady in Waiting")
- **Three are unhappily dating** (Kay Freestone in "Make Me a Perfect Murder," Dr. Joan Allenby in "Sex and the Married Detective," and Lauren Staton in "All in the Game")
- **Three are single or estranged, and gladly not dating** (Viveca Scott in "Lovely but Lethal," Nora Chandler in "Requiem for a Falling Star," and Abigail Mitchell in "Try and Catch Me").

Only two women are happily married. Lilian Stanhope is with Nickolas Frame, her soulmate husband, as children playing together and performing on stage together. Without momentary lapse, the two stay together until the end, when they are arrested. Vivian Dimitri loves her husband so much that she becomes enraged, obsessed, inconsolable, and bent on revenge for his death in prison. Blaming the arresting officer, Columbo, and the witness who testified against her spouse, she turns depraved. These examples, though, are unlike most of the female villains. The three other married wives kill their husbands, just as the three unhappily dating villains slay their boyfriends. To be fair, Vanessa Farrow inadvertently killed her menacing ex-husband in self-defense. The other half of the female villains represent various types of singledom: divorced, widowed, and never married. This means that they are agents of their own destiny, which, for them, includes prison.

Among the fourteen female killers, only one is a mother or is shown as a mother, though the same is true with the male villains: there are only two fathers. Dr. Marshall Cahill (Jose Ferrer) in "Mind over Mayhem," is in a protective relationship that drives him to murder. The same is true with Fielding Chase (William Shatner), the possessive and controlling paternal figure in "Butterfly in Shades of Grey." As a biological mother with the maternal drive to protect her daughter, Lauren Staton (Faye Dunaway) in "All in the Game" plans and executes killing the deceitful, philandering Franco, with Lisa as her accomplice. In an ultimate sacrifice, Lauren protects her daughter from the hardships of imprisonment. Indeed, her maternal connection to her adult child is strong. The other example of nurturing expressed in the absence of her ward is in "Try and Catch Me," with Abigail Mitchell avenging the murder of her niece, whom she clearly loved. Again, her niece was a grown woman. Audiences are not privy to scenes of caring between them, only with the legacy of Mitchell's calm wrath at her niece's injustice. With the other twelve female villains, the correlation between being a killer and being childless is absolute. In "Ransom for a Dead Man," Leslie Williams is a stepmother similar to the kind found in fairytales: with a touch of evil. There is no warmth to her character, affection or concern about her stepdaughter, and, in fact, she pushes her back to school overseas as soon as she can.

During the baby boomer's generation of adult viewers, the vilification of a woman starts with her rejection of society's expectation that she be a loyal, supportive wife and mother in the home. Generally, her life would be private in the domestic sphere in unpaid service to each of her family members across generations. Thirteen out of the fourteen killer women have careers or career aspirations that are explored once those who encumber their freedom and opportunities are eliminated—one of the men in their lives. *Columbo*'s femme fatales are primarily focused on adult lifestyles in public spheres, which are the vicarious fantasies that viewers at home can imagine living from their ordinary lives. Importantly, the more conventional viewers continue to live in their homes, while the famed villains are sent to prison; this is the morality tale.

Only two women killed other women. Nora Chandler, in "Requiem for a Falling Star," inadvertently killed her personal assistant when she was trying to kill a blackmailing gossip reporter. However, Viveca Scott of "Lovely but Lethal" murdered two blackmailers; though the first was in the heat of anger by accident, the second was calculated: a laid-off chemist who stole the chemical formula for a promising new anti-aging cream that would save her struggling company (Martin Sheen) and her competitor's secretary, who'd been her paid informant but presented grand demands. With blackmailers and ultimatum makers, sympathy is created for the murderers by offering them few options besides eliminating the coercive extortionists. In these cases, the murderers are part villain and part victim, which creates ambivalence in viewers toward the criminals, as discussed in the previous chapter on *Columbo* murderers. *Columbo*'s murderers garner sympathy through other acts of wrongdoing committed against them, or through a lack of premeditation in their crime. For instance, Abigail Mitchell in "Try and Catch Me" kills her niece's husband because she cannot bear the thought of him getting away with murdering her niece. Six of the femme fatales killed their husbands or lovers who were philanderers or abandoners after using them. While Lilian Stanhope in "Dagger of the Mind" accidentally killed her employer, Sir Roger Havisham, she is not a murderer by nature, though she is far more concerned about getting caught than with Havisham's death, which leads to a cover-up homicide. In other words, sympathies can shift throughout the episodes from less so to more so, depending on the villains' alibis, cover-ups, framing of innocents, or killing innocents.

Columbo–*Femme Fatale*

Certain differences emerge when comparing Columbo's approach to female suspects with his treatment of female witnesses. Some examples of witnesses are the smart and cooperative widow Norris (Louise Latham) in "Double Exposure," the distraught, alcoholic ex-wife (Collin Wilcox Patton) and the heedless but respectful secretary (Gretchen Corbett) in "Exercise in Fatality," the murdered nurse's dingy and flirtatious but obliging roommate (Nita Talbot) in "Stitch in Crime," and the lovely and vulnerable suspect's wife (Geena Rowlands) in "Playback." With the female witnesses, Columbo is always polite and gentle-mannered in an old-fashioned way. He is not slyly flirtatious, relentlessly interrogating, craftily belittling, or disingenuously flattering with them. His inquiries are carefully presented but expeditious, comforting but openly reliant on their knowledge and observations, sensitive but resolute, and, ultimately, collaborative with the shared goal of pursuing justice for the deceased.

In contrast, Columbo's relationships or personas with the female villains all share the element of duplicity in terms of him secretly suspecting them but not letting on that he does. However, the manner in and reasoning for which he projects a lack of suspicion varies among four relationship strategies: "Doting Devotee" (which he does with the males as well), "Treats 'em Like a Lady," "You're Not Crazy," and "Stupefied by the Woman Executive." While developing descriptive categories is useful for analyzing and identifying patterns of communication, relationships, and interaction, Columbo employs multiple strategies, with one predominant over the others.

"Doting Devotee"

The Lieutenant butters up the celebrity with excess praise and recognition of their talents or successes, placing them up on a pedestal from which to look down on the working-class cop. These celebrity female foes include Lilian Stanhope in "Dagger of the Mind," Nora Chandler in "Requiem for a Falling Star," Grace Wheeler Willis in "Forgotten Lady," Vanessa Farrow in "Columbo Likes the Nightlife," and Viveca Scott in "Lovely but Lethal." However, this kind of self-deprecating and devotional behavior is also used with the celebrated male suspects to put them at ease with him. What is different about the detective's approach with women is that he uses flirtation, flattery, or both, communication behaviors that distract the villains in a gender-specific way: relaxation. So, the murderers relax their guard because, if the investigator is doting on them for their beauty and femininity, he appears less likely to suspect them of murder. He expresses an excess of what would be appropriate signs of approval, appreciation, admiration, attraction, or the like from a high-ranking police officer to a person of interest in a homicide investigation. In turn, Columbo fashions a persona who is not likely to think outside of gender roles and expectations of women as nurturers, harmonizers, and passive supporters to all in their lives; in other words, they are safe from his suspicion.

In "Try and Catch Me," Abigail Mitchell (Ruth Gordon), a mystery novelist, is almost universally viewed as sympathetic by *Columbo* fans (Columbophile and others), who appreciate the writer's grief over the unsolved murder of her niece by her greedy and emotionally vapid nephew-in-law. Angry at the police department's impotence in bringing about justice for her niece, she delightedly lures the young, avaricious man with promises of inheritance in her newly rewritten will. Locking him in a walk-in security vault, he suffocates to death after running out of oxygenated air. Lacking blood loss and violence, the passive but desperate *modus operandi* is fitting for the diminutive, mature, and otherwise affable and light-hearted murder mystery novelist. Regarding her successful writing career, Columbo douses Mitchell with excessive accolades for her prolific documentation of fictional cases and her terribly effective fictional detective. Upon Mitchell's insistence on the Lieutenant sharing his vast investigative experience in homicide,

Columbo agrees to speak at a lecture she is giving on crime solving. While most celebrity murderers accept praise and adoration from the detective, few return the doting treatment back to him. She is playful with Columbo the whole time, teasing him, exchanging deductive reasoning and detection strategies, treating him with formal respect and embellishing her accolades about his brilliance. At the moment of capture, there is a shift from exaggerated performance to genuine affinity, evidenced by the two sincerely exchanging mutual sympathy, regret, and high praise.

"Treats 'em Like a Lady"

Columbo enacts gentlemanly politeness, taking care of the "weaker sex"; he shows worry for the "little ladies," holds his hand/arm out for them, and holds the door for them. Exaggerating traditional male paternalism with the mature or reserved women attackers, Columbo exudes gentlemanly manners observable in the following episodes: to Beth Chadwick (Susan Clark) in "Lady in Waiting" (during the first act in which he appears, before her transformation), Ruth Lytton (Joyce Van Patten) in "Old Fashioned Murder," Grace Wheeler Willis (Janet Leigh) in "Forgotten Lady," and Abigail Mitchell (Ruth Gordon) in "Try and Catch Me." Along with a noble man's approach, the detective may express personal worry for the fragile, grieving survivor of the murder victim, treating her with "kid gloves," like she is also a victim, when, in fact, she is the villain. With the especially attractive female suspects, the Lieutenant appears to be captivated by their beauty, clumsily appealing to the traditional value of a woman's desire for male attention and attraction to them to secure their sense of self-worth on heterosexual men's terms. However, these vixens do not need it or want it, though some do play along with his attentions in order to avoid breaking his pronounced spell of magnetism. Examples of such vixens include Viveca Scott (Vera Miles) in "Lovely but Lethal," Kay Freestone (Trish Van Devere) in "Make Me a Perfect Murder," Dr. Joan Allenby (Lindsay Crouse) in "Sex and the Married Detective," and Lauren Staton (Faye Dunaway) in "It's All in the Game."

Perhaps the most explicit reference to treating a female suspect like a lady appears in "Old Fashioned Murder," in which head curator Ruth Lytton never marries and manages her pride and joy: a family-run museum. However, her brother has promised to dissolve the financially failing institution, despite his sister's pleading. She is stoic in demeanor, asexual in presentation, matronly in style, and stuck in a time past. Investigating the double homicides of her brother and a supposed burglar, the detective respectfully enters her older home containing obvious remnants of past wealth, interacting with her and her sister in old-fashioned charm and conversation. The setting hardly feels like twentieth-century Los Angeles; it's more like an old southern home. Columbo accepts Ruth's offer of tea service, and he graciously thanks her for it, almost as if he

FIGURE 18: Screenshot: Columbo with Lauren Staton (Faye Dunaway), both cozy at a diner, playing their parts with some personal engagement. Vincent McEveety (dir.), "It's All in the Game," *Columbo*, 1993. Universal Television.

were her gentleman caller, which is what Ruth expects or, at least, desires. While not a gentleman of wealth and social standing, Columbo inhabits the role of a gentleman in understated pleasantries and manners befitting his refined and well-spoken female company.

Moreover, the ending epitomizes the high culture world of art, history, artifacts, and refinement, in which ambiguous speech replaces unpleasant, explicit truth words such as "homicide" and "murder." In such contexts, communication takes the form of doublespeak that simultaneously shrouds upsetting details from those sheltered by harsh realities while establishing the terms of those realities with the unsheltered. During the final scene, Columbo demonstrates to Ruth, with indirect references that nevertheless clearly communicate to her, that he has the evidence to prove she murdered her brother. All the while, in the presence of this conversation, Ruth's flighty and sheltered sister Phyllis Brandt exasperates, "Lieutenant, I have no idea what you are talking about." In a type of code understood by only Ruth and Columbo, the two speak freely and negotiate terms: that Ruth's murder of long ago is out of consideration, but that Ruth will make a confession for the recent murders to avoid a trial. As a final vestige of her old life, Ruth fluffs her hair for her exit to make the permanent public appearance from her home and requests, with ladylike reserve, "Lieutenant, may I take your arm?" Offering his arm with reverential eye contact, like a suitor at a formal ball, Columbo replies, "It's my pleasure, Miss Lytton." And they walk out of her home to the police vehicle.

"Clueless Comforter"

In several episodes, the female villains project a vulnerability and emotional instability to which Columbo responds by offering abundant condolences and commanding his subordinate police officers to escort, drive, or otherwise take care of them. With embellished states of shock, grief, or anger, the murderesses elicit relationships with the detective that convey harmlessness and lack of motive to kill, demonstrated by highly reactive emotionality to the death of the murder victims. In turn, Columbo plays the sensitive, compassionate consoler and caregiver to the supposed "secondary victims" of the homicide. In "Lady in Waiting," Beth Chadwick initially presents a peevish, passive, and subjugated adult sibling of a tyrannical brother, whom she shot while mistaking him for an intruder, so her story goes. At first, the Lieutenant reassures Beth of her innocence in the accidental homicide and shows sympathy for her when she tells him about the whole family's lifelong, chauvinistic control over her as the younger and female sibling: the deceased authoritarian father and complicit mother, and, more recently, her degrading, restraining, and infantilizing older brother. In truth, Beth had had enough of their subordination and constrictions and snapped, resorting to murder. Beth made an immediate transformation from understated and quiet-spoken Beth to "the mouse that roared," updating her fashion and hairstyle boldly, ostentatiously featuring her wealth, and commanding control over the family's corporation with an arrogant, heavy hand, just like her father and brother had before her (Susan Clark in Dawidziak 76).

In an act of desperation and to avoid imprisonment, Beth pulls a gun out on the Lieutenant. At the end, he talks her out of shooting him in a calming, respectful and gentlemanly way, treating her like a lady who does not have it in her nature to kill him. He recognizes her panic and despondency in the anguish of the moment, an animal cornered by her own predator. Despite the fact that she has just turned a gun on him, he soothes her with calm reasoning in terms of what would be against her own best interest, reassuring her that things will be ok.

In "A Bird in Hand," Delores McCain (Tyne Daly) appears entirely unsettled and grief-stricken when the Lieutenant arrives at the house, the crime scene. She plays a new widow on the brink of emotional collapse, trying to hold it together by self-medicating, and she is unreliably incoherent. In fact, throughout the episode, Delores's demeanor is highly nervous, intoxicated by alcohol, and emotionally needy until the last act of murder and attempted cover-up when

COLUMBO, WOMEN OF HIS INVESTIGATIONS, AND THE EQUAL RIGHTS MOVEMENT

FIGURE 19: Screenshot: Beth Chadwick (Susan Clark) and Columbo soon after she mistakes her tyrannical brother for a burglar and fatally shoots him by accident. She is already irritated but has so much more questioning to endure. Everett Chambers (dir.), "Lady in Waiting," *Columbo*, 1971. Universal Television.

she suddenly exhibits glimpses of control over herself and her mental state. Unhappily married, alcoholic Delores McCain (Tyne Daley) projects a nonthreatening, unaware, desperate-for-attention, pleaser-without-a-plan type of woman. However, she is having an affair with her husband's nephew, Harold McCain (Greg Evigan), a wooing gambling addict and con artist who is desperate to pay back threatening loan sharks with his aunt's money. In turn, Delores runs over her husband to free up her husband's finances and help her trusted lover with his debts. Naïve about his charms, Delores is disillusioned when she discovers that her much younger lover and dependent is romancing other women, incurring more debt at the casino all night, and taking advantage of her generosity. The scorned woman takes revenge in a hastily plotted fatal shooting of her disloyal companion. Except for the work party, during which she is larger than life as a diva, Delores portrays her murderous acts as crimes of passion by a neurotic on tranquilizers. However, the denouement depicts the murderer and the investigator abandoning their respective façades of innocence and cooperation. Delores reveals a smirk when Columbo initially confronts her with the insubstantial evidence of her two homicides. In this moment, however, Columbo promptly reveals his knowledge of her calculated campaign of homicide and innocence without treating her like a fragile cat in the rain; instead, he treats her like a killer. Right after, her victorious smirk of duping delight drops to a defeated foe's frown when the Lieutenant clarifies, with some delight himself, the possession of substantial evidence to prosecute her for the second murder.

Another example of the reassuring relationship with the female villains includes Vivian Dimitri in "Rest in Peace, Mrs. Columbo." Vivian is a vengeful, grieving widow who misplaces blame for her murderous husband's fatal cardiac arrest in prison onto the Lieutenant, who arrested him for homicide years previously. Redirecting her grief into revenge, Mrs. Dimitri plans to kill Mrs. Columbo so that he feels her devastating pain in losing a spouse. After the police fake Mrs. Columbo's death to keep her safe, Dimitri redirects her venom- fueled plans to kill the detective with a jar of poisoned lemon marmalade. Though Mrs. Dimitri's anguish is murderous, Columbo maintains the role of a compassionate sharer of grief, even while she anxiously awaits his expected death. Despite the fact that he knows Vivian poisoned the jar of marmalade she deliberately serves him, Columbo remains calm and sure that his police officers have switched the poisoned jam for a new, untainted one. Despite Mrs. Dimitri's plans to avenge her late husband by murdering him, Columbo remains cool, deliberate, and polite. The Lieutenant's innate and experiential comprehension of human psychology keeps his focus on the object of rational investigation of the villain and her homicidal acts. He keeps her close by acting ignorant of her malice with the pretense of their being kindred spirits as widowed spouses and him genuinely caring about her. Without having *ad hominem* vengeful attitudes about Vivian and her trying to kill him, Columbo sticks to the issue, the cause, the job, explaining on several occasions, "I never take it personally."

With Grace Wheeler Willis in "Forgotten Lady," Columbo is aware of her fluctuations in lucidity, mental escapism to her past stardom, and floating memory. Instead of interrogating the suspect, the detective treats her like a woman with a brain disease. Grace is obsessively nostalgic, has unrealistic career projections, and reruns her films daily for immersive, imaginative transport into her cinematic past. He expresses adoration for her brilliant career and talents, appeasing her vanity, while he continues to conduct an investigation about the *modus operandi* of her husband's murder, disproving his apparent suicide. As she does not seem to remember killing him, she is not elusive with the Lieutenant. In fact, she invites him to come back to her home for special viewings of her films. She behaves almost as if Columbo is a new friend and not investigating her as the prime suspect. In her mind, there is no murder to investigate.

While he pursues his homicide investigation, finding Grace to be the able-bodied murderer of her husband, his inquiries involve her career-long dance partner, who willingly takes the credit for the man's death. Motivated to stall the legal system long enough for her to die or be unfit to stand trial, Ned prevents Grace from experiencing prison detainment during the final month or two of her life. With ambiguous feelings about the victim's culpability and prosecution, Columbo accepts the loving dance partner's false confession, projecting the eventual dismantling of that confession, though not before the forgotten Grace dies from her brain illness.

"Stupefied by the Competent Woman Executive"

Playing the male chauvinist with the high-powered executives, the investigator acts out paternalistic attitudes of attenuation regarding the value of their career accomplishments. The sexism projected by the detective shows him to be stupefied by the powerful, public figures' departure from traditional female sex roles. Columbo acts as if he presumes women cannot be demanding and scheming corporate executives, creative and courageous founders of competitive businesses, cut-throat lawyers, or strategic agents of their professional lives. They cannot simply because they are women. He pretends to underestimate them, citing their female natures as incompatible with murder. As the "good ole boy," Columbo overreacts when he encounters a woman suspect who is not a homemaker, nurturer, or dysfunctional grieving widow/boss, expressing astonishment and conviction that such women are very unusual women, indeed.

In "Ransom for a Dead Man," Leslie Williams (Lee Grant) is a brilliant and beautiful tort lawyer who fatally shoots her boring husband and constructs an abduction scenario with a ransom request, as if he were still alive, to cover up the murder. By any standard, Leslie Williams is extraordinary, and Columbo reinforces her ego by asking with amazement, "You fly a plane?" Simply and steadily, Leslie responds with a factual, "Yes." Still in wonder, Columbo asks, "By yourself?" Again, Leslie gives a short, definitive affirmative with direct eye contact: "Yes." Still, incredulous, Columbo queries, "No kidding?!" Repeating the Lieutenant's exact wording of his exclamation in the function of a question, Leslie adjusts her tone to declare the verity of her ability to pilot a plane: "No kidding!" While closely watching the Lieutenant's browsing through her home, she flirts with the egotistical and condescending lead agent of the FBI team investigating the abduction and ransom case, allowing the LAPD, local police, to "feel perfectly free to stay" while they do their jobs. Leslie plays the damsel in distress, worrying about her missing husband, soft and demure, deferring authority and experience to him, while he returns the relationship with overly optimistic consolation to not upset the emotionally reactive woman. When Columbo remarks on her unusually calm constitution during the chaos of waiting for a ransom call, Leslie checks her demeanor and solely attributes her calm exterior to the security provided by the agent and his team. Multitasking with her brilliant mind and steady nerves, Leslie checks in with the meandering and inquisitive local detective in the next room and then volunteers to cook the men dinner as a delightful hostess with unexpected composure. Pensive, having watched Leslie answer her husband's staged call, Columbo notes to the lead agent about her emotional disconnection, "unique woman [...]. She's an exceptional woman."

She is a disliked stepmother and suspected of her father's demise. She is basically a cold, cutthroat attorney, strategic but lacking empathy: "you have no conscience," as Columbo says to her during the episode's denouement. In "Ransom for a Dead Man," Leslie is confronted by her husband's teenage daughter from a previous marriage during the night before his body is found. Since Leslie has sent her stepdaughter Margaret (Patricia Mattick) to a Swiss boarding school, she sends her a telegram regarding her father Paul's abduction, and hostage-ransom predicament. In response, Margaret arrives at their magnificent home, suggesting, "Let's drop the polite charade, Leslie. I hate you as much as you hate me, maybe more. And you don't have to play the martyred stepmother to me anymore. I've outgrown that." Clearly, Leslie has a substantial history of negligent parenting, a lack of feeling for her husband's daughter, and an absence of maternal desire entirely, which both differentiates her from conventional women and vilifies her character as apathetic toward a daughter whose father is missing. Further, Columbo is keen to recognize the futility of flirting with a woman disconnected from any need for male reassurance. In sum, her villainy is projected through her incongruently calm, controlled, and unemotional behavior during her husband's supposedly life-threatening situation; her lack of maternal responsibility or sincere caring for her stepdaughter; her motivation to murder because of ennui and self-serving greed; and her total lack of conscience for killing her husband and Margaret's father. Among the best villains, she is a mastermind of evildoing who, in fact, understands human nature and suspects early on that Columbo's bumblings are just a façade to disguise his brilliance and dupe her.

Kay Freestone (Trish Van Devere) in "Make Me a Perfect Murder" is an overlooked professional because of the "boys club" antics denying qualified, hardworking, dedicated women promotions. More specifically, her West Coast TV executive boss, Mark McAndrews, for whom she has worked tirelessly, applying her intelligence and hard work to secure his promotion and relocation to New York

City, is also her secret lover. When he learns of his promotion, McAndrews dumps her, refuses to take her with him professionally, and even denies her the job in California that he is leaving behind. As Kay is a young, conventionally lovely, feminine woman, Columbo approaches her with flattery about her appearance, a softer speaking voice, subtly patronizing her authority at the television-and-film studio, and displaying false and inflated amazement with her advanced skills and knowledge about film production technologies and processes. While her killing of MacAndrews is premeditated, it is rooted in deep personal rejection, abandonment by her partner in all senses, disappointment in what she thought was true, and fear and anger over the career devastation. Despite the compassion many viewers have expressed for her lot, Columbo comes on especially heavy. He targets her sense of culpability with speeches that criticize her deception and obligate her confession in ways that are uncharacteristically overbearing and unsympathetic to her life circumstances. He relates to her like an imperious father, doling out judgments, demands, and punishments. Finally, he takes advantage of her generally kind and professional nature with relatively intense microaggressions that ruthlessly break her down, like a bully going after the weak one.

FIGURE 20: Screenshot: Husband-murderer Leslie Williams (Lee Grant) calls Columbo out on his folksy pretense. Richard Irving (dir.), "Ransom for a Dead Man," *Columbo*, 1971. Universal Television.

In some cases, the villainous women's egos demand respect and even deference, and so he gives them the opposite, depreciation, to throw them off-guard. Leslie Williams in "Ransom for a Dead Man," Beth Chadwick in "Lady in Waiting," Viveca Scott in "Lovely But Lethal," Joan Allenby in "Sex and the Married Detective," and Vanessa Farrow in "Columbo Likes the Nightlife" (2003) exemplify unusual women that stupefy the Lieutenant. In part, his misogyny imparts lesser credibility on his position as an investigator of a homicide, suggesting a diminished ability to identify women as the potent murderers. Also, he patronizes them by suggesting they need his help or other men's guidance. He diminishes their creativity, initiative, intelligence, and business savvy by assuming there is a man behind their success. In order to maintain their façade of innocence and cooperation, the villains choose not to fight in the battle of the sexes with him. Instead, for survival, they maintain cooperation, at least for a time, until he outstays even a fake welcome.

In "Sex and the Married Detective," an attractive sex therapist Dr. Joan Allenby (Lindsay Crouse) witnesses her partner engaging in an affair and kills him in revenge. Several factors amalgamate to produce her unique villainy as well as her tactical offense in sparring with the investigator. In particular, Allenby continually uses the topic of sex therapy and sex with his wife to stump him, make him uncomfortable, and throw him off of his focus on the homicide case. She is not flirting with him, or trying to seduce him. The sex therapist clinically questions the modest detective, instigating a personal conversation with him about his intimate life with Mrs. Columbo, which appears to be awkward for him to do. Perceiving his obvious embarrassment as he blushes, stammers, loses his train of thought, and performs closed body language, Joan prods the wriggling, prudish Lieutenant into further discomfort, or, at least, seemingly so. As long as the murderous therapist holds the conviction that her tactics are effecting the Lieutenant's disorientation, she is not as guarded against the underestimated investigator. In fact, she smiles while toying with him, fooled by his façade of sexual naïveté and traditional distress with the subject of sex in conversation, especially with another woman. While some amount of sex talk may be customary among male friends, such an inquiry with an attractive, sexy woman is alien territory, though audiences do not know to what extent, if at all, the Lieutenant experiences anxiety or is just exhibiting the pretense to subdue her hyper-vigilance. Certainly, her lively banter and affability subside when she realizes that his "one more thing" implicates her as the murderer. As a woman, Joan's indulgent probing into the Lieutenant's intimacy amuses her, which is a mild form of *Schadenfreude* since she believes him to be ill-at-ease and works to further his distress. However, the great detective, well versed in psychological games of purposed duplicity, encourages her sense of superiority and power over his demeanor by enacting inadequacy on the subject of sex.

In "Rest in Peace, Mrs. Columbo," Vivian Dimitri (Helen Shaver) blames her husband's heart attack in prison on the arresting officer, Lieutenant Columbo, and on the business partner who informed on her desperate husband's racketeering and homicidal crimes, Charlie Chambers (Edward Winter). After killing Charlie out of revenge, Vivian turns her attention to the Lieutenant by planning to violently vanquish his wife, perhaps the most malicious motive of all *Columbo* villains. If Mrs. Dimitri was not irrationally seething with rage and misplaced bloodlust, audiences might be more inclined to be sympathetic toward the grieving widow. Even so, her behavior and internal monologue manifest as a deranged, obsessively vindictive character incapable of interpreting her husband's arrest and fatal heart attack in prison as anything other than a direct result of Columbo's maleficence. Unevenly and illogically, Vivian overlooks her husband's murder of an unappeasable client, victimizing him, though she vilifies the judicious Lieutenant who is simply doing his job without personal vendetta. Her reasoning is fallacious, her emotions are absurdly exaggerated for the situation, and her perception of her husband shows blind love without critical judgment. Mrs. Dimitri is a sick and dangerous woman.

Another outstanding manifestation of wickedness served by Vivian Dimitri is that she projects "duping delight," a term coined by Paul Ekman to describe micro-expressions that accompany lying: specifically an increase in eye contact and smiling. From The Body Language Project, Christopher Phillips expounds on the rationale for these micro-expressions that are inappropriate for the situation:

> One is that smiling happens more often because the liar is experiencing pleasure with the act of lying which has been extensively proven through research on psychopaths, con-men and pathological liars, the second says that a smile is in fact due to stress and embarrassment which causes a stress smile. An increase in eye contact is also explained in terms of a desire to measure the efficacy of the lie. The liar holds eye contact to watch for signals of disbelief in his counterpart to allow him to calibrate his tactics accordingly. So by this reason, the liar holds eye contact more than truth tellers in order to gauge how well his lie is being pulled over on his victim and to revel in joy as his ploy washes over his victim.
> ("Duping Delight, Eye Contact And Smiling")

Other signs of duping delights include raising one's voice pitch, speaking louder and/or faster, nodding more frequently, and an inordinate presentation of gestures. While the subtle, secret grin on villains' faces, pleased with themselves for ostensibly getting away with deception, is a typical characteristic or behavior, Vivian Dimitri cannot control her countenance at all. Furthermore, Vivian's villainy is amplified by the repeated close-up camera shots of her celebrating each act of duplicity, which advances her evil agenda of revenge. Examples include when

Mrs. Dimitri knows she has put Charlie in harm's way, after she kills Charlie, and when she shows confidence that Columbo believes her alibi.

Female Accomplices

In addition to these formidable female adversaries, several women have acted as supportive accomplices to the primary killers, both males and females, encompassing a range of relationships.

"Prescription Murder" (1968): Joan Hudson

At the start of the series, Joan Hudson (Katherine Justice) is a patient and mistress of Dr. Ray Flemming, the wife-murdering psychiatrist in "Prescription Murder." After Flemming kills his wife, Hudson assists with his cover-up by impersonating his wife as the two board an airplane bound for Mexico to celebrate the couple's ten years together. As an actress, Hudson employs her professional skills by faking an argument with Ray and storming off the plane, leaving the psychiatrist to vacation to Mexico on his own and establishing the robbery-murder cover story. Resolute in refusing to divulge information that would incriminate the man she loves, Hudson resists the rare pressure of an emotionally intense interrogatory moment, replete with accusations and threats, enacted by the otherwise calm and indirect Columbo. Convinced that Flemming loves her, too, Hudson refuses to cooperate with the Lieutenant, except to observe an enactment of her own suicide by the LAPD for Ray's benefit. Having witnessed the recovery of, presumably, Joan's body from a swimming pool after an apparent suicide, Dr. Flemming talks with Columbo about the absence of evidence the police have against him, especially now that his mistress is dead. Taking the bait Columbo offers about the great emotional loss at Joan's death, Ray admits no great loss, expresses disregard and lack of love for her, and clarifies that his relationship with her was merely instrumental to his plans. Over hearing his admission, Joan experiences a cruel awakening and crushing disappointment, which elicits her confession as his accomplice. Hudson's knowledge of Flemming murdering his wife serves to bring on the complacent, loveless therapist's arrest. More importantly, in terms of viewer–villain relationships, the trap exposes a loathsome villain who is completely narcissistic. Starting with his strategic marriage to wealthy Carol and ending with his indifference to Joan, Ray uses others to serve his intentions with no conscience, ethical boundaries, or emotional loyalty.

"Suitable for Framing" (1971): Tracy O'Connor

Rosanna Huffman plays Tracy O'Connor, an aspiring artist who acts as accomplice to art collector and critic Dale Kingston (Ross Martin) in "Suitable for Framing." Huffman's help is risky and gruesome. After Kingston kills his uncle for his art collection, she stays with his uncle's dead body to keep it warm, obscuring the time of death. Firing a shot for the security personnel to hear while Kingston makes a dramatic appearance attending an art show, Huffman secures his alibi. Unfortunately for her, Kingston eliminates her in an "auto accident" as a loose end, reneging on his promises to her of mentorship and patronage. Huffman's greatest weakness is her career ambition through illegitimate channels, clouding her judgment, morality, and decency for an advantage. Ultimately, her worst judgment is in thinking Kingston is loyal and a man of his word.

"Dagger of the Mind" (1972): Lilian Stanhope

In "Dagger of the Mind," married Lilian Stanhope (Honor Blackman) had been playing the part of a doting love interest on the sly with her and her husband's career benefactor, Sir Roger Havisham (John Williams), until he realizes that she has just been acting. Depending on Havisham's financial backing of their London play, Shakespeare's *Macbeth*, Lilian Stanhope and Nicholas Frame (Richard Basehart) are confronted by Havisham, who intends to rescind his funding and close the play before it has opened. During a physical scuffle between the men, Lilian unintentionally kills Havisham by throwing a cold cream jar at his head to disrupt the fight. In doing so, her husband and co-star assumes the supporting role as accomplice to her manslaughter. However, when Frame takes up the part of primary murderer in killing the blackmailing butler (Wilfrid Hyde-White), Stanhope becomes the accomplice to the staged suicide. Maintaining a calm exterior with the authorities, despite Columbo's recurring inconveniences, Lilian weathers the police presence like a pro. However, undercutting their mutual accompliceship, Nicky Frame degrades mentally into a madness that parallels Shakespeare's Macbeth. To which, Lilian sobs in desperation, admitting that Havisham's death was an accident. Neither Lilian nor Nicholas are monstrously villainous; they are like "children," as Stanhope remarks about actors. They are singular in their vision to return to the stage in glory and scheme with a charade to gain the funding needed to do so. However, the moment things change is when Nicholas is convinced that the only way to deal with a blackmailer who knows their secret is to kill him. This is when Frame's childishness becomes madness and villainy, while Lilian's efforts to cover up the fake suicide-murder is tarnished with maleficent self-interest.

"A Deadly State of Mind" (1975): Nadia Donner

In "A Deadly State of Mind," Nadia Donner (Leslie Ann Warren) agrees to cover up the accidental death of her abusive husband by her lover and psychiatrist-hypnotherapist Marcus Collier (George Hamilton). Acting against her better judgment, the new widow is complicit in backing her lover's alibi, though her unstable nervous condition makes her unreliable. As described in the previous chapter, Collier influences her through hypnotic suggestion, convincing her that she wants to go swimming by jumping off of a high-rise balcony to the pool on the ground, thereby killing herself. As Nadia is irresolute, attention-dependent, and highly impressionable, Marcus takes advantage of her weaknesses and fears to protect his career and life. Visibly neurotic, Nadia wants to please Marcus, but she is not accomplice material; she is a terrible liar. Hardly villainous, Nadia meets a sad fate, further vilifying the great manipulator, Collier.

"A Trace of Murder" (1997): Cathleen Calvert

Cathleen Calvert (Shera Danese) in "A Trace of Murder" co-conspires with her lover, Patrick Kinsley (David Rasche), to eliminate her husband Clifford (Barry Corbin) and the restrictive terms of their prenuptial agreement. Rather than killing her husband, which would make them the prime suspects, their plan involves her lover killing a man suing her husband. In turn, Clifford would be the most likely suspect with a strong motive for murder in the criminal investigation. Cathleen plants evidence on her husband, and the pair frame him with the murder. With her husband in jail, Cathleen would be free to live with her lover in financial security. Cathleen's contribution as an accomplice to murder is completely nonviolent and relatively negligible. Her culpability lies in shifting the blame for the murder from her killer-lover to her innocent husband. Her villainy is her apathy for her husband's fate. Should the schemers have succeeded, Clifford would have lived the rest of his life in prison for a murder he did not commit.

"Columbo Cries Wolf" (1990): Tina, Chateau Model/Nymph

"Columbo Cries Wolf" is set on the grounds of a *Playboy* mansion type of chateau for the men's magazine called *Bachelor's World*, co-owned by Dian Hunter (Deirdre Hall) and the cavalier rogue and photographer Sean Brantley (Ian Buchanan). Dian is tired of Sean's wasteful spending on the chateau, the models living there, and expensive parties that drain the profits from the partnership. After Dian's publicity stunt disappearance, which she planned with her business partner, she is even more determined to sell her majority share of the magazine at the newly inflated price to a media mogul. However, Sean refuses to give up his control of the company. Breaking Dian's neck is his means to retaining his part of the empire as well as hers. To cover up his being the last to see Dian alive, Sean asks his latest "nymph of the month," Tina (Rebecca Staab), to take Dian's car, wave to the security cameras, and leave the chateau premises disguised as Dian. Orchestrated by Sean, Tina doesn't realize she is playing the accomplice to Dian's real murder. Her participation is minor and, ultimately, ineffectual since Columbo recognizes her immediately from the security camera's video. In other words, her participation as an accomplice is inadvertent and without violence or harm. Rather, it speaks to Sean's manipulation and motivation to maintain his extravagant existence at whatever cost of human life.

"Death Hits the Jackpot" (1991): Nancy Brower

This episode represents the murder of a lottery winner, Freddy (Gary Kroeger), for profit by his conniving, soon-to-be-divorced wife and his devious uncle, who are having an affair behind his back. Predicated on some notion of love or lust, Nancy (Jamie Rose) and Leon Lamarr (Rip Torn) scheme to deny Freddy his winnings, though Freddy wants to deny his soon to be ex-wife Nancy any part of the winnings as well. As accomplice, Nancy performs several functions: setting up a fake phone call that gives Leon an alibi, maintaining Leon's secret about his murdering Freddy, and supporting Leon's claim to the lottery winnings. Without Nancy, this scheme would not work, and, without Leon, Nancy would not benefit either. They need each other, but, under the pressure of the investigation, answering all of Columbo's questions, and retelling their stories, their relationship foundation—based on lies and deceit in the first order of their affair—crumbles, resulting in their turning on each other. Perhaps the lesson here is that extramarital affairs do not produce strong, healthy and mutually supportive relationships that can withstand imposed stress.

"Columbo Likes the Nightlife" (2003): Vanessa Farrow

Vanessa Farrow (Jennifer Sky) is the primary, though accidental, murderer of her ex-husband in "Columbo Likes the Nightlife." Fearing mob retribution, she and her boyfriend, nightclub owner Justin Price (Matthew Rhys) hide the body. Witnessing this transaction with photographs as evidence, a lascivious gossip journalist blackmails the two. For the second murder of this blackmailer, Vanessa serves as an accomplice to Justin, who extinguishes the threat in a staged suicide. Though an actress by trade, Vanessa makes a nervous suspect, failing to discourage the Lieutenant's investigation. Until Columbo finds the corpse of Vanessa's mobster ex-husband under the glass dance floor of Price's club, the actress is highly anxious, particularly about the Lieutenant's enduring inquiries. Neither murderous nor an effective accomplice, Vanessa made choices to marry and divorce a mob man, likely enjoying the power and creature comforts the lifestyle afforded her, a beautiful but struggling and little known actress. However, Price and Farrow hang in together until the corpse can no longer be denied.

"All in the Game" (1993): Lisa Martin

In "All in the Game," Lauren Staton (Faye Dunaway) and her daughter Lisa Martin (Claudia Christian) are charmed and swindled by the same financial opportunist-playboy, Nick Franco (Armando Pucci). In fact, when Lisa promises to tell her wealthy mother that he has been dating both of them simultaneously, Franco cuts her cheek, threatening to kill her if she disrupts his wedding plans with Staton. However, mother and daughter band together with Lauren murdering Franco and Lisa helping with the cover-up, which was purportedly caused by a burglar at his apartment. While Lauren's daughter is highly motivated as a part injured-party seeking revenge, her involvement is to collaborate with her mother, who resolutely kills the threatening, opportunistic scoundrel. Their familial bond successfully delivers the murderer and accomplice relationship until the end of the episode.

In genuine love, Staton's commitment as a mother to protect her daughter from the antagonistic Franco as well as from incarceration is a unique element and consequence of murderer–accomplice relationships in *Columbo*. They protect each other, with Lauren taking full responsibility for the victim's death, sparing her daughter. In several cases, murderers fail to protect their accomplices, attempt to frame them, or kill them outright. Their knowledge and assistance are critical but also threatening to the killer's fear of getting caught. In some cases, these female accomplices protect and support their male lovers who use them without the bonds of genuine love. As long as they are useful in protecting their innocence, the murderers let them live. In "Columbo Cries Wolf," the killer is caught too soon after the accomplice's attempt to impersonate the victim. So, we won't know how their depraved relationship might have played out. All in all, the women protecting their killer lovers are extensions of women in supportive, nurturing, and self-less roles for the benefit of others. *Columbo* shows how their self-sacrifice and dependence on these murderers is a dead end.

Columbo Plays the Underestimating, Traditional Male Chauvinist

"Lovely But Lethal" (1973)

Viveca Scott (Vera Miles) runs Beauty Mark, Inc., a cosmetics company whose products are in every woman's home. With sales dropping, she's counting on a miraculous new beauty cream created by her chief chemist to boost sales and overtake her rival, David Lang, who is charmingly played by Vincent Price. However, the chemist's assistant (Martin Sheen) steals the formula. Scott attempts to negotiate with him but, in a rage, knocks him over the head with a heavy microscope, killing him.

As Columbo investigates the murder of a chemist recently employed by Beauty Mark, Inc., he meets the lovely founder of the cosmetic empire, and immediately reduces her role to beauty object—the face on the products made by this "lady's business." After crime scene observation and some background research about the deceased with the Human Resources department, the detective arrives at a photo shoot for a lipstick ad, bumbling around aimlessly in the backdrop of the studio. With his typical overuse of apologies, Columbo interrupts the photographer's work, which company founder Viveca Scott (Vera Miles) is supervising: "I must have gone in the wrong way. I'm sorry." When he has failed to appropriate the target's full attention, he affects more disorientation and calls out, "Miss Scott, right?" in a harangue that incontestably interfers with the photographer, models, and Scott. Again, he piles on the social pleasantries: "I'm sorry. Forgive me. I didn't mean to intrude." All the while, Columbo amicably but unstoppably advances toward Scott with an assault of praise about the studio, the office building, her empire, and her role in his personal hygiene. Annoyed, Scott asks, "Do I know you?" Columbo responds with exceeding and unsophisticated adoration of Scott's status as the deserving, long-time reigning queen of beauty: "You don't know me, ma'am, but I sure know you. Every time I shave, there ya are. It's a pleasure." Post women's civil rights movement, Columbo uses an old-fashioned choice of "Miss Scott," as opposed to "Ms. Scott," to refer to her unmarried status, thereby negating her identity as professional mogul. Further, he commits a social indiscretion by being too familiar with the cosmetic queen, inviting himself into her private affairs as a total stranger. These gestures begin to establish a particular type of simple-minded inspector, one who is prone to superficial celebrity worship and who has traditional, male chauvinistic views, speech, and behaviors. Later in the episode, Scott indicts him by challenging his "masculine double standards."

Projecting an intellectually dull fanatic, Columbo overwhelms the cosmetics founder/killer with inappropriate personal drama at the workplace, forcing her off-guard before presenting his police identification and his raison d'etre.

With a quick mention of her own office staff having sent him to her, Columbo validates his presence in the private photo session. With a conspicuous whisper and invasion of her personal space, the Lieutenant leans in close to the glamorous woman, positing a fake command-question, "Do you have a minute?" as if Scott really has a choice to speak with him or not, and as if he was confiding in a close associate. With his head down, but looking up into her face, Columbo projects the humble civil servant as he announces the murder of one of Scott's employees. Though she describes the dead chemist/her former lover/and blackmailing industrial thief as merely an insignificant acquaintance, she properly expresses sympathy in a diminutive fashion, pitying the "nice young man's," and the "poor boy's" demise.

Relaying a story about having been prevented from accessing a chemistry laboratory to ask about the victim, the detective emphasizes his astonishment at the high level of security in a cosmetics company: "You know, they wouldn't let me in, like Fort Knox around here. I had no idea you had such top secrets in a nice lady's business like this." The Lieutenant's comment projects a naïve simpleton, who discovers for the first time the high level of competitiveness in the beauty business, the potential threats of espionage regarding trade secrets, and the extreme security measures taken to protect them. Simultaneously, Columbo projects unfamiliarity with both the magnitude of the cosmetics industry's procedures and operations as well as Scott's market-immersed status in a patronizingly, sexist manner that secures his persona as an "old school good ole boy" stereotype. In effect, Columbo constructs himself to be less threatening to Scott because his traditional and worshipful perspective may prevent him from seeing her as a likely suspect. In turn, Scott merrily dials the telephone while reassuring him of his importance at her domain: "I can fix that, Lieutenant." Confident that the admiring and paternalistic Columbo won't discover any evidence against her, she decrees, "You can go anywhere you want, ask anything you want. We have no secrets from the police." In granting Columbo full access to all of the company's facilities and personnel, Scott portrays the socially expected behavior of an accommodating, feminine host to his traditional male persona. However, she does so while exercising her authority as Beauty Mark, Inc.'s head executive. In response, the detective covertly praises Scott for her compliance to his will as a sign of her predictably good character, which he somehow knows omnisciently—another move to control an acquiescent "lady" that quashes the real woman with her own volitions and power. Within the context of the women's movement for work opportunities and equal pay, the tension is palpable, watching the beauty giant play the hostess role at her own business with a condescending, less successful, and intrusive man: her fake, public smile, her rigidly upright posture, her uncharacteristically submissive demeanor, and her controlled, short sentences spoken with a sales associate lift that reassures one that the customer is always right.

Further ingraining his relationship of over-familiarity with the queen of glamor, Columbo stands too close to the suspect, an act that may, in other circumstances, justifiably result in a backwards step from her or a demand for him to step back. Transgressing social boundaries of personal space as practiced by Americans, Columbo strategically creates tension and subtle dominance. Further, he belittles her accomplishments, high social status, and her womanhood with the following remarks as a patriarch: "You know, I got to tell you honestly. I feel like I know you for 100 years. I feel like you're a member of the family. I mean you're like, like a Lydia E. Pinkham." Dumbfounded by the unflattering age implication and wild comparison, Scott stutters utterances, stalling to develop a response to this nonsense. With a look of distaste, she digests the analogy he makes to a famous "quack": "an iconic concocter and commercially successful marketer of herbal-alcoholic 'women's tonics' meant to relieve menstrual and menopausal pains" during the mid to late 1800s (Holbrook 63). After some stammering, Scott swallows the discrediting implications. Managing a forced smile and a flustered "Oh, well, thank you," Scott simulates appreciation for the ignorant reference, thought to be meant mistakenly as a compliment. With a knowing smile and direct eye contact with Scott, the Lieutenant enjoys the impact of his offenses, realizing that her guilt is what prevents her from fittingly rebuking him for the affront. However, from Scott's point of view, she has succeeded in projecting a persona of a woman unlikely to commit murder. This certitude is evident in her newly relaxed composure and friendly concern about the police Lieutenant wasting his time investigating the murder at her facility.

Stripping away that confidence, the Lieutenant walks away and unexpectedly returns to share an important fact from the crime scene investigation. Indirectly implying her possible culpability, Columbo plays a tactical ambush, inductively stating his hypothesis: "It might not have been a murderer. I think the killer was a woman." Again, the gender issue emerges in the detective's language use, distinguishing between a woman who kills and a typical murderer, presumed here to be a male. Divulging crime scene evidence of a "doodle" on a television magazine made with a woman's black eyebrow pencil, the Lieutenant identifies the magazine on which she proposed dollar amounts to satiate the blackmailing victim (Martin Sheen) who stole the formula for a "miracle" wrinkle cream from their lab to sell to the highest bidder. Such evidence instantiates a motive for killing him. Now startled by this incriminating find, the gorgeous unnatural redhead listens impatiently to the details Columbo puts forth, but not without disruptions—a cough, waiting for a sneeze, or the like—prompting him to expediently finish his

FIGURE 21: Screenshot: Viveca Scott (Vera Miles) as the glamorous beauty mogul and killer stifles the urge to dismiss the insulting working-class detective who just admits the cosmetic industry has "come a long way since hair curlers and face grease." Jeannot Szwarc (dir.), "Lovely but Lethal," *Columbo*, 1973. Universal Television.

point. Asserting some expertise on women using eyebrow pencils to write notations, Columbo refers to his wife doing so when writing grocery lists, being "the only pencils she can find in her purse." He accusingly points to Scott's purse, which happens to hold the incriminating jar of miracle cream. By associating the same practice of using the makeup stick as a writing utensil, Columbo downgrades the glamorous CEO of her own cosmetics empire to the status of a domestic maven. *Columbo* fans know that his mysterious but, certainly, beloved Mrs. Columbo supplies him with a pencil every morning. In turn, she has no need to use an eyebrow pencil with which to write. Knowing his character's devotion to his wife from other episodes, audiences know that he acknowledges his wife's minor quirks but isn't critical of them. Nonetheless, Scott recognizes the offensive implication and diverts the insinuated attack on her alibi by informing him that "redheads don't wear black eyebrow pencil." At this scene's end, Columbo plays perplexed about this cosmetic norm, and Scott smiles in duping delight.

In particular, this approach is demonstrated during multiple interviews with witnesses in "Greenhouse Jungle" (1972). One such example is with the murder victim's former secretary and alleged lover, Gloria West (Arlene Martell). Obviously nervous and self-conscious with the policeman, Gloria is defensive about offering information that would fuel gossip about the deceased Tony (Bradford Dillman). To quell her worries, Columbo qualifies his intentions: "Miss West, I'm not here to hurt you, and I believe everything that you tell me. I just think you can help me, and I'd appreciate it if you would cooperate." During a subsequent interview, the deceased widow Kathy Goodland (Sandra Smith) indignantly defends her continued affair with her gold-digging boy toy, Ken Nichols (William Smith). Upon the detective's approaching her sailboat at a marina, Kathy assumes the worst from Columbo when she demands, "Just what are you trying to imply?" Embarking on the vessel with purpose, Kathy reproaches the detective again with a rhetorical question, "You still don't approve of my lifestyle, do you? I told you before; I really don't care what you think." Emerging from the boat's cabin below deck, Ken asks, "Where did he come from?" With heavy sarcasm, Kathy retorts, "Homicide, of course. Oh, they handle morals now. He's objecting to places I go." To rectify Kathy's misunderstanding, Columbo shakes his head and directly explains, "No, ma'am. That's not true." In his effort to clarify a few "little things," the detective asks about her whereabouts during the time of her husband's murder. Reactively, she pronounces her long drive with Ken and rebuffs what she assumes is his petty moral disapproval.

However, the investigator surprises her by presenting the opposite of her presumptions: "You know, Mrs. Goodland. You are a very unusual person. You're not a hypocrite, and I won't be bothering you anymore with these things." Taking the wind out of her defensive sails, so to speak, Columbo removes any doubt that he judges her negatively, neither for her romantic choices nor her forthrightness about them. In fact, he offers high praise for her integrity, which has helped him on the murder case; after all, doing his job is what concerns him. Using his substantial understanding of typical human behavior as well as deviations from it, Columbo identifies suspects and dismisses innocent associates of the murder victims. Once he recognizes a witness's innocence, Columbo shifts from his contrived façade of antipotency to his authentic character of astute investigator. Indeed, his plain questions and artless demeanor with witnesses allow him to overcome their guardedness, facilitate their cooperation, and advance the murder investigation.

The following Part 2 and chapters describe and codify Columbo's rhetoric of inquiry.

PART 2

COLUMBO'S METHOD OF INVESTIGATION

7

Crime Scene Investigation and Ratiocination

Before delving into his manner of questioning, it is useful to understand how Columbo analyzes crime scenes, identifies inconsistencies, interprets them, and associates his theories with motives, cover-ups, and suspects. Like Auguste Dupin and Sherlock Holmes before him, the Lieutenant engages in ratiocination, but clearly relies on abductive reasoning in his investigative method more than his predecessors. More specifically, abductive reasoning is "a form of logic based on observation, hypothesis, and confirmation [...] [requiring] the use of background knowledge to draw conclusions. Therefore, cultural context and beliefs become part of the interpretive process [of clues]" (Weiss iv). Recognizing Lieutenant Columbo's abductive prowess, Sue Trumbull posits that much of his interpretation of crime scene clues involves his sense of human nature—what makes sense or doesn't make sense, particularly in the presence of contradictory factors. The detective does not have a degree in deviant behavior or cognitive behavioral psychology, or forensic psychology. He has twenty-plus years of experience carefully observing people, paying attention to the details of each case: the unexpected elements, the variety of motives for committing murders, and the qualities underlying interaction with guilty suspects. For the last point, he has interviewed countless suspects who cover up their crimes, frame others, feign obliviousness of the implications, construct façades of ignorance and unfamiliarity with the victims, and participate in cooperative and, sometimes, collaborative investigations. As a matter of course, Columbo often claims to have identified the killer before any evidence is discovered, even upon first meeting the suspect. His process of investigation shapes his pretense of antipotency as does it his strategy of questioning, inclusion of the suspect in the investigation, timing of his false exits, and pace of projecting inferences from the evidentiary clues.

In "Requiem for a Falling Star," the detective performs the "doting fan" approach to a celebrated actress and suspect who, in turn, entertains his intrusions in a good-natured manner. Nora Chandler (Anne Baxter) is being blackmailed by her estranged husband Jerry Parks, who is also a gossip columnist. He holds an unflattering secret about her past and blackmails her with using it if she does not give him a lump of money. In the meantime, Jerry has also been romancing Nora's secretary for continued access to the star's secrets. In desperation, Nora puts an explosive device in the blackmailer's car. Inopportunely, it is the secretary driving it; she is killed by mistake. Unable to establish any motive for the woman's murder, Columbo pursues suspects close to her such as the victim's lover, Parks, who has an alibi, and her employer, Nora, who seems to have an alibi as well. Doting on Nora as an ostensible fan of the career actress, and involving his wife, an even bigger fan, via telephone, Columbo soothes the guilty suspect with unprofessional expressions of fondness as distraction.

While Nora is on the sound stage, enacting her role as a fictional detective, the Lieutenant approaches a gentle-mannered, male Assistant Producer. In a nonthreatening, working-man-to-working-man sort of way, Columbo inquires

FIGURE 22: Screenshot: Once again, Columbo is suffocating the celebrity suspect Nora Chandler (Anne Baxter) with exaggerated and unprofessional attention, which stresses the actress's overly polite demeanor with the investigating Lieutenant. Richard Quine (dir.), "Requiem for a Falling Star," *Columbo*, 1973. Universal Television.

about the contents of Nora's thermos, implying that liquor is likely in it. In a generalized presumption about actors taking the edge off with spirits, Columbo acts the part of a huge fan of Nora's, intending no criticism by the question. Hooking onto the bait, the set assistant defends Nora's honor by clarifying how she is not a heavy drinker at all. In fact, despite the immediate circumstance of just having given her a swig, the assistant emphatically argues that he only gives her this type of drink on the rare occasions when she feels particularly under pressure. Evidenced by her heavy perspiration and frenetic movements, Nora's uncharacteristically high stress level becomes apparent to Columbo. With a subdued and sly grin of delight at this discovery, Columbo learns how to read her uncharacteristic signs of anxiety. However, atypical apprehension is likely indicative of human nature under investigation. Otherwise, what else would jolt Nora out of her usual calm, controlled demeanor? With the certitude of having witnessed Nora place a bomb in her husband's car and her assistant mistakenly dying in the explosion, audiences know that Nora's nervous demeanor is caused by her culpability in the presence of the police detective.

Another example of the Lieutenant's abductive reasoning is at the crime scene of the final episode "Columbo Likes the Nightlife." Columbo amusingly, disgustingly, and closely examines the body of the apparent suicide victim, having hanged himself by jumping from his third-story apartment. The investigator leans close into the corpse's face to study and sniff the body's marred but well-groomed condition, transgressing the taboo of the abject dead body, which often triggers disgust and horror. Encouraging a slightly sickened and resistant police officer to do the same, Columbo receives confirmation of his observation while also mentoring a good cop. Through close examination, the detective gains knowledge about the victim's condition prior to his falling from the third-story apartment. Arguing from probability, the Lieutenant articulates the incongruity of deliberately jumping out of an apartment window just after elaborately grooming oneself. More specifically, the alleged suicide victim would know that the blood splatter and body mutilation from hitting the pavement would only camouflage his cleaning, trimming, and deodorizing efforts. In fact, it does, save for the Lieutenant's willingness to get his hands dirty. Clear to Columbo, these incongruities, coupled with common sense, suggest that the suicide is staged.

Another sample of such incongruity is in "Suitable for Framing" when the Lieutenant queries Dale Kingston (Ross Martin) about the murder of his uncle and theft of valuable art pieces. The murderous nephew casts blame on his uncle's wealthy ex-wife who never cared for art. As an art critic and collector, Kingston considered the original paintings to be priceless as well as worth a great deal monetarily in terms of an insurance claim. In contrast, his ex-wife was bored by the art world, as Columbo discovers during an interview visit to her home. Without financial need to sell stolen art nor the notable interest in collecting art, the ex-wife is an illogical choice as a suspect, since she possesses no discernible motive for this type of crime. The lover of art, by contrast, desires the paintings as well as the insurance payout for them. Therefore, Kingston's avoidance of admitting such obvious likelihoods signal faux denial of the crime, namely, a failed attempt to displace guilt on another.

A particularly revealing example of Columbo's perception of minute details and drawing meaningful inconsistencies from them is in the series' first feature-film pilot: "Prescription Murder." While investigating the wife's recent murder in the master bedroom of the luxury apartment she shared with her husband, Columbo observes the husband arriving home after a trip out of country without calling out to his wife, "Honey, you here?" His argument is that he, himself, would have called out to his wife if he were returning after days away. The detective interprets this omission through "common sense" or in light of general tendencies, "human nature," within a purportedly strong marriage. After all, the couple projects happiness during an anniversary party several nights before. Intuitively, Columbo surmises that the psychiatrist-husband-murderer's omitted greeting to his spouse, first, suggests that their relationship is not as happy as he professes, and/or he may already know she is dead. The detective rationally moves from the observation stage to the hypothesis stage in his probabilistic interpretation of behaviors, present and absent. Columbo's observations at crime scenes and among suspect and witness interactions are vital to a solid foundation of effective rhetorical inquiry and detection process.

8

The Working Cop's Habit of Asking Questions: A Rhetoric of Inquiry

LT COLUMBO: *Hey, I'm sorry. I'm making a pest of myself.*
KEN FRANKLIN: *Naw! [sarcastically]*
LT COLUMBO: *Yes, yes, I am! I know, it's because I keep asking these questions, but I'll tell ya, I can't help myself. It's a habit.*
(*Columbo*: "Murder by the Book" 1971)

LT. COLUMBO: *Can I ask you something?*
LAURA STATON: *Why do you ask if you could ask? You're gonna do it anyway.*
(Faye Dunaway, *Columbo*: "It's All in the Game" 1993)

As the show *Columbo* is not representative of the action-adventure genre, the events of each murder investigation are objective-driven inquiries to discover relevant crime facts and victim details such as his or her failures or scores, conflicting relationships, financial history or security, romantic affairs, vendettas, and the like. Disguised as innocuous questions within informal conversations, the investigator's inquiries present less as official police business and more as friendly interest in the case's specifics and the suspect's accomplishments. Despite his powers of observation, tactical persona, and sound reasoning, Columbo's method of detection relies heavily upon the implementation of various types of questions to advance the rhetorical actions of the investigation (hypotheses, leads, conclusions, traps, arrests, etc.). With every question, Columbo serves a rhetorical function that goes beyond eliciting specific information not only to solve the puzzle. In addition, he makes tactical moves to provoke certain emotions, instills false security in the suspects so they let their guards down against his investigation, and prompts reactive action to real and fake leads in the case. His indirect style of conversation manifests a nonthreatening persona and encourages relationships with the suspects. Of course, his designs are specific to each interview and each suspect. Hence, I describe his method as rhetorical inquiry. The following section illustrates how questions are powerful, communicative, and relational acts.

Columbo's *Leading and Misleading Questions in Rhetorical Inquiry*

Many make the mistake of assuming that those issuing declarative statements, telling others what to do, are always in the powerful subject positions. On the contrary, others, like Columbo, recognize the directive, persuasive, and relationship-building powers that stem from questions phrased that are appropriate to the situation, audience, purpose, and delivered at exactly the right time (*kairos* being the Ancient Greek rhetoricians' term addressing the opportune time for a rhetorical act). The rhetoric of asking purpose-directed questions is an active communicative act, not a passive one. Certainly unlike silence, complicity, or plasticity in form, questions are assertive and steer the exchange with others. Most pertinent here is that questions within the information-gathering interviews are a detective's stock and trade with secretive villains. In fact, asking the right questions to the right persons has valuable applications, as outlined by the nonprofit organization of persuasion-focused philosophers, ChangingMinds.org:

> Questions provide *control* because they put the asker in charge of the conversation, exerting social obligation to *listen* and to *respond* with technical or personal *information* from which the asker can learn. Especially if one is careful with the phrasing and timing of questions, one can exhibit interest in the other, prompting them to disclose pertinent background details to facilitate *bonding* and the development of *persuasive tactics*.
> ("The Power of Questions")

In application, the Lieutenant's barrage of questions suspends the suspects in his presence, interrupting their lives, requiring them to listen and respond, holding them to their promises of assistance during the investigation. Even if he noncoercively inquires, the culprits know they have no choice but to play along with the Lieutenant in an excruciating psychological contest of endurance and hyper-vigilant self-censure. In the following section, numerous question tactics are identified and discussed in terms of their role in the Lieutenant's investigative method.

Asking questions is a fundamental prerequisite for uncovering information and effecting subtle persuasion. Several theories exist, projecting taxonomies of types of questions, purposes of questions, and functions of questions within various career, civic, and domestic contexts. The Lieutenant demonstrates the power of asking questions. From the independent scholars at ChangingMinds.org, a range of question types are discussed in terms of how they can deliberately shape one's relationship with others and pursue persuasion.

Open Questions are "for long and detailed answers" that are more successful when suspects are not censuring their illuminating stories or explanations. Open questions gather general information and initiate conversation. With the cavalier and curious villains, Columbo commences his relationship with open-style questions, such as "I'm Lieutenant Columbo of the LAPD. And you are?"

Clear, Closed Questions "seek short, simple, and unambiguous answers" that may reveal a minute fact or clue to the crime. "Where were you at 7pm last night?" "Were you close to the victim?" "Did you know he wasn't well?"

Action Requests are "questions that influence for action," such as obligating a suspect to assist in an investigation: "Would you help me? It would be an honor."

Echo Questions "repeat what they say as a question," showing your attention to their words and gaining clarification or confirmation, if needed. An example is when the Lieutenant reiterates, "Are you telling me that [...]?" Echo questions operate like declarative statements, but in the form of interrogatives. In doing so, the speaker emphasizes surprise in terms of the information offered, and disbelief with either the verity of the news or the exceptional nature of the circumstances conveyed. If disingenuously asked, the speaker may be constructing an effect of *aporia*, manipulating the listener to see him as naïve, inexperienced, unsophisticated, unformidable—antipotent, even, in his role.

Provocative Rider Questions "wind them up with a secondary question" after giving an innocuous first question that has put suspects at ease. Columbo's first sentence in "Negative Reaction" bears hyperbole in self-deprecation, which relieves the suspect of their initial guardedness towards the Lieutenant. Then, suddenly, Columbo's focus shifts to questioning a contradiction of action by the framed and murdered victim. Analyzing the sequence of events with the double-murderer Galesko (Dick Van Dyke), Columbo projects puzzlement over the incongruity of newly released ex-con Deschler wasting what little money he has on expensive taxi cab rides when he ends up renting a car. As Deschler's act of renting a car after undoubtedly spending a fair sum on cab fares appears nonsensical and impractical for his situation, Columbo challenges Galesko hypothetically with that improbability so that he can watch the lying, opportunistic killer argue against his interpretation of incongruity. If successful, Galesko achieves his double aim: to succeed in the framing of Deschler, and to avoid being brought to justice for his wife's murder; if unsuccessful, the detective looks elsewhere for the real suspect. The logical progression is for Columbo to seek another suspect for the woman's murder—the suspect with the certitude and directing the blame elsewhere. Therefore, in two sentences, a speaker moves from general comment or side note to a surprising and alarming interrogation that implicates the other speaker in the conversation.

Rhetorical Questions: "Questions without answers" or with obviously known answers, which speakers do not expect an answer to, nor do listeners expect to say, for instance: "That must have taken a lot of courage?" While the courage to perform the action in question is certainly required and not doubted or debated, the speaker emphasizes the point about the doer's outstanding courage. Further, that courage may surpass what the speaker thinks he or she would be capable of calling forth in a like situation. Finally, some speakers use the rhetorical question for the heroification of a courageous subject and the simultaneous devaluation of themselves.

Elenchus *and* Aporia *are Translations from the Greek*

Socratic Questioning is a method of questioning introduced by Socrates to elicit learning (from students, or other dialoging subjects). Both Socrates' and Columbo's primary mode of interaction concerns a series or system of purpose-driven questions (a rhetoric of inquiry) with necessary participants in a dialogue toward truth-construction (dialectic). Further, the philosopher-teacher and the philosopher-detective exhibit themselves similarly, both with traits of "an unkempt appearance" and "distracted behavior" (Madigan). While there are some overlaps in terms of Columbo's use of inquiry to engage suspects in cooperation to discover the killer, the investigator's application differs from the teacher's. The Socratic approach depends on the teacher refusing to just give students the answers. Socrates would adopt a persona of intelligent ignorance by responding to the students' questions with counter-questions that challenge overgeneralized applications of definitions, conditions, and circumstances of concepts. In turn, Socrates would facilitate male students' learning by asking questions that challenged what they knew and how they knew it. As Yip Mei Loh explicates in a reading of Plato's *Theaetetus*, Socrates analogizes his role as an educator to that of the goddess Artemis as a *maeutik* ("midwife"). His "techne," or practice of knowledge-seeking, is not to "procreate" wisdom (*episteme*, knowledge, facts) but to enable his students "to be pregnant in their minds and bear spiritual works" (404). In fact, Socrates, as written about by Plato, requests that Theaetetus not expose his method of teaching, in part to learn more with them, and in part to enable his students to be fertile in their intellectual explorations of truths. Moreover, he attentively listens to arguments made by students and identifies errors in logic, mistaken notions about subject particulars, exceptions to accepted general rules, fallacious logic (faulty reasoning to argue or make one's case), assumed premises (preconceived assumptions about a subject one is studying), and faulty conclusions that disprove their positions (a technique called *elenchus*).

In "The Socratic Elenchus," Gregory Vlastos differentiates Socrates' use of "indirect elenchus" from a philosophical method known as "standard elenchus." While we established that indirect *elenchus* is practiced by Socrates with his students, dismantling their arguments without offering counterarguments, standard *elenchus* aims "to establish the truth or falsehood of any particular thesis," which is a principle philosophical method used by Socrates in Plato's early works, the dialogues (711). Well-practiced in both, Socrates implements indirect *elenchus* to stimulate intellectual enlightenment, and standard *elenchus* to argue a point of truth or knowledge. The paradox of Socrates' mentoring his students' philosophical reasoning is that experience of each lesson typically culminates in their being in a state of *aporia*—puzzlement, impasse, doubt, or uncertainty. Designed to express and produce *aporia*, Socrates illustrates fallacious reasoning and inconsistencies that challenge the student to judge and analyze the issue for themselves instead of relying on the product of standard *elenchus*, an accepted truth (Cohen 163). Indeed, the lesson recognizes that philosophical knowing is often elusive, due to the many particulars that resist the universalization of any tenet. For example, *sophrosyne* is arguably a virtue in a speaker and a useful tactic for making appeals to socially superior individuals. However, the Socratic dialogue regarding *sophrosyne* illustrates that temperance, reserve, and humility are not always the best characteristics to call upon: in war, for instance, when one side wants to intimidate the other. Many situational factors are variants that undermine absolute knowledge of something being true in all circumstances. Within public political disputation, Socrates may initially have used indirect *elenchus* to unravel another speaker's fallacious reasoning, but then enacted standard *elenchus* to make his arguments clearly, persuasively, and truthfully.

In many ways, the policeman is in the position of the Socratic student, eagerly journeying to the truth behind the mystery of the crime. The suspects are the ones who possess the awful secret of their crimes and refuse to grant that insight to the detective. Their objective is to maintain the detective's inaccessibility to definitive, condemning evidence against them, that is, to maintain their perceived innocence. However, the villains are not teachers of Columbo; they are his adversaries who self-preservingly perpetuate the Lieutenant's *aporia* regarding their crimes. During conversations with the suspects, Columbo may be suspicious of a character but he will not indicate it, instead pretending to be without a clue, or feigning suspicion of another character of the murder. Since we do not have insight to his thoughts, only his actions, he withholds his hypotheses or suspicions from the resistant villains and, in turn, to viewers as well. While audiences have witnessed the crime in the opening scene of each episode, and know who committed the crime, they do not know what the detective thinks, producing a degree of *aporia* in audience and villain alike. Put another way, the show creates what storytellers call suspense for how the investigator discovers the truth, which is *Columbo's* ultimate objective.

Fake Questions: Ask but Don't Tell

A fake question is a category of inquiry in which the asker already knows the answers, but nevertheless wants to assess what others know and think, or indeed whether they are speaking the truth. Fake questioners facilitate reactions of confirmation, agreement, compliance, surprise, dishonesty, disturbance, resistance, or the like. Accordingly, the asker can confirm or gauge the other's perceptions of and feelings toward the subject. In "Fade in to Murder," William Shatner's two-tiered character as an actor under suspicion (Ward Fowler) and a television detective character (Lieutenant Lucerne) openly acknowledges the reason a homicide detective would be present at the television studio following the death of one of the show's executive producers, Clare Daley. Fowler immediately recognizes that the Lieutenant is conducting a murder investigation, and astutely observes the falsely innocuous Columbo "stumbling around, asking silly, fake-innocent questions" as opposed to poignant questions in a "routine investigation." While Fowler is onto him, Columbo's use of a fake question works when entering a situation incognito to assess the social dynamics and discover information. Gaining awareness of his surroundings, the victim's known associates, and their relationships with her, the Lieutenant effectively listens, comprehends the situation, and adapts his discourse and persona for the occasion. As a result of this displayed acquiescence from Columbo, both the LAPD Lieutenant and fictional Lieutenant Lucerne agree to their fake cooperation in solving the television producer's murder case as co-investigators engaged in ratiocination.

Fake Questions: Tag Questions

Another type of fake question Columbo uses is a "tag question," functioning to achieve acquiescence on a minor point of action or fact. Like a rhetorical question, for which the answer is obvious, logical, and jointly accepted by all parties in a conversation, tag questions are designed to gain compliance regarding a seemingly trivial accommodation. One can add tag questions or fragments that are positively or negatively phrased into statements. Examples include, "You're not from around here, are you?" (negative statement with a positive tag), which expresses a hypothesis and elicits a confirmation or refutation of that theory. The next example is "At 10:45am, you were at the bank, isn't that what you said?"

(negative statement with positive tag), which expresses minor doubt about one's recall of the matter, seeks confirmation or denial, and prompts further discussion about the person's location and timeframe in question. These tag questions enable two respondents to comprehend the situation and facts, awarding opportunities for the Lieutenant to clarify alibis, for example.

Examining "Lovely but Lethal," Columbo inserts his presence into the daily routine of suspect and CEO of Beauty Mark, Inc. cosmetics, Viveca Scott (Vera Miles). Clearly having done his homework before entering the active workplace, the Lieutenant contradicts himself by first stating his desire to be nonintrusive and stay out of her way, but, then, doing the exact opposite: following her around the office and her beauty farm business, looking over her shoulder, and asking one distracting and disruptive question after another. With the qualification that he would not be in the way, expressing clear awareness that being in the way is universally unwanted behavior, Columbo obliges the suspect into permitting his invasive surveillance by implying that a refusal would be unreasonable. Since appearing unreasonable contradicts the villain's façade of cooperation with the Lieutenant, she allows his demanding presence with a strained smile to further forge her compliant persona with the increasingly intrusive investigator. More specifically, Columbo meets up with Scott while snooping around her "fat farm" business for women's weight reduction and health revitalization. Viveca addresses a few of his basic questions about the nature of the facility, curtly entertains his patronizing and disingenuous inquiries about the cost of the program for his wife, "Only $200 a day," and loses patience with his time-consuming exaggerations of pseudo amazement with her "women's business." Scott attempts to dismiss the tenacious detective by nervously checking the time on her wrist watch and exasperating, "Well, you can see I really do have a tight schedule. So, if you didn't have something to say, I really must be going." Turning to face Scott directly and gently restraining her by holding onto her forearms with his hands, Columbo commands her attention with patronizing, gentlemanly control, "Oh, listen, ma'am, you don't worry about that. Now, you go about your business. I'm not going to interfere with your schedule. You do whatever you have to do, and I'll just tag along. Don't you worry about it." In this scene, the Lieutenant performs a totally accommodating, innocuous, "good old boy" who refuses to take no for an answer, insisting on accompanying her for every moment. He insists on following her about her business as a benevolent presence. Such manipulated complicity forces suspects to contradict themselves in order to maintain their innocence of the crime. Tag questions can result in an unsuspecting and resistant person inadvertently admitting to something secreted. At this later stage in the investigation, Columbo heightens his interferences, creating the earnest, clueless, but stubborn detective façade that figuratively suffocates the villain.

Probing Questions to Elicit Information

Probing Questions are designed to establish more intricate details of the crime, the victim's relationships, and the context. For example, in "Fade into Murder," when Columbo is trying to understand the nature of the suspect's relationship to the victim, he asks the deceased's husband a series of probing questions: "Are you saying that you didn't want to pay him that money?" "I still don't understand. You and your wife are partners. Isn't it in her best interest to not give him all that money?" "Forgive me for asking this, sir. I seem to remember stories that at one time they were pretty close. Are you suggesting that their relationship was still pretty close?" By the end of this inquiry, which is designed to obtain key information about the victim's relationships with the usual suspects, he discovers pertinent details that guide his pursuit of further inquiries and evidentiary clues.

Probing Questions to Incite Hypothetical Reflection

Hypothetical Questions are used to gauge an individual's creative imaginings about situations that the listener has purportedly never experienced. During the investigations, Columbo asks hypothetical questions to assess the villain's thinking about the victim, or the factors related to the murder but in a nonthreatening way, as the question is posed as hypothetical. The following is an example of a hypothetical question designed to encourage suspects to divulge their point of view: "If you were the killer, would you have stabbed the victim?"

Probing Questions to Effect Critical Analysis of Situations

Reflective Questions ask the listener to reflect on the situation and present responses based on reflection rather than short, gut reactions. In "Fade in to Murder," William Shatner plays Ward Fowler, an actor who plays Lieutenant Lucerne on a television police drama, and who kills his blackmailer. Columbo engages a willing Fowler in a philosophical dialogue about the four possible suspects of the murder victim, of which he is the most likely. In a brilliant, meta-detective exchange, Columbo-Lucerne and Columbo-Fowler dissect crime scene evidence and, in turn, Fowler's own probable culpability:

FOWLER: "There are only four people who could have killed Clare."
COLUMBO: "You mean the four people who knew where Claire Daley was going to be that night?"

FOWLER: "Exactly, and only one of those is instantly associated with make-up, wardrobe, and props."

COLUMBO: "Well now, let's see. . ... What do you think?"

Bringing out the possible culpability of Fowler into the discussion may suggest that, if Fowler were guilty of the crime, he would rather deflect such suspicion or not address it entirely. Therefore, the logical conclusion would be that his innocence allows him to rationally, as a detective, discuss the possibility of his own culpability and then to dismiss it as an impossibility or, at least, improbability. However, the Lieutenant plays along with Fowler's hypothetical deductions, not overtly showing that he does, indeed, suspect him. At this point, Columbo doesn't have condemning evidence to prove that Fowler killed his blackmailing producer. Both Columbo and actor Ward Fowler (William Shatner) know this; both characters sustain their amiable repartee, which delays the inevitable arrest until the Lieutenant discovers undeniable proof of the murderer's identity.

Deflective Questions

To redirect conversations away from undesired topics, askers can use deflective questions as a strategic form of rhetorical inquiry. When Ward Fowler prematurely directs the analysis of "likely suspects" to accuse himself, Columbo redirects the conversation by asking, "Who ever said that Ward Fowler is under suspicion for murder?" By doing so, the Lieutenant is able to control the pace of the conversation, slowing it down to avoid accusation before hard evidence is discovered. Obviously, the Lieutenant asserts via interrogative mode that Fowler need not worry and can relax, since the investigation of his manager's murder is not focused on him. However, Fowler knows the game, and that the odds are stacking against him.

The next chapter focuses on a standard method of investigation used by the Antipotent Detective: to obligate, intrude, insist, bother, tell inane stories, disingenuously flatter and apologize, and use the famous false exit, all in order to irritate and fluster the suspects progressively so that they inadvertently reveal self-incriminating information, confess, or become ensnared by their own lies.

9

Killing Them Softly: Irritating the Suspects in Seven Modes

As a key procedure in his investigations, Columbo rhetorically and physically badgers the suspects with repeated intrusions and questions. Importantly, this rhetorical strategy in the form of inquiry functions only in the presence of other factors. First, the suspects have to be arrogant enough about the commissioning and cover-up of their "perfect crimes." Second, the devious murderers with enormous egos and assumptions of entitlement are certain that their superior intellects will derail and outwit any challenges posed by the less educated, lower-class civil servants investigating them. Third, the killers' hubris is so central to their characters that it allows them to stay available, doing business as usual, and to disregard and underestimate the efficacy of the Antipotent Detective's inquiries. Instead of trying to escape and get out of town, the suspects conspicuously go about their lives, go to work, entertain friends and family at their homes, and work out at the club, all the while making no adjustments to their lifestyles despite the serious and extraordinary event in their lives: murder of a close associate, relative, or friend. Synchronously, the egotistical murderer collects social data in observation of the investigator's benign affectation to reformulate an equally misleading self-presentation of innocence and desire to catch the killer. In the case of accidental killing—manslaughter—anxiety is more present in the villain's character and behavior. Strategically, the villain offers suggestive and often concocted "evidence" to elicit the investigator's doubts about other characters' credibility, goodwill, plausible opportunity, behavioral likelihood, and overall culpability. Fully investing in a fake partnership with the Antipotent Detective, the villain feigns co-commitment to solving the case by acting as a good samaritan for the greater good.

Taking advantage of their charade, Columbo assumes the Antipotent Detective persona. To initiate a relationship with and the investigation of all clues and suspects, Columbo uses praise, modesty, and appreciation. However, this escalates progressively through the episode, becoming overabundance of flattery of the suspects, excessive false modesty, unwarranted apologies, and gratuitous expressions of gratitude with his

FIGURE 23: Screenshot: Ken Franklin (Jack Cassidy) is a quintessential villain being annoyed by the ever-present and dutiful Lieutenant. Steven Spielberg (dir.), "Murder by the Book," *Columbo*, 1971. Universal Television.

repeated, automatic, Elvis-like "Thank you very much" for every minute assistance. While Columbo's tactics of irritating the suspects can aggravate the viewers, the approach serves to wear down the defenses of the resistant culprits.

Obligating the Suspect with Appeasement Pressure and the Extrication of Any Threat

When offering praise, admiration, and need for the suspect's contributions during early scenes of each episode, the clever Columbo builds a cooperative partnership in the investigation. This rhetorical transaction involves the detective soliciting the known associate's cooperation, an effort that depends on the suspect's belief in the detective's low efficacy. More specifically, the suspect is invited to share expertise—what he or she knows about the crime scene, the victim, possible suspects and motives—and experiment with hypothetical *modus operandi* as related to the confirmation or disputation of stated alibis. Moreover, the suspect is enlisted to engage in the ratiocination of all case details, which is met with Columbo's incongruent enthusiasm and lack of suspicion, as a police officer. Behaving more like an admirer than an astute investigator, the star-struck detective prods the villain with exclamations, "Would you? Oh, that would be an honor, sir/ma'am. Wait 'til I tell my wife!" As an overly polite and respectful devotee, who seems to lack pride and poise, the Lieutenant incongruously displays no ego to protect and offers unbridled affirmation of the suspects' merits.

Having an obsessive nature, Columbo cannot sleep when details of a case don't make sense or clues to the killer's *modus operandi* and motive have not been discovered. Detective fiction critic George N. Dove refers to this often-used detective genre convention as a favorite hermeneutic structure: "the instance in which something keeps nagging at the back of the detective's consciousness, something he or she cannot identify at first but which later proves highly significant" (89). The convention is integrated into *Columbo* by way of repetition; throughout each investigation, there is something that is not right, is out of place, is incongruent. Further, Dove explains how the detective expressing intuition about a case is a convention that helps draw readers into solving a mystery alongside the investigator. In turn, the audience's shared sensation of discord transitions into suspense for what threat will come next.

Being bothered by little details that result in him not sleeping, Lieutenant Columbo projects obsessiveness in an earnest mission to do his job, prove a murder, and serve justice. Both the villain and the detective practice moderation and self-control,

FIGURE 24: Screenshot: Arrogant surgeon and killer Dr. Barry Mayfield (Leonard Nimoy) can barely tolerate Columbo's question. Hy Averback (dir.), "A Stitch in Crime," *Columbo*, 1973. Universal Television.

retaining their façade for their respective desired outcomes. On the one hand, the villain avoids self-incrimination and maintains innocence of the crime by acting as an aid in the investigation and feigning the intent of bringing the murderer to justice. On the other hand, by often purporting to suspect someone else, Columbo elicits the villains' calm assurance that the investigator is nowhere near solving the cases. In other words, both implement rhetorical performances of cooperation with each other. At the moment of offering help, what the villain does not know is just how completely involved with Columbo he or she will be in this investigation.

Irritating the Villains: Use of Excessive Flattery and False Modesty

False modesty works effectively with excessive flattery in affording a potency-oriented individual scope to create and manage an antipotent persona. Columbo uses both to his advantage. False modesty manifests in Columbo's discourse whenever he refuses to accept credit where credit is due, conspicuously diminishes the degree of his own accomplishment in question, or reflexively turns discussions to the villain's merits, who are undeserving of excessive high praise. While deflecting credit or praise from himself, Columbo praises the villain for his or her achievements, home, or the like. Complimenting is a rhetorical action designed to reduce social tension in an interlocutor who perceives a threat or competition from another interlocutor. By demonstrating sincere appreciation for the villain's successes, Columbo implements the underclass ancient Greeks' sophrosynic tactic of elevating the value of the power class, which works to appease and disarm the defensive interlocutor's resistance to them. Designed to create cohesion, appeasement strategies placate "the authority in an uncontested concession," reassuring the superior that "their authority remains intact" (Trexler 3–5). Importantly, concessions made by the authority only seem to cede superiority to a minimal degree, nevertheless allowing power over the subordinates to be maintained. As a legitimate enforcer of the law, Columbo uses copious appeasement behaviors to reinforce his contrived persona of a bumbling, self-deprecating detective, to empower the suspect. While sincere praise effects trust and cooperation, excessive, disingenuous flattery may feel hollow and undesirable to internally secure individuals. However, prominent thinkers, from Aristotle through to contemporary psychologists have acknowledged that narcissistic, high-ranking buffs luxuriate in exaggerated accolades that further fuel their delicate sense of security, position, and authority. In a TV roundtable discussion about "The Most Dangerous Match" episode, Noel Murray describes the Lieutenant's strategies of flattery with some hyperbole:

> Columbo keeps flattering Clayton, raving about the chess champion's memory, and saying things like, "I got a cousin up there in Albany, he wears big thick

glasses and he thinks you're the greatest thing in the world," even while Clayton is dismissing the lieutenant's inquiries and questioning the integrity of the Los Angeles Police Department.

While part parody and part critique, Murray's comment illustrates the Lieutenant's hyper-focus on playing his humble part, regardless of the condescension he receives thereafter. Essentially, such a status-bolstering rhetorical act distracts the villain from the Lieutenant's main purposes, revealing enough incriminating evidence to force an force anarrest or a confession. Some examples used by the Lieutenant with various villains include: "Amazing, sir." "I should have thought of that myself." "You did it again, sir. You read my mind." "My wife is not going to believe this." "Would you mind giving me your autograph? My wife is a huge fan." While a degree of admiration is genuine—after all, they are smart, sophisticated, and successful characters—the higher degree of fandom that Columbo acts out has comic effect as well as having the purpose of building common ground and bonding with the strangers, opponents, and adversaries. Further, the Lieutenant's solicitation of the villain's help with the case is reasonable; after all, the villain knew the victim. Unfalteringly, the Lieutenant stays on course with his unstoppable process of rhetorical inquiry into seemingly trivial details, which, taken together, amount to serious pestering of the suspects.

In "Negative Reaction," Columbo depicts scholarly interest and tenacity when he buys, reads, and enquires about the killer photojournalist's published books. To the suspect's astonishment, the investigator has counted the number of photographs in a particular collection of imagistic stories of San Quentin Prison, nine of which were of the recently deceased patsy blamed for the wife's murder. Further, in an effort to recreate the killer's writing of a ransom note, Columbo fixes his attention on the incongruous fact that it has allegedly been constructed of letter clippings by the deceased patsy in a hotel room devoid of any shreds of paper. With a pile of newspaper cuttings on his desk, Columbo demonstrates the implausibility of cutting and pasting letters for the ransom note without leaving a mess of paper clippings. He claims to have tried multiple times, even with his wife, but to no avail. Initially, the suspect fails to see "the problem," and frustratingly demands, "What is your point, Columbo?" However, his berating countenance falls when hearing the lucid argument against him.

Irritating the Villains: Repeated, Disingenuous Apologies

If genuine apologies for missteps, offenses, insults, or the like can heal a relationship, an onslaught of disingenuous apologies are without meaning and only serve as an affectation of social decorum. While Columbo utters words of apology, he does so out of automatic and feigned politeness when bothering suspects. In any given episode, Columbo says, "I'm sorry" between ten and fifteen times. Like an unconscious reflex, a profusion of phony apologetic messages automatically accompany imposing rhetorical inquiries that are vexing to the villain. Other typical expressions of empty regret include "I hope you don't mind," "Sorry to bother you," "Hope I didn't interrupt anything," "Please, bear with me," "I don't mean to be a pest," and the like. They operate as polite niceties that assume assent, permission, or pardon for the intrusion or violation of privacy. The expectancy inherent in Columbo's nominal expression of regret is clear in the fact that he generally does not wait for a response from the villain. Like in the quote from Lauren Staton (this book 138), Columbo asks for permission to ask a question when he will ask it regardless. As Columbo obsesses over his own agenda that involves the villain, he speaks his business immediately after the "I'm sorry," without a beat, disregarding the recipient's wishes. When villains are at the end of their patience and hear "I hope you don't mind," some begin to lose control over their faux cooperation as plotted personae and snap back, "Yes, I do mind." At that moment, the Lieutenant knows he is successfully irritating the villain.

Irritating the Villains: Wasting the Suspect's Time

Another way that the detective flusters his suspects is by making it clear that he is stealing the villain's time without regard for their personal boundaries or privacy. Several behaviors convey disrespect for the villain's time. First, distracted attention in the midst of a dialogue indicates that Columbo is no longer listening to either a villain's answer to a question he himself posed, or is not listening to a question posed by the villain, who expects everyone's full attention. The lack of focus on the suspect triggers their hubristic and supercilious demands that Columbo not waste their time with his banal considerations and inattentiveness. Moreover, Columbo's silence and lack of attention toward the villain undermines the murderer's power. If he's not listening, the privileged villains are being neglected or ignored, and, therefore, not wielding social dominance. While the murderers would rather the detective leave their homes or offices or social places, his appearance requires at least feigned interest in the interruption.

A painful example of the Antipotent Detective dragging out a short drive home, which would test the patience of even the most meditative individuals, is when he asks an arrogant murderer to follow him. Leaving late at night from the crime scene of the symphony concert hall in "Murder with Too Many Notes" (2001), the Antipotent Detective advises that the maestro Finlay Crawford (Billy Connolly) has had a few drinks and should be very careful driving home so as not to be pulled over and arrested for driving intoxicated: "I've got an idea. Why don't you follow me home on nice, quiet streets, and, if anything happens to you, I'll take care of it." The Antipotent Detective offers no rational alternative to Crawford with his neighborly, small-town consitution, casual language replete with contractions, and basic common sense. As a rhetorical action, Columbo ingratiates the suspect into accepting his kind offer of protection and help, driving home behind his beat-up Peugeot via quiet streets, nice and slowly. With backfiring noises, weak idle, and uneven canter, the Peugeot moves desperately slowly as Crawford's impeccable luxury sedan follows smoothly, quietly, but resistantly. As the self-assigned leader in this short caravan, Columbo tediously assures the plotting, narcissistic murderer's safe arrival at home at the cost of the conniving conductor's limits of tolerance within a context of obligatory gratitude.

For what feels like an eternity in broadcast air time, Columbo meanders in a slalom fashion, driving noticeably below the speed limit, being passed and honked at by annoyed motorists. The irritation heightens for the arrogant, competent, and efficiency-oriented murderer as the Antipotent Detective further stalls the voyage by periodically pulling his car to the side of the road and getting out to talk to the incensed Crawford about maddeningly folksy, and inane details, such as his wife going to a museum near the suspect's home, obvious points of direction, and excessively polite, unreasonably concerned discourses that project his faulty leadership in getting Crawford home. The scene is brilliantly farcical as a bicyclist on a beach cruiser amiably rings a bell while passing the flabbergasted Crawford, who is white-knuckling the steering wheel. This scene takes Crawford's frustration up a notch when the Peugeot ceases its ambling gait, and the detective exits his vehicle, announcing "Bad news, sir." At this unlikely and unfortunate situation of a cop running out of gas, Crawford exasperates, "What the fffff...!" Undaunted, Columbo opens the back door, putting the murder victim's things into the back seat while fake-asking, "Would you mind if I put these back here?" as if Crawford has a choice of rejecting the request already in action.

With rolling eyes, clenched jaw, and frantic slaps on the steering wheel, Crawford is beyond flustered and yells, "That is it! I am on my way!" However, when the detective asks if the conductor has a phone, the comic irony of a police officer needing a phone to get help breaks his tension for the moment, bursting into a cackle of madness over the absurdity, "You are something. You really are something, Columbo." Then, in a pronouncement of poetic surrender, Crawford exclaims, "Ah, I am resigned to my fate." While the conductor accepts that he cannot hurry or control this ride home, his patience is further taxed when he must give the nerve-grating but ever-pleasant "Mr. Columbo" (having fully bought into the Antipotent Detective persona) a ride home in his own vehicle. The final injury occurs when Columbo, seemingly without consideration for the pristine condition of the luxury sedan, places a dirty gas can on the upscale car's leather back seats. Actor Billy Connolly vividly animates the excruciating restraint needed to sustain his façade of calm and appreciative cooperation. Characteristically, the Antipotent Detective constructs suffocating intrusions and delays, all facilitated by the suspect's guise of friendly accessibility and cooperation, and renders the otherwise controlling and confident murderer impotent in managing their own time.

Eventually, the two arrive at the maestro's mansion, and Crawford is trapped still with the aimless detective until help arrives from the precinct. For the Scottish composer, the worst is that he must continue to restrain his desperation for ridding himself of the irritating detective; in fact, he must play hospitable host to the good-natured but infuriatingly inept investigator of the crime he has just committed. After finally arriving home at his wit's end, Crawford urgently swigs another glass of scotch, offering a glass to Columbo to maintain the appearance that he is innocent and helpful with the investigation. Perhaps, this scene can be said to consitute villain abuse via Antipotent Detective, but it nevertheless seems like justice with a highly villainous premeditating murderer such as Findlay Crawford. Even for the *Columbo* genre, this scene ranks as one of the zaniest and best examples of the Antipotent Detective's strategy of wasting a suspect's time in order to irritate them.

Unbeknownst to Crawford, the can of gas the Sergeant brings to the house for Columbo's car is part of the Lieutenant's charade; in fact, Columbo has roughly half a tank. The sneaky Lieutenant shushes the Sergeant, whispering that he shouldn't tell anyone about this. Indeed, this brief exchange among colleagues confirms the contrived antipotency shrouding the scheming detective. Here, viewer and villain suffer alike, though Crawford does not experience the catharsis that viewers are gifted.

Columbo's faulty attention span, combined with his disregard for his subjects' lives and privacy, agitates these presumed members of American high society, and reasonably so. Further agitating to the villains is that, during these moments of distraction, Columbo reflects on damaging implications for the villain, which stem from trifling details. Relentlessly, the professional snoop visits the villains' homes, workplaces, churches, sacred funeral services, and celebrations. Operating with a subtext of usurping their power, the Antipotent Detective invades any space considered sacred by the villains with the authority of the law, yet in the pretense of haphazard and socially unaware investigative procedures. Like a pest, he permeates all breathing spaces, night and day, with his "suffocating presence" (as Paul Galesko in "Negative Reaction" phrases it), wasting their precious time.

FIGURE 25: Screenshot: The murderous maestro Findlay Crawford (Billy Connolly) has just been through an ordeal, courtesy of the Antipotent Detective. Patrick McGoohan (dir.), "Murder in Too Many Notes," *Columbo*, 2001. Universal Television.

Irritating the Villains: Circumstantial Speech and Storytelling

Using the term "circumstantial speech," behavioral scientists describe indirect speech patterns in which "an individual delays reaching the point by introducing unnecessary, tedious details and parenthetical remarks. Circumstantial replies or statements may be prolonged for many minutes if the speaker is not interrupted and urged to get to the point" (Watson 136–37). Associated with Obsessive Compulsive Disorder, the symptomatic traits are patient distraction, decentered responses to questions, and emphasis on circumstances that are not germane to the inquiry. Certainly, these communication behaviors describe Columbo's social interaction with the villains. From each villain's perspective, the detective is "a funny little man" who discredits himself as the lead investigator with frustratingly indirect and verbose discourses. However, the tactic of implementing circumstantial speech patterns results in "mission accomplished" for the Lieutenant. Typical prompts from villains exhibit their waning patience with the detective: "Would you get to the point?!", "What does this have to do with ...", "All right, Lieutenant. What's the meaning of this?" Columbo eventually gets to the point but via an indirect route, which signals a disorganized mind and thought process.

An obvious dimension of his investigative approach and character, the use of circumstantial speech in storytelling has three rhetorical functions. One is that this disorganized narrative style portrays a scattered mind, which reassures the condescending villains of the detective's lack of intellectual prowess and the implausibility of his solving the case. Therefore, the villains become more confident in their own security, innocence, and freedom. Second, the lengthy ramblings take up the suspects' time, which aggravates them. Third, Columbo's long and winding stories of his wife, extended family members, and personal experiences serve as a means of bridging the wide social gap between him and the villains. However, he tells the stories knowing that the elitist villains resist any kind of comparison with him, which would undermine their sense of superiority. Instead of creating familiarity through the reciprocal self-disclosure of personal history with the investigated subject, the evil masterminds roll their eyes at the dull, average life of the proletarian detective.

Columbo expert Mark Dawidziak suggests that the contradictory personal stories across the *Columbo* series support the reading that they are strategically invented to further the eponymous detective's persona as folksy and unsophisticated—his persona of antipotency. Whether the stories are "true" to the Columbo character or are fictional background stories told by the alter-Columbo to make particular impressions on the villains, the Lieutenant's drawn-out and seemingly pointless narratives effect high levels frustration amongst the villains. As the murderers pretend to be interested in the circular, repetitive, digressive, and trivial storytelling to placate the detective, their restrained arrogance percolates to the surface amid the distress. Particularly when they have had to repeatedly suffer through them, the suspects react with increasing irritation, citing lack of time to listen, attempting to get away from Columbo unseen, avoiding any communications with him, or vainly beseeching him to "Get to the point, Lieutenant!"

Irritating the Villains: Doggedly Hounding Them for a Melt Down

Regular viewers of the show have seen the process of the Lieutenant wearing down his suspects until they make a mistake or fall into a trap. On the one hand, he is ever-present or relentlessly returning. On the other hand, he crowds their personal space like a parasite. In Figure 26, Columbo is in a small car with suspect Charlie in "Last Salute to the Commodore," but the car is not as small as he makes out. This invasion of personal space would offend even the average American, who enjoys a larger comfort zone than many other cultures; when the Lieutenant, of a lower socio-economic class, therefore invades the personal space of Charlie, his actions cause especial offense.

During "Prescription Murder," the detective explains to accomplice Joan Hudson (Katherine Justice) his method of investigation with suspects:

LT. COLUMBO: Miss Hudson? I hope you understand that this is only the beginning. In a way, I feel sorry for you, because from now on, I'm going to do everything I can to break you down. Do you understand? Doctor Flemming made one mistake and you're it. You're the weak link, Miss Hudson. Now, you surprised me today, because you were strong, but there's always tomorrow and the day after that... and the day after that... and sooner or later, you're going to talk to me. Until you do, you're going to be questioned. You're going to be followed ... and you're going to be hounded ... and Doctor Flemming can't do anything about it. You're on your own, Miss Hudson, and I'm going to get to him through you. That's a promise.

In this passage Columbo, in no uncertain terms, explicates his procedure of incessant presence, needling inquiry, and perpetual surveillance, i.e., stalking. What is especially unsettling about this exchange is Columbo's uncharacteristic anger,

FIGURE 26: Screenshot: Columbo crowding suspect Charlie Clay (Robert Vaughn). Patrick McGoohan (dir.), "The Last Salute to the Commodore," *Columbo*, 1976. Universal Television.

forcefulness, and stated intention of performing a harmful and methodical hunt for the truth at the accomplice's expense. This practice of confrontation and intimidation ends with this first film. Only in a couple of subsequent episodes are there confrontations with principally offensive, maliciously narcissistic, and dismissively inciteful villains: "A Stitch in Crime" and "Exercise in Fatality." Yet, these moments are provocations by the villains, which differ significantly from the Lieutenant's provocation of the manipulated accomplice, whose crime is facilitating a cover-up. An act of direct harassment in a "shakedown" of a relatively innocent, though delusional, witness suggests an element of the hard-boiled mode initially adopted by the show's creators. Starting with the second film, "Ransom for a Dead Man," this character trait is immediately dropped from Lieutenant Columbo's profile. Watching that scene after seeing the whole series of episodes strikes me as oddly aggressive for the otherwise gentle but deceptively Antipotent Detective, who refuses to carry his sidearm and avoids fighting all together.

Irritating the Villains: False Exits: "Oh, and One More Thing"

Described as his "signature interrogation technique," the false exit is a method of asking questions after the suspect thinks the interview with the Lieutenant is over and they are temporarily safe in his absence. The false exit proceeds as follows: "Columbo conducts a seemingly innocuous interview, politely concludes, and exits the scene, only to stop in the doorway or return moments later and say, 'Just one more thing'" (Brandon). He rethinks the departure, turns around to face the villain, and asserts that he almost forgot, or just remembered, that he has one other question, point of contradiction, or bothersome detail that does not make sense to him. The expression varies only slightly from episode to episode. But whenever the suspect seems to be rid of the Lieutenant, Columbo turns with a bemused remark, something like: "Oh, there's just one more thing ..." (Bounds). Generally, this supposed afterthought follows an inquiry he makes with the villain about a trivial detail.

However, rhetorical scholar and teacher Jay Heinrichs links the Lieutenant's false exit questions or pronouncements with another key rhetorical device:

> The TV Columbo's big technique wasn't the leading question (what detective doesn't ask leading questions?). It was the last-second question, after his victim thinks the interview is over. "Oh, I almost forgot...." Columbo's real rhetorical technique was KAIROS, the art of timing.
>
> ("Ask Figaro")

While Columbo shares with other great detectives a range of questions designed to reveal the details of the case, the unique tactic is also part of his antipotent persona. In other words, sustaining his absentminded, disorganized, and non-accusatory façade, the Lieutenant acts as if the question or discovered detail just occurred to him at that unplanned moment. Conversely, this timed tactic conveys information to the killers that implicates them without directly incriminating them. Therefore, the killers know that the investigation is gaining momentum in their direction, which is stressful, but they remain confident that the distracted detective has not applied ratiocination to the clues in a way that incriminates them in the homicide.

While each suspect feigns innocence and a desire to help Columbo with the investigation, their acquiescence is what allows the Lieutenant to repeatedly pester them with the minutest of details, forcing them to answer just one more of his seemingly unplanned, unprepared, and unscheduled questions:

> Columbo's most irritating technique was to leave a room and then return, with a befuddled look on his face. Scratching his head, he'd say "Just one more thing ..." and ask a seemingly innocuous question. The killer, by then eager to see the last of this annoying fellow, would quickly answer, and later find out that the question was not so innocent after all, when Columbo returned to say "You're under arrest."
>
> (Madigan)

Each suspect's irritation and anxiety peak once they realize that Columbo's ratiocination of the clues culminates in an inference of their own guilt.

In "Prescription Murder," a mentally unstable man recently discharged from the army confesses to killing Mrs. Flemming. At the station house, a rare setting for the show, the Lieutenant interviews him while Dr. Flemming observes at Columbo's request. Releasing the disturbed but clearly innocent man, Columbo and Flemming agree that the confessor was lying, knew only as much as was reported in the newspapers, and mistakenly described the nature of the strangulation of the victim. What is clear in this scene, among others, is that the Lieutenant and the psychiatrist share a great deal in how they conduct their business: their jobs demand that they are good at analyzing human behavior, using their intellects, and being on-call all hours of the night. Flemming replies to Columbo with clear annoyance, asserting the pointlessness of the questions the detective has been asking about him instead of his wife's killer. Defensive and critical about Columbo's investigative approach, Flemming retorts by mocking the detective and reinforcing his primary concern: "What do my reading habits have anything to do with any of this? You've been concentrating on everything but the man that broke into my apartment. Or is this some new type of police procedure?" The psychiatrist challenges Columbo's misdirected approach, but is clearly agitated as a result of his scrutiny. Indeed, Flemming has identified the Lieutenant's unique procedure of conducting criminal investigations. As audience members who know that Flemming is the murderer, the scene amusingly confirms that the good Lieutenant is right on track. In this scene, Columbo does not accuse the suspect; he only provides evidence or rational explanations to propel the inquiry.

The impact of this technique can be alarming, as the detective presents trivial clues that suggest the suspect is to blame. The false exit enables the badgering Columbo to either gauge the suspect's culpability response to yet another question, pose another theory, or solicit another favor from the miserable murderers who want nothing more than for him to go away. Through the maddening pace and intensity of investigation, Columbo drives the killers to exasperation with his relentless rhetorical inquiries, wearing them out so they make a mistake that will cost them their freedom and status. Eventually, Columbo wears out his welcome, inspiring a pronouncement along the lines of "arrest me or get out."

When Villains Realize that the Lieutenant is onto Them

The following examines how Columbo sparingly uses inquiry to reveal something about a significant clue to the crime, dispel a cover story's credibility, or even dispel his suspicions about the suspect. These tend to occur at the end of the second third of the investigation. With varying degrees of insight, the Lieutenant discloses to his suspects that he has greater knowledge and expertise than he has been feigning up to that point. Unbefitting the early stages of the investigation when basic crime, motives, possible suspects, and alibis are established, the "I almost forgot" or "Just one more thing" is used when information is discovered that contradicts a suspect's stated claims, relationship status, alibis, or the like. The effect on the suspect is unnerving to their sense of control over the lead detective and confidence of remaining unknown as the killer.

Having established a practice of hounding the suspects, this tactic is shown to work because the villain is caught off-guard, enabling the investigator to confront the suspect with "a jarring question of inconsistency about either the crime scene or the suspect's alibi" (Brandon). Since they are in a temporary relaxed state due to Columbo's announced departure, the menacing question, accusation, or fact elicits a more natural reaction than when the villain is bracing themself in self-defense. The false exit serves three different micro-functions: to ask a question that may seem trivial but, if answered with honesty, is significant; to offer newly acquired information about the crime and method that shows Columbo advancing his investigation; and, in some cases late in the investigation, to directly articulate the damning nature of the evidence against the suspect at hand. If the latter happens, the villain will generally terminate their guise as assistant-to-the-investigation and withdraw into self-preservation mode.

In the first two-hour pilot film, "Prescription Murder," the psychiatrist-murderer asserts confidence that the murderer cannot be caught because of the extraordinary intelligence of the criminal who has plotted every move, committing a murder impervious to detection. In carefully noted disagreement, Lieutenant Columbo explains the playing field between police and criminals to his suspect, the psychiatrist Ray Flemming (Gene Barry):

> You're probably right. He sounds just too clever for us. What I mean is, you know, cops, we're not the brightest guys in the world. Of course, we got one thing going for us: we're professionals. I mean, you take our friend here, the murderer. He's very smart, but he's an amateur. I mean, he's got just one time to learn. Just one. And with us, well, with us, it's—it's a business. You see, we do this a hundred times a year. I'll tell ya, Doc. That's a lot of practice.
> ("Prescription Murder")

By examining the average level of expertise murderers and police officers have in terms of committing crimes and covering them up, Columbo implies the argument that law enforcement has an advantage over one-time killers. His use of "our friend" to reference the "unknown" murderer diminishes the power that Flemming has exerted in killing his wife.

During a conversation with the suspect, maestro conductor Alex Benedict, Columbo argues against the theory that the pianist Jenifer Welles committed suicide. Having hypothetically accused the murderer of killing Jenifer Welles via an exhortation of their M.O. and the fact they had the opportunity to do so, Columbo asserts the legitimacy of investigating her death as a homicide. Walking away to let the conductor take his nap, Columbo makes a false exit:

> Oh, just one more thing. I know that you don't agree. I have at least convinced my superiors that Jenifer Welles was murdered. It was not a suicide. And they've officially assigned me to the case. That's my specialty, you know—homicide.
> ("Étude in Black")

Rarely does the Lieutenant call attention to his substantial expertise and experience in law enforcement with his suspects. Doing so undermines his method of deliberately being unpretentious, unimpressive, and underestimated. However, he does use the revelation sparingly and at strategic moments to give the suspects pause. This is a turning point in every investigation; Columbo reveals his poker hand to the suspect, and the cards add up to a threat that he does not believe their cover story. He is not as antipotent as he has previously conveyed, and he will pursue the suspect until the case is closed. Understandably, from the point of revelation onward, suspects are reticent to give the great detective open access to their lives. Their guard is up, the detective's pestering makes them angry, but Columbo is onto them with a growing body of suspicious coincidences, plausible motives, intelligent speculations, and/or circumstantial evidence. Nevertheless he needs proof, and they know it.

In "Try and Catch Me" (1977), bestselling mystery novelist Abigail Mitchell (Ruth Gordon) has avenged her beloved late niece's mysterious murder on a short sailboat ride by killing the man responsible, her niece's husband (Charles Frank). She could not let him get away with it and steal her inheritance. The charming banter about fictional mystery investigations and the "real" police detective's investigation is lighthearted and carries throughout the episode. However, the Lieutenant makes a serious discovery about the suspect's grief over the death of her niece. He acknowledges how difficult it must have been to lose someone she so loved, especially when she was "cheated" out of life at such a young age. In response to Columbo's show of empathy, the crime writer smiles in delight and expresses, "I'm beginning to be very fond of you, Lieutenant. I think you're a very kind man." While the Lieutenant has established a simpatico with the grieving writer, he warns her that there are limits to his kindness: "Don't count on that, Miss Mitchell. Don't count on it." The policeman's caution foreshadows her arrest in that, despite understanding why she killed her nephew-in-law, he has to obey the law. Nevertheless, Mitchell does appeal to Columbo's kindness by asking him, "I don't suppose you would be willing to make an exception in my case, an old woman, harmless all in all, under the circumstances, your kindness. . .?". To a fault, Columbo almost never strays from being a professional in service to the legal justice system, regardless of his personal feelings about the suspect. Miss Mitchell must face the courts.

Special Cases of Direct Confrontation: The Lieutenant Gets Mad

Sheldon Catz summarizes the debate among *Columbo* viewers as to whether the few times that the Lieutenant gets angry at the suspects is intentional pretense or if the detective is genuinely angry with the murderers:

> Among the many fascinating aspects of *Columbo*, one that generates more attention than most is the question of those few times when the Lieutenant loses his cool. Is it for real? Is he faking it as a new approach to unnerve the murderer? Perhaps the reason this question is so intriguing is that it touches on the deeper unknowable issue of what is actually on Columbo's mind? . . . Some people have

suggested that Columbo's explosions are part of his act because they come late in the episodes, after his usual methods have not produced results.

(Catz 274)

Catz makes a good argument for Columbo faking his venom with Joan Hudson (Katherine Justice) to get her to break emotionally and reveal her lover's murderous act. On the one hand, he also points out that the Lieutenant of this first pilot film evolves to be a nicer and more patient character, discontinuing this strategy after its first use. On the other hand, Catz explicates Columbo's sincere anger at Milo Janus in "Exercise in Fatality," because Janus is arrogantly indifferent to his deceased business partner and his ex-wife Mrs. Stafford's misery. Also, Dr. Barry Mayfield in "A Stitch in Crime" murders a witness to shift the suspicion for his killing a nurse off himself and onto a recovering addict friend of the nurse's. In both cases, innocent people are harmed while the Lieutenant is investigating the initial murder and attempted murder, which, arguably, would cause the detective frustration and antagonism toward the festering villains.

However, for this project, why the Lieutenant shows anger, strategically or sincerely, is not the main concern. Rather, the effects of his anger on his suspects and on his relationship with the suspects are primary. More specifically, the outbursts reveal an angry, frustrated man who is done playing the Antipotent Detective, and is determined to catch the murderer, accusing them directly with full authority and intellectual prowess (potency). At the hospital where Mrs. Stafford is recovering from near-fatal alcohol poisoning, Columbo runs into Janus in the waiting area with a man and a woman sitting there:

JANUS: How is she? They won't tell me a thing.
COLUMBO: What do you care?
JANUS: What's that supposed to mean?
COLUMBO: You don't care whether she lives or dies. As a matter of fact, she's drinking because she thinks you're responsible for the death of her husband. And you want to know what? So do I!
JANUS: I warned you at my office. Don't you. . .
COLUMBO: I checked your alibi for the time before you got to the house. It doesn't wash.
JANUS: First of all, I don't need an alibi. Secondly, I was at Parker Motors.
COLUMBO: You said they were closed when you got there. The fact is, they've been open every night until 9:00 for the past

	month. (*distraction with a magazine*). That's right! (*He lights his cigar*)
JANUS:	Your health program didn't last very long.
COLUMBO:	Long enough.
JANUS:	You know something, Columbo? You're a devious man.
COLUMBO:	That's what they tell me.

With a drop of all pretense, this short, quick scene reveals Columbo as both the detective of the LAPD and a man who is compassionate about Mrs. Stafford's emotional and physical suffering as related to this cold, arrogant, dismissive, apathetic, profiteering murderer. Plainly and vehemently, Columbo indicts Janus for his role in her condition as a sensitive and broken woman, and reveals his astute, questioning mind and careful research practices in establishing the small details that unravel Janus's alibi with Parker Motors. His emphasis with "that's right!" exposes his intelligence and tenacity, qualities which enable him to analyze crimes, motives, opportunities, and character. Janus is speechless at the discovery of the real Columbo behind the pestering little man, out of shape and with an unhealthy lifestyle, having feigned a resolution to change. Instead, the Lieutenant is the outstanding police officer who has earned his rank and cares about people who are hurt, whom he protects and serves. Knocked off-guard, Janus realizes he was wrong about him, believing his persona, and indicts the Lieutenant with a strong criticism of character that directly contradicts his persona as having an obtuse, trusting, and trustworthy nature. To this indictment, the detective shamelessly acquiesces, "guilty as charged." In a rare moment, Columbo definitively reveals the truth about his duplicity as the Antipotent Detective.

In "A Stitch in Crime," Dr. Barry Mayfield (Leonard Nimoy) is the young, brilliant, and fearless up-and-coming heart surgeon whose older but more conservative mentor, Dr. Edmund Hiedeman (Will Greer), needs heart surgery, which is performed by him. When the loyal and conscientious nurse Sharon Martin (Anne Francis) suspects dissolving stitches were erroneously used in Hiedeman's surgery—which required permanent stitches to hold the tissue repairs—she investigates the materials with the company. Martin suspects that the ambitious, impatient, emotionless, and narcissistic Dr. Mayfield has made such a mistake purposely to gain both power and funding for their prototype research. Throughout the investigation, the Lieutenant suspects Dr. Mayfield, who remains cool and steady, throwing a fancy party the day that Martin's body is discovered in the parking lot at the hospital. As is typical of the show's villains, Mayfield entertains discussions about the crime with the needy detective, generally disagreeing with him on any detail that may incriminate himself. Even among *Columbo* villains, Mayfield is a paragon of arrogance, dismissive superiority, self-serving murder, and total emotional unavailability. Columbo goes to see Sharon Martin's friend, Harry Alexander (Jared Martin), a recovering heroin addict staying clean and turning his life around. Directly after the visit, Mayfield kills Alexander with an overdose of the drug, in order to cast suspicion on him for Sharon's murder.

Taunting the detective with the fact that only he and another of the nurse's friends know about Alexander, Mayfield places doubts on her friend as a suspect, whom Columbo dismisses as a most unlikely suspect: "I think she knows less than she says." Then, Mayfield cavalierly challenges the Lieutenant to imagine what possible motive he would have for killing Sharon, exiting with duping delight. After a long monologue, during which Columbo explains all that he has learned about surgical sutures, Mayfield bursts into maniacal laughter, belittling the Lieutenant for believing his "foolish" theory about how the wrong sutures were used as a means of murder. While in mid-hysterics, Columbo takes a coffee carafe from Mayfield's desk and shockingly and uncharacteristically slams the desk with it, immediately deflating Mayfield's obnoxious and callous laughter. Resolute and definitive, the investigator pronounces his knowledge to Mayfield: "I believe you killed Sharon Martin, and I believe you are trying to kill Dr. Hiedeman." Unlike the shock expressed by Milo Janus discussed earlier, the surgeon does not falter or pause for a minute. Instead, fearlessly, he patronizingly judges and taunts his adversary further: "Lieutenant Columbo, you're remarkable. You have intelligence, you have perception, you have great tenacity." With calm certitude and sheer audacity, Mayfield leans forward toward Columbo. "You've got everything but proof." With a surgeon's cool demeanor under the pressures of life and death, Mayfield luxuriates in his security, power, and unrivaled preeminence.

As a disruption to the menacing doctor's certitude of safety, Columbo warns, "You better take good care of Dr. Hiedeman because if he dies, we're gonna have to have an autopsy, aren't we? I mean, we're gonna have to know whether a heart attack killed him, or whether it was just dissolving suture." This scene is a head-to-head confrontation with the Lieutenant lifting the veil of his antipotent persona and ending his passive, indirect interactions with the suspect. The scene reveals more than just the fact that the Lieutenant's theories about the crime are directly rooted in certainty about Mayfield's guilt. It shows the lengths in research, questioning, or the like to which he goes in order to learn what he needs to understand about the situation at hand. Perhaps, most importantly, the scene reveals the true Columbo: sharp and committed to protecting the affable, innocent, and vulnerable Dr. Hiedeman. He is capable and primed to catch the homicidal physician in his murderous, self-promoting scheme. In sum, he is a formidable upholder of the law and of justice.

10

Columbo Closes the Case: Capture and Consequences

This chapter addresses the episodes' denouements, whether the Lieutenant catches the villains in a self-incriminating act that leads to a confession, constructs a trick to make them believe there is evidence that they must eliminate, or the rare occasions when there is an attempt to kill Columbo, which he thwarts. Importantly, this chapter raises questions about the ethical implications of the detective's devious investigative methods.

Some of the most satisfying *Columbo* episodes portray the master detective tricking the murderer into giving themselves away, revealing the truth of their culpability for the murder or murders. The con is risky because it relies on the murderer falling for it, though the deception tends to involve wild cleverness. In the final act, Columbo hones in on the smallest of details, which unravel the suspect's alibi, or he fabricates a story about a nonexistent clue, which is the suspect's property, left at the crime scene in order to spurn their retrieval of the object. In each case, Columbo successfully misleads or manipulates the suspect to perform a misstep, an act of self-incrimination, so they must surrender to the legal consequences judged befitting of their crime. Significantly, several epiphanies occur for the villains: that they have not committed the "perfect crime," that they are not as brilliant as they thought, and that the Lieutenant has bested them, and/or they were mislead to believe in Columbo's charade of antipotency. Perhaps the greatest epiphany is that this seemingly antipotent working cop is the one who has the power to take away their freedom, life of luxury, and pride over possessions and social stature. Not only was his authority underplayed as a Lieutenant detective of the LAPD, but his nature, accomplishments, and intensions behind his rhetorical inquiries were falsified, shrouded, or, at least, obscured with antipotent behaviors and communications. Ultimately, Columbo's conniving façade that he puts up for the suspect outperforms the villain's duplicity as innocent of the crime. Such is the consistent outcome of the cat-and-mouse game between them.

Reasonably, collaborations between detective and killer are unusual, to say the least, and also completely counterintuitive. While sense can be made out of the "keep your friends close and your enemies closer" line of reasoning, most detectives follow Sherlock Holmes's science-based investigations by tracking down forensic reports, and interpreting trace evidence from crime scenes, victim's persons, and the killer's own bodily proofs of commission of the crime (Knight, *Form and Ideology*; Skaggs). After all, guilty persons are better off not helping an investigator prove their own culpability for legal prosecution. "Say nothing except to a lawyer" is the conventional wisdom for persons of interest. However, in *Columbo*, the villains assume their own superiority, and therefore assume with erroneous certitude that they can talk with the Lieutenant, their enemy, without giving themselves away. The roles that both detective and suspect play are dishonest; the suspect's personae enables the Lieutenant to patiently ensnare them in their conjured alibis, inconsistencies, and falsities, which are performed before the investigator's watchful attention. Meanwhile, the criminals maintain a false sense of relaxed confidence, superiority in their ability to perform the "perfect crime," and in the effecting of elusiveness as the guilty party. However, as the episodes advance, the plot thickens, as the saying goes, with Columbo coming on stronger, with greater insistence and directness in his rhetorical inquiries of the murderer. At this point, the killer relinquishes the assistant role to the detective and presents aggravation and intolerance to Columbo's continually encroaching interrogations. Both verbally and nonverbally, the criminal's obvious anxiety and indignation toward the homicide investigator are blatant. As Columbo strengthens the case against the killer, the façade of collaborator is dropped, and, in turn, an honestly adversarial relationship is acknowledged, especially with the rogue's realization that Columbo has been playing dumb all along as a misleadingly benevolent and inconsequential predator. By the end of the episode, Columbo has taken an apparently minor discrepancy in the murderer's story and fashioned it into the noose with which he will hang the suspect. If the suspect is a magician, the Lieutenant uses a magic trick. If the crime was done by knowledge of movie special effects, Columbo uses similar special effects to construct the cons (Bounds). As Columbo delivers the final blow or the ultimate reveal, the episode reaches the conclusion, often featuring a weary yet agreeable criminal, cooperatively leaving the scene with uniformed cops.

So the murderer accepts defeat, sometimes in bitter indignation, or sometimes ironically aghast by a sense of betrayal by the Lieutenant. Exceptions to this generic Columbo-killer relationship and plot ending include instances when the villain and the detective-hero share mutual respect and general fondness for one another, resulting in reluctant capture from both parties. Some examples include Faye Dunaway in "It's All in the Game," Ruth Gordon in "Try and Catch Me," Johnny Cash in "Swan Song," Donald Pleasance in "Any Old Port in the Storm," Theo Bikel in "The Bye-Bye

Sky High IQ Murder Case," and Janet Leigh in "Forgotten Lady." Though these are chiefly reluctant villains, sympathetic to varying degrees, the detective remains objectively firm with the law and denies any killer a "get away free" pass. The Lieutenant performs his job with blind precision, abdicating any exercise of clemency for them, regardless of the circumstances, which can be viewed as a humane point in the sympathetic villain's favor. Arguably, Columbo's goodness as a man-hero is bolstered or moderated by his policy of noninvolvement in the justice system's outcome in this drama–fantasy police procedural. By refusing to wield power for or against anyone due to his personal feelings, the detective's character is fixed over the decades of his career. Viewers imagining Columbo on their criminal cases would have to reconcile certain arrest and prosecution under the law, without exception.

Until the start of the third part of each episode, the detective and villain do a deceptive dance of appeasement. However, the investigator's increasingly specific questions grow more unanswerable for the villain, who is struggling to maintain his or her faux innocence. In fact, it is during this third part that the investigation more directly targets the villains' knowledge of and relationship with the victims, uncovering possible motives and opportunities that previously eluded Columbo because of their irrefutable alibis. At this late stage of the investigation, the suspect may be aware of the detective's suspicions, deceptions, manipulation, and intent to arrest him or her. Therefore, all cooperation is revoked, anger replaces aggravation, and the suspect testifies to the detective's calculating hunt for their capture. In some cases, Columbo insists that the resistant and highly irritated suspect help him "one last time" to re-enact the murder to discover some clue about the commission of the crime. Other times, the villain acts on misinformation given by the Lieutenant, which results in their self-incrimination such as in "Death Lends a Hand," in which the purposeful blackmailer but accidental murderer, played by Robert Culp, goes to the trunk of his car to retrieve the contact lenses of his victim that were never there in the first place. The deceitful detective lures the killer into giving himself away based on a lie he tells about the certainty of damning forensic evidence.

In "Prescription Murder," the detective facilitates a progression in the investigation of the psychiatrist and wife-murderer Ray Flemming. By orchestrating and performing a ploy with the help of a female undercover police officer who doubles, from a distance, for the loyal and resistant actress and Ray's co-conspirator Joan Hudson, Columbo convinces Flemming that Joan has committed suicide in his pool. Looking at what appears to be her dead, floating body, Flemming smiles in delight, realizing that no one can prove his culpability for murdering his wife. Having finally convinced a reluctant Hudson, the only witness to the crime, to listen carefully to a conversation, Columbo traps the guilty psychiatrist into admitting he never loved "the girl." Relying on the arrogant murderer's excessive pride and insolence, Columbo turns his hubris back onto him for the snare. Infuriated and deeply hurt by his disingenuous affection and manipulation, Joan Hudson agrees to testify against the narcissistic killer–shrink, which is the evidence Columbo needs to secure arrest and probable conviction.

In a third type of trap, Columbo again uses the villain's hubris but, in these cases, he strives to trigger their inflated sense of self regard for their own expertise. In such a set up scheme, Columbo presents what he knows about the means of the murder or its concealment, but deliberately employs a mistake that only an expert would recognize. In "Negative Reaction," after much questioning, badgering, and nitpicking Paul Galesko about his wife's homicide, Columbo calls the hostile and condescending photographer to the station to present evidence against him. Enacting sincerity and conviction, Columbo demonstrates how an incriminating photograph has been manipulated in reverse, revealing a clock with Mrs. Galesko's true time of death on it, and, thereby, destroying his suspect's alibi. However, Galesko's expertise in photography and compulsion toward superiority and bravado compel him to correct the investigator on a misstep in developing the negative into an enlarged photograph. He urges the investigator to locate the negative in the back of the camera that the murderer used to take the original photo. To expedite the clarification of how Columbo failed to develop the picture properly and, in turn support his alibi, he goes to the collection of cameras in the evidence room's shelf behind where the detective sits. After immediately identifying the exact camera among twelve cameras at the secure police station, Paul opens the back of the camera for the negative. Immediately, the Lieutenant commandingly points to each of the three of the police personnel in the room with them, asking repeatedly, "Did you just see what happened?" In each case, the individuals affirm that they recognize it. By immediately identifying the correct camera with the correct negative of Mrs. Galesko being held hostage, the prize-winning photographer incriminates himself in the absence of any substantial proof. Furthermore, few killers throughout the show are quite as aghast as Paul Galesko to discover that they have fallen prey to Columbo's persistent, dishonest tactics, which result in underestimation of the investigator. In particular, Galesko is beside himself, recognizing how the Lieutenant's trap depended on his own mammoth ego, which drives him to correct others, and which gave him away. He simply cannot fathom how off his perception of the detective has been. Certainly, Galesko is not a sympathetic villain, especially after killing and framing a good natured ex-con trying to change his life for the best. However, his total disillusionment exposes the extent of Columbo's manipulation of him, begging the question...

Columbo: Virtuous or Villainous?

The Lieutenant's investigative methods prove to be effective in garnering evidentiary clues from the murderer and other persons of interest in the investigation. However, his method of doing so relies on deceit in the construction of a common and unremarkable persona, family history, and cognitive process, in order to elicit the information and cause suspects to underestimate him. Further, he is relentless in the pursuit of the killer, never swaying from his duties for any reason, suspect, or situation. Certainly, his dedication is a virtue, but his tactics are not always virtuous:

> I love tryin to pick the exact moment when Columbo figures out who the murderer is—even if he doesn't know anything else yet. It's like a boa constrictor. He finds the killer early in the episode and just wraps him/her up slowly, squeezing down on them in scene after scene.
>
> (Brune)

Above, Drew Brune's response to Andrew Bowden's blog article about *Columbo*: "A Deadly State of Mind" highlights an ethically gray area of the Lieutenant's charade with the villains. Brune's comparison of the detective to a boa constrictor celebrates the devious, predatory, and, perhaps, villainous elements of Columbo's figurative suffocation of the suspects during his investigation. In person, some of the villains have described him in unflattering ways that suggest ambivalence toward his character, calling him on his bluff. To recall, in "Ransom for a Dead Man," Leslie Williams confronts the Lieutenant on his disingenuous façade as a simpleton, his possession of a "bag of tricks," and *modus operandi* of successful "jugular" attacks, figuratively speaking. Each of these metaphoric descriptions has aggressive nuances with little counter argument from the Lieutenant himself. Ray Flemming in "Prescription Murder" diagnoses Columbo's deliberate practice of "compensation, adaptability" to effect underestimation and surprise. Additionally, when Milo Janus in "Exercise in Fatality" accuses the Lieutenant of being "a devious man," he admits that reputation. As evidenced by the following disparaging remarks, the Lieutenant isn't always endearing as a hero: "I never liked Columbo, chiefly because there is something mean and snide about pretending to be stupid when you're not" (Yancey 86). Another writer praising the authentic and relaxed PI of *The Rockford Files* makes a morally critical comparison between the two detectives: "He's kind of like *Columbo*, if you didn't want to punch Lieutenant Columbo in his artificially self-deprecating face" (Henne). Obviously, the Lieutenant's fake façade grates on these viewers and critics because he lacks transparency with the audience and villain, and he is therefore deemed unlikable in the hero role. On the one hand, like an antihero, Columbo displays a mixture of admirable and self-sacrificing traits in the cause of justice, though he uses underhanded methods characteristic of villains. On the other hand, he employs deceptive techniques in character much as undercover cops must implement. While undercover cops are incognito to blend into criminal environments, Columbo's appearance is of a proletariat, signalling him to be an outsider among the wealthy culprits. Perhaps the most significant difference between the novel and how the show's creators adapted the villain and detective characters and interactions is in the narration. As narrative point of view is limited in the show, a single Columbo film seems to address viewers like suspects; they receive selected information and crafted façades. However, after familiarity with the series builds, viewers experience the accumulated history of his secret nuances and rare conversations with witnesses or professional colleagues. Even so, viewers are not just witnessing the "cat and mouse" game between suspect and investigator; viewers know the killers but are being teased with little insight into the "familiar" detective-hero, as are the suspects. With the novel, readers get to know the criminal and the detective. In the television show, audiences get to know the criminals and have a range of spectator relationships with them (from antipathetic to sympathetic), but audiences are not Columbo's sidekicks or confidants. The narration keeps Columbo's knowledge and strategies from watchers' access, which suggests a potential threat to any citizen. For instance, Columbo fans in the numerous social media groups have commented, "I wouldn't want Columbo on my case." His relentlessness, duplicity, and some well-planned deviousness are acknowledged eventually by all suspects.

With duplicity and cunning, Columbo leverages the villains' huge egos and pretenses of innocence and caring for the deceased to solve homicide cases, but with a cost to his hero status. If the detective hero uses villainous tactics to ensure due process in the legal system, is justice served ethically? Socrates would interject with questions about moral or correct action having universal application. *Columbo* presents a competition between tricksters, which viewers take pleasure in watching play out to its conclusion. Lieutenant Columbo's obsessive nature presents itself when he relentlessly hunts the suspects, going beyond realistic "due process" and into emotional exploitation, as is his means of winning or closing a case. While Columbo's force of rhetorical queries in antipotency cause no physical harm, are they ethical in the sense of being fair, respectful, or reasonable? While working on "the right side of the law," the Lieutenant's dubious strategies of excessive deference, apology, incompetence, confusion, etc. are comparable to the murderers' strategic performance of *aporia* in not knowing, being innocent of the crime, and wanting to help.

From a pragmatic point of view, the Lieutenant must close the cases, as that is his job. If he does not, he loses sleep, his singularly focused and genius mind ruminating until the little loose ends are resolved. Is it obsession, like a mental disorder, that he cannot stop himself feeling? Is he so thoroughly goal-oriented that solving the puzzle is a compulsion? As predominantly single, domestic or workplace homicides, the killers react or plan to eliminate a threat or obstacle in their lives, or take revenge on someone who personally hurt them. Therefore, the argument that his motivation is related to public safety is weak, though it is not to posit that the murderers would not kill again. The central point is not whether killing others is always justifiable or ethical, nor is this argument leading toward excusing the villains for taking a life. The issue relates to how our hero–detective uses rhetorical methods as an ethical investigator, a good man. Instead of occupying the traditional hero role in the *Columbo* narrative, the Lieutenant portrays aspects of the anti-hero, though he is operating completely within society as a highly ranked police officer and not as an outsider. Further, the detective's mysterious character constructs a spectator relationship in which viewers are engaged in an intriguing but passive observation of the much smarter investigator at work.

The compelling incongruity with such a character is his totally compliant relationship to the law as a Mensa-level genius and brilliant mastermind. With the sympathetic villains who killed by accident, by passion, or with justification for self-preservation, the short-sighted view of justice undermines his razor sharp intellectual abilities that are limited or suppressed by the legal justice system that has been developed over centuries by less intelligent people than himself. There is a gap in logic for a genius to have complete faith in or obedience to a code of human-made laws, practiced fallibly in the court system by humans, where felons are punished in a system of dangerous incarceration, their sentences decided through biased human judgment. At this point, disbelief is no longer suspended. Indeed, the charge of pursuing this philosophical debate to completion is like Socrates' students making simplistic claims but being unable to prove the universal truth of them. Alas, it is beyond the scope of this work and the *Columbo* series.

What can be established is that Columbo, in falsifying what he knows, who he is, and also how he sees himself in relation to the arrogant, entitled criminals, mars his role as "good guy" somewhat, by his own villainous tactics of deceit and manipulation. After all, to be described as "devious": this is a character judgment about one's use of unfair and treacherous skills to achieve one's goals without regard for the well-being of others involved, or with design to harm them. While Columbo deploys his rhetorical inquiries and actions for the cause of legal justice (which is good for the community) and the pursuit of excellence and a reliable reputation, his duplicitous means do challenge the Aristotelian concept of the good person, or goodness in a person: the individual who essentially has the three basic qualities of "good sense, good moral character/excellence of soul, and good will" (Aristotle, *On Rhetoric*, book II, ch. 1, 9–10). A basic tenet of Aristotle's rhetoric and ethics is that a person's good character may be "the most effective means of persuasion he possesses" (*Rhetoric*, book I, ch. 2, 12–13). Spectators see the detective portray himself as a good man with the suspects, which includes his feigned naïveté, trusting and absentminded nature, appeasing interactions, sensitivity to presumably grieving persons of interest, empathy for the victim, and slow but dedicated investigative process. In other words, the Lieutenant constructs a persona of harmlessness that temporarily cloaks the threat of his flawless arrest record. Predicated on the premise that arrogant villains tend to let their guard down when they are in the presence of those whom they assume are inferior, Columbo acts antipotently. Also, self-inflating characters can take advantage of those they deem inferior—bullies, for instance. Therefore, adopting a self-deprecating identity with the egotistical villains is sound rhetorical practice for taming the arrogant beast. But it still does not refute the general consensus in the police department that he is "devious," which matters when the villain is sympathetic.

Columbo: *The Denouement*

In the denouement, Columbo's persona of antipotency is exposed, revealing his rhetorical deceit throughout the investigation. At the same time, the villains' personae of innocence and cooperation with the police is dismantled. Most villains are beyond surprised to realize that Columbo has been not only a pest but a formidable adversary who cunningly manipulated them into disclosing themselves as murderers. They do not try to run or escape capture, as *Columbo* is not an action police drama. Likewise, the denouement in *Columbo* episodes does not feature an investigator who is gloating, self-righteous, or angry as the culprits are being relocated for booking at the police station. Despite enduring a steady stream of insults, disrespect to his authority, and mocking laughter from most of the suspects, the Lieutenant exhibits sophrosynic relationships even while pronouncing their inevitable arrest. While confirming the presence of condemning evidence against them, the Lieutenant remains respectful as a good winner in the face of their fate. With sensitivity to the gravity of his power in the legal process, Columbo often concludes with his head down in regret for the villain's prognosis, "I'm sorry, sir." These scenes end quietly with Columbo requesting that his police officers proceed with the arrest of the astounded, even betrayed, speechless villain. Without hubris, the detective is tired but sure that the job was done right. Unceremoniously, he prepares to go home. As a matter of course, the villains realize that they have been bested, not only by Columbo's duplicity and substantial intelligence, but also by their own hubris. Ending each episode, the seemingly common hero attains justice for the victims and consequences for the privileged killers from Los Angeles, the city of false appearances, and acted roles, just one more time.

While numerous critics have mentioned the socio-economic class conflict between the honest working-class, "Everyman" hero–detective and his consistently arrogant old-moneyed, privileged villains, the show's creators insist that they did not set out to make a social critique against the upper class so much as to invent character relationships of contrast (Levinson and Link 93). Each must enter the other's unfamiliar world to not only participate in the rhetorical process of the murder investigation but to develop a substantial level of intimate familiarity with the other. In doing so, the Lieutenant gains the knowledge needed to shape his duplicitous personae of ineffectuality that lures the cautious, vigilant killer out of defensiveness, dissonance, and into false confidence and consonance. Synchronously, the egotistical murderer collects social data in their observation of the investigator's benign affect, using it to reformulate an equally misleading self-presentation of innocence, co-commitment to solving the case, and dependable deference to the authority of the justice system, as a civil servant to the greater good. Their role-play strikes crisis mode when the villain begins to recognize Columbo's pretense of inferiority. The Lieutenant diminishes his highly strategic rhetorical ruse until he has identified enough condemning evidence to close the investigation. In the climactic moments, the villain is trapped in his or her deception and guilt, suddenly fully aware of Columbo's use of fabricated ineffectiveness to serve their own capture. Conventionally, the denouement portrays a reluctantly defeated villain acknowledging having been bested by the more intellectually capable and powerful police Lieutenant.

I think that the aspects of this book that may disturb ardent *Columbo* fan readers is the rhetorical inquiry into the Lieutenant's character as a "good man." In the end, he is still a good man, but with shades of villainy that disrupt a reading of Columbo as a pure hero. While this may seem disrespectful to the most loyal fans, my book makes a case for the detective's complex dimensions of character: as a servant of the law, brilliant thinker, loving husband and dog owner, obsessive personality, and devious con and manipulator. Columbo plays a villain to catch a villain. What keeps Columbo out of the ethical deep waters is that we as the viewers don't exactly know to what extent he is faking his ignorance, trusting nature, and manipulative understatedness. As a long time *Columbo* fan, newsletter/fanzine reporter, and expert, Sheldon Catz addresses this "myth" about the investigator's supernatural brilliance and calculatedness by pointing to a lack of sufficient evidence about the exact nature of the detective's intellectual ruminations (xviii). In turn, viewers never truly know Columbo; rather they observe what kind of man he really is by his actions, dialogue, and behaviors that are shown in the show. With Columbo's internal character being mysterious, viewers are target audiences for the performance of antipotency as much as the villains. While some loyal *Columbo* viewers argue that they feel well acquainted with "the good detective," much is left hidden from the spectator's as well as the villain's view. Therefore, for some spectators, the viewing experience can involve ambivalence about the investigator, with mixed feelings of frustration, annoyance, uncertainty, surprise, as well as intrigue, fondness, admiration, and delight.

PART 3

COLUMBO'S LEGACY IN POPULAR CULTURE AND ACADEMIA

Descendants of the Lieutenant manifest in numerous venues and media. Columbo appears in artists' renderings of the detective of which there are hundreds with more still being created. Featured in various fan-based and auction websites are art works done by Peter Falk of his character. The work includes paintings, drawings, sculptures, wood carvings, imitative performances, caricatures, and the like. Further, writers have created short stories about the Lieutenant, inspired by Richard Levinson and William Link's popular fiction. Truly, *Columbo* lives on, posthumously. In fact, William Link, the surviving co-creator of *Columbo*, published a collection of short stories about the Lieutenant seven years after the last broadcast of original episodes in 2003, giving fans more cases for Columbo to solve. Besides the obvious profit motive, commercial memorabilia are designed to extend the viewing enjoyment of the show and character beyond the film into viewers' daily lives. Examples include the *Columbo* board game, t-shirts, license plate frames, autographed publicity pictures and scripts, coffee mugs, fake Columbo police badges and identification cards, to list some examples. Serving fans as reminders of their favorite character and expressing his importance to them, even today, customers, male and female, go to costume shops or order costumes and props online to dress up as the iconic detective, wearing a tan raincoat, holding a real or prop cigar. Bringing their favorite detective to life, people don the costume, scratching their heads in search of pencils and repeating key phrases such as "Oh I almost forgot," "Oh, by the way," "One more thing," "Am I bothering you?" and the like. Fans masquerading is a testament to the continued relevancy of Columbo and *Columbo* for viewers and their ongoing desires to live vicariously as the investigator, even for a short while.

11

Television Detectives Influenced by Lieutenant Columbo

According to television crime show researcher Ric Meyers, the 1970s television market was saturated with detective shows. However, CBS program producer Quinn Martin didn't heed the warnings against making another. This time, Martin would make it a "mature" private investigator, an "elderly Columbo," and co-producer Fred Silverman came up with choosing a "foxy grandfather type," having "the character doing 'schtick,' You know, drinking milk and things like that" (Meyers 181). Further, Meyers explains, "*Barnaby Jones* (1973–80) was initially conceived as "an 'old Columbo' (both detectives were unassuming and seemed less capable than they were) ...."

While both shows featured the commission of the crime during the opening sequence, they differed in the remaining 60% of their episodes: *Columbo* focuses on the detective's investigation while *Barnaby Jones* is about the villain's cover-up of the crimes (Meyers 182). Also, the police Lieutenant was a seemingly absent-minded but persistent homicide detective working "in the realm of the rich, who are not like us [viewers], while the more direct private investigator 'invaded the world of the middle class [...]' 'our next-door neighbors [like us]' [...] 'nicely dressed, seemingly civilized folks who were actually amoral monsters'" (180). The two shows were both about local or domestic crimes, mostly murders, and carried themselves gently, quietly, intelligently, with working-class wisdom and undeniably firm resolve.

Pursuing the same question of homage, *Columbo* scholar Sheldon Catz notes several "Columbo Offspring," television series that have been influenced by Levinson and Link's successful show and character, citing a list of amateur detectives: Levinson and Link's other hit murder investigation series, *Murder She Wrote*, featuring professional mystery novelist Jessica Fletcher (Angela Lansbury) who finds herself caught in murderous cases by chance (CBS 1984–96). Others that Catz notes include *The Cosby Mysteries*, with retired criminologist and forensics expert played by the arguably formerly lovable comedian Bill Cosby (NBC 1994–95); *Matlock*, with the southern gentlemanly lawyer in Atlanta played by the affable, aged country boy

Andy Griffith (NBC 1986–92, ABC 1993–95); and *Diagnosis Murder*, with chief of internal surgery played by the esteemed Dick Van Dyke (CBS 1993–2001) (Catz 374–75). Certainly, these shows and many others offer a range of golden-age mode detectives, some of which have quirks, self-effacing characters, and deceptively unassuming façades with actual skills and knowledge that catch killers. Also, Catz includes suspended police detective Adrian Monk (Tony Shalhoub) as the eccentric, obsessive-compulsive, germ-fearing consulting detective in the series *Monk* (2002–09) (374–75) and the NYPD detective Robert Goren of *Law and Order: Criminal Intent* (2001–11). In the next section, the latter detective is compared with the Lieutenant.

Law and Order: Criminal Intent: *Detective Robert Goren*

Law and Order: Criminal Intent's Detective Robert Goren (Vincent D'Onofrio) has a manner similar to the Lieutenant during police inquiries: a tilt of his head and earnest, nonthreatening expressions, asking so many trivial questions from a pointless position of curiosity, and relentlessly returning with more inquiries. While some methods of rhetorical inquiry overlap between the two offbeat, New York City raised, urban detectives, the shows are created within different subgenres, which call for distinctions: police action drama mystery with Goren closing cases via intense interrogations in the squad room versus inverted mystery, police detective light drama with fantasy and comedy. On at least two occasions, actor Vincent D'Onofrio responded to fan tweets asking about his thoughts on the connections between his Detective Robert Goren and Peter Falk's Columbo: "I wish I was that good. Peter Falk was an amazing actor" (27 February 2017), and "I loved Columbo and would sometimes celebrate that with adding a lil something from that iconic character" (19 March 2017). Hearing from the actor himself clarifies the question of whether we can consider Goren a descendent of Columbo. While D'Onofrio admits to mimicry, Professor and research blogger Amelie Hastie differentiates the shows' genres via their lead detectives—emotionally dark NYC Goren against the light-hearted, Golden Age-style detective of luxurious Beverly Hills:

> I think Goren's role within the detective unit (we never see Columbo in a police station) and the seemingly emotionally unstable element of his own "bumbling" mean they don't seem to textually line up for me, either. Plus, I think Falk plays Columbo with a real sense of humor—and that the fictional detective himself has a sense of humor. That's partly what invokes such affection for him.
> (Hastie)

Law & Order: Criminal Intent is a police drama mystery with two partnered detectives of the New York City Police Department: Robert "Bobby" Goren (Vincent D'Onofrio) and Alexandra Eames (Kathryn Erbe). Produced by Dick Wolf

FIGURE 27: Screenshot: Det. Robert Goren (Vincent D'Onofrio) and Det. Alexandra Eames (Kathryn Erbe) pretending to be coworker-friends of the deceased to get information from associate mothers watching their children at the park. Jean de Segonzac (dir.), "Privilege," *Law and Order: Criminal Intent*, 2007. Wolf Film, NBC Universal Television.

FIGURE 28: Screenshot: Paul Hanlon (Robert Culp) gets worn down by the persistent Lieutenant. Jeremy Kagan (dir.), "The Most Crucial Game," *Columbo*, 1972. Universal Pictures.

and developed by René Balcer, *Law & Order: Criminal Intent* premiered on NBC on 30 September 2001 and continued with its seventh season on USA Network on 4 October 2007, ending its tenth season on 26 June 2011. Further, the show was "shot entirely in and around New York City," taking "viewers deep into the minds of its criminals while following the intense psychological approaches the Major Case Squad uses to solve its crimes" (The Futon Critic). On USA Network's promotional website, the Columbo-like investigator is described in action:

> When Detective Robert Goren is at a crime scene, nothing is overlooked. With a broad intellect and cunning instinct that borders on brilliance, this modern-day Sherlock Holmes brings an unparalleled level of scrutiny to the job. However,

it's in the interrogation room that Goren truly displays his genius. By virtually entering the mind of the criminal, Goren examines every possible angle of the motive. Operating on just the thinnest shred of evidence, Goren can break down even the boldest criminal into an impassioned confession.

(USA Network)

Despite his genius, Goren is unpopular with his colleagues due to his moody, cryptic, and unsubstantiated "hunches," while the eccentric Lieutenant is well-liked, respected, and trusted, though operates alone most of the time. Goren's emotionally wounded detective has periods of spiraling out of control with insubordination and even relationship disruption with his devoted partner, Alexandra Eames. While at times destructive to relationships, Goren's mental instability elicits good information from suspects under interrogation about the particularly disturbing major crimes. Other times, Goren acts quirkier than he is, much like Columbo acts less capable than he is. Further, Columbo is not emotionally volatile nor presented as having personal tragedies or personal triumphs. The LAPD Lieutenant conventionally inquires calmly at suspect's homes, workplaces, recreational facilities, airports, and the like, stalking them relentlessly. Otherwise, the calm and dogged detective appears to have friendly, neighborly conversations about the crime with suspects at locations typically outside of the squad room. With more vulnerable and frightened suspects or witnesses, Goren strategically uses a Columbo-like approach: a seemingly sympathetic, unfamiliar, and suspect-dependent approach to investigating suspects' personalities, alibis, abilities, resources, relationships to the victims, and possible motives.

In the episode called "Phantom" (2002), suspect Charlotte Fielding just arrives at the interrogation room, outside which detective Alexandra Eames turns to Bobby Goren privately, "Ready?" with Goren delighting, "Let's play." Like Columbo, Goren has a way of engendering candor, even unintentional candor, though both in and out of the "interrogation room." Responding to leading questions, the person of interest continues to talk with Goren and Eames about her humble beginnings before stepping into her identity as the wealthy socialite Charlotte Fielding. At the end of the interrogation, Fielding acknowledges having been caught by the detectives' verbal snare to reveal more than she wanted to: "I fell right into your hands—good cop, bad cop. I forgot all cops are bad cops." She calls them on their deceitful, questioning tactics designed to soften her reluctance to disclose any details about her boyfriend, who is the real suspect of their murder case.

Further in the "Phantom" episode is the discovery that Fielding's boyfriend is living a double life with another unsuspecting woman: his wife and their kids. Goren and Eames employ a ruse at the residence of the suspect to confirm that the identity of the woman untangling a wind chime on her front porch is the target's wife. She is interrupted by the detectives' inquiry, "Tessa Rankin?" Using the ruse of an investigation involving her husband's car, Eames executes a rhetorical inquiry, requesting trivial details while Goren completes Tessa's task with the wind chimes. His act serves to distract the suspect's wife with the ordinariness and general helpfulness of his attentions. As he untangles the last strand, Goren praises Tessa for having a good system of communication with her husband that involves leaving a message on his pager for a call back rather than her calling a direct landline to an office. Maintaining his persona of ignorance about their relationship, Goren plays innocent and placating, "Is that what he does when he travels overseas?" Through indirect rhetorical inquiries and responses to information provided by Tessa, Goren leads her to see her husband's deceit. Goren victoriously strikes the untangled wind chimes, and gives a knowing smile for having just discovered the means by which the suspect maintains his double life in secret from his wife. Upon returning to Tessa and Jerry Rankin's home with a search warrant, Goren plays the role of comforter while knowingly inquiring about her late father's suspicious death. Doing so enables Tessa to offer new details relating to a seemingly unrelated subject that warrants sensitivity and compassion, which garner her confidence. As a result, Goren repositions himself as Tessa's protector against her opportunistic husband with a pattern of suspicious ties to murder and financial acquisitions.

Other Columbo-isms include Goren enacting antipotency: adopting a passive and nonthreatening persona with Jerry by avoiding eye contact, taking his suit jacket off, and showing no visible firearms. However, Goren takes risks of personal danger and is, indeed, vulnerable to this impulsive killer. Further crafting his persona as someone who relates to Jerry's life burdens of unreasonable expectations and responsibilities, Goren exonerates him of his responsive crimes and deceits: "How you've been caught up in the tentacles of circumstance. Everything has been done to you." By reflecting Jerry's own self talk of self-victimization, Goren appears to be successfully calming the delusional man with strategic submissiveness, comforting Jerry with reinforcements of his credo, "I didn't have any choice." Maintaining a submissive affect with emotionally unstable, desperate, and volatile Jerry, Goren moves from simpatico to a discourse of heroification to lull the killer into consonance. In contrast to Detective Goren from the police procedural genre, the Lieutenant's confrontation of suspects happens only at the end and without being in danger himself, as *Columbo* is not an action police drama but a cerebral one.

In the eighteenth episode of the first season, "Yesterday," Eames and Goren enter the corporate world of a head office in a high-rise office building to interview the controlling and arrogant supervisor and suspect of the murder in recognizable Columbo style. Here, Eames and Goren are the unwanted inquisitors, and the suspect, Jay Lippman, maneuvers to rid himself of the interlopers. Unfortunately for Lippman, Goren recognizes the often-played social maneuver of getting someone to leave a place. The suspect walks toward the door and speaks in a low voice, making himself difficult to be heard and, thereby, draws conversants to the intended destination: out the door. Comprehending the suspect's controlling character and devious communication tactic, Goren expresses his observation: "I like how you did that, making me cross the room by keeping your voice down." While denying the accusation of doing that deliberately, Jay gives a tense, fake smile. Pushing further and with potency, Goren refutes his denial, "Come on. It's the classic Sicilian gambit. To get me to the door." Contrary to Lieutenant Columbo's persona of antipotency, Goren postures but politely, assuring the suspect that he is aware, smart, in control, and not easily manipulated by him: "We're done, anyway. Thank you for seeing us."

While Columbo would not be so direct and confrontational with a suspect until the denouement, Goren and Eames perform a quoted Columbo false exit of "Oh, by the way." Adopting the method, the pair of detectives turn to walk out of the door, but then halt in the door frame. Turning back to face the slightly unnerved suspect, Bobby Goren employs a signature Columbo phrase, followed by a rhetorical question: "Oh, by the way, you don't want to know why we are asking about Morrissey?" Like Columbo, Goren articulates his observations of uncommon or incongruous behaviors, often sparking understated defensiveness from the guilty. Later in the investigation, the detectives arrive at the Lippman residence with a search warrant for financial forensics about her husband's activities, obliging the innocent Mrs. Lippman to reveal incriminating evidence before turning to exit with polite gratitude. Pausing at the door, Goren performs the Columbo "just one more thing" false exit by conveying their commitment to solving the murder with transparency, "One more thing .... If you want to tell your husband we were here, by all means, we have no secrets from him. The more he knows, the better it is."

Like Columbo, Goren triggers suspects' reactions tactically by controlling the conversation's circumstances and duration to agitate their inflated egos. In the police interrogation room, Goren hypothesizes with Jay Lippman that he has likely suffered under the control of his dominant, drug addict college friend, Morrissey, rationalizing his murder. Using this bait psychology, Goren challenges Lippman's sense of superiority over the late college roommate with exaggerations of decades-long victimization at the hands of the deceased. No longer able to contain his condescending feelings and indignancy about the murder victim, Lippman inadvertently blurts out an arrogant, self-justified confession. In other words, Goren, like Columbo, uses his knowledge of human nature and of a suspect's psychology to lead criminals to revealing damning information, despite their intention to remain mostly silent to protect their best interest. The transition to the county jail cell is a short one from the dingy, bare police interrogation room. The implications of an ominous fate abound, while Columbo's suspects are shown, conventionally, leaving escorted, often without handcuffs, from their homes into a mysterious and generally not depicted future of prosecution and punishment. The *Columbo* killers' fate is like the vague fantasy of living happily ever after in fairytales. The after is not shown because the story ends there, as it does for suspects in *Columbo*, who are presumably living unhappily ever after.

Contrary to *Law and Order: Criminal Intent*, *Columbo* is humorous, and, more specifically, the Lieutenant is the object of many of the jokes. Detective Goren is very serious, and, when he is joking, the humor is characteristically sardonic and about the case at hand, offering brief moments of distracting relief. Unlike the Lieutenant, Goren is literally self-critical and critical of those in his surroundings, not humorously self-deprecating. He is brooding and has depression and trauma, in opposition to the Lieutenant, who is lively, positive, and with a mostly blank slate for a personal life. As confirmed previously, *Columbo* is not a police procedural but could be categorized as a dramedy, blending dramatic and comedic features, situations, dialogue, and happy endings of restored order. Conversely, *Law and Order: Criminal Intent* is a realistically oriented, urban police procedural with the depraved violence related to policing major crimes. *Columbo* has fantasy components such as a cop who refuses to carry a sidearm, has an expired safety certification and a shabby vehicle, fears blood, and is accompanied by an occasional dog sidekick. All of these components emphasize the intellectual puzzle and playful elements of the show. After all, if he doesn't carry a gun, he cannot have shoot outs. If his car is in disrepair, he cannot participate in car chases. If he cringes at the sight of blood, viewers do not see blood. In terms of a final interrogation, Columbo does not conduct one in the same style as Goren with both confrontational and misleading sympathy approaches.

Instead, Columbo's style is indirect and does not put the villain into an ominous official police interrogation room. Instead, his inquiries seem frustratingly disorganized without a point, going nowhere, keeping killers guessing about the investigator's knowledge, abilities, and suspicions. Finally, if his part-time sidekick is a dog, there are only one-way conversations with amusing nonverbal expressions from a floppy-eared, droopy-eyed, short, and lazy dog. In fact, Columbo's lack of a partner and internal monologue leaves audiences guessing or waiting for clarity about the detective's actual discoveries, theories, and plans, watching his actions unfold before their gaze, much like the murderers do.

Lieutenant Columbo's Possible Future

After a publicized 24-hour Twitter exchange about *Columbo* between actor Mark Ruffalo and screenwriter Gary Whitta, Ruffalo announced that he would gladly play the detective role:

I've always been a huge fan of the television series. I thought Peter Falk was magnificent in his crumpled genius. He is an Everyman often finding crime in places where he is despised. I really can't wait to get on the rain coat, practice my squint and say the immortal line, "Oh I almost forgot, just one more question."
(Sternberger)

In *The Guardian*'s TV and radio blog, reporter Graeme Virtue published an article about the unofficial discussions regarding a possible remake, film adaptation, or other extension of *Columbo* in mainstream cinema in which he argues, "A reboot of *Columbo* is a fantastic idea – apart from one enormous flaw." While Virtue warns against taking *Columbo* to the big screen, he encourages Ruffalo to play the Lieutenant on television in a similarly extended time format. "Columbo is as rich a character as Sherlock Holmes." However, just as actors' portrayals of Sherlock Holmes and Dr. John Watson have distant nuances, and the script writers' and directors' plots and narratives vary considerably, so might Ruffalo's reincarnation of Falk's Lieutenant in the company of a full film production company and crew. On the online blog *The Columbophile*, curated by an anonymous writer called

FIGURE 29: Mark Ruffalo in *Zodiac* and Peter Falk in *Columbo* look alike. Tom: "Mark Ruffalo As 'Columbo'?....Yes Please!!" *The Last Reel*, 17 July 2014, 4:24 p.m., thelastreel.blogspot.com/2014/07/mark-ruffalo-as-columboyes-please.html.

Columbophile, fans debate about whether or not to reboot the show at all and if Ruffalo would be well-suited for the Columbo role that is so intimately associated with Peter Falk. While Universal Pictures has not yet given permission for a *Columbo* update, many fans are hoping for it.

Spoofing the Lieutenant

The traits that are exaggerated or spoofed are similar among the print and video texts: Columbo being unintelligent and disorganized, and inadvertently, or, rather, deliberately annoying suspects (and perhaps some viewers as well). In January 1973, *Mad Magazine* published their animated parody called "Clodumbo," by writer Lou Silverstone and illustrator Angelo Torres in homage to the 1971 *Columbo*: "Death Lends a Hand" with Robert Culp as the villain. The comic genius is best explained by webzine author Lisa Philbrick as she humorously illustrates one of the Lieutenant's stock investigative methods, incessantly pestering the suspected murderer:

> The story opens with Clodumbo annoying the hell out of the Police Commissioner and the rest of the department [who are] wishing for a homicide so Clodumbo can go and annoy somebody else. […].And like Columbo on the series, Clodumbo aggravates Dr. Culpable to the Nth degree. Only, unlike Robert Culp, who played the guilty party with aplomb, Dr. Culpable was innocent and ended up confessing to a crime he didn't commit, just to get the pestering Lieutenant to leave him alone!
> (Philbrick)

In 1989, writer Dick Debartolo and illustrator Angelo Torres reprised the "Clodumbo" parody in *Mad Magazine*'s satire "The ABC Misery Movie." Satirizing Columbo's signature investigative style, Clodumbo reveals the key to his success with suspects: "I badger the witness! I use a lot of cunning ploys! And I badger the witness! I'm rather sneaky in my ways! And did I mention that I like to badger the witness?" (DeBartolo 27). At the end, the suspect swims into shark-infested waters to escape Clodumbo's pestering. When Clodumbo follows him in a rowboat and warns him that a huge shark is coming, the man says, " 'Thank God!' It'll be a much less painful death than dealing with you!" Both mock Columbo's method of frustrating, irritating, and aggravating the suspects in a supposedly benign and unintended manner while also portraying the efficacy of that agitating stratagem not only on the suspects but also on viewers.

Two memorable video comic sketch parodies also exaggerate the Lieutenant's methodical "bothering" of suspects. For example, on *The Tonight Show with Johnny Carson*, the host Johnny Carson and the Mighty Carson Art Players act out a sketch featuring a couple who are the villains, planning a getaway to Paris after executing a "full proof caper" and murder. Almost safe and heading for the airport, the two are interrupted by Carson as the monotone, rambling Lieutenant Columbo: "I hate to bother you at 4 in the morning.... I'd like to ask you a few questions, if you don't mind, of course. I don't like to bother people, if they don't mind. You don't mind, do you?" With impertinence, the villainess retorts, "Well, what's this all about?" In hyperbole, Carson-Columbo answers, "Well, I wish I knew, ma'am. There are certain things not clear in my mind ... you know, can't sleep at night." Carson employs similar but exaggerated Columbo-isms: monotone, circumstantial speech that evokes *aporia* in being cognitively disoriented, asking questions that seem meaningless and aimless, adding nonrelevant information, and projecting cluelessness about the suspects. After the villain couple stresses their usual willingness to cooperate with the police, Columbo continues to speak quickly, aimlessly, repetitively, and without a clear point, "Most people don't want to be bothered. ... I'm the last one to bother people. ... won't bother you anymore."

FIGURE 30: *Screenshot: The Mighty Carson Art Players, Peter Leeds and Sandy deBruin, in a spoof skit "Columbo," bothering suspects until they are driven mad and desperate.* The Tonight Show with Johnny Carson, *1975. Carson Production, NBC Productions.*

For a moment, the detective leaves the home after the third false exit, the female villain expresses agitation, "He's beginning to get on my nerves." The male villain responds with exaggerated underestimation of the inspector's cognitive abilities, "Oh, forget it. He's just a dummy in a raincoat." Then, of course, Columbo makes his way back into the room, but now he does so through impossible locations: the closet, a window, the wall safe, a file cabinet drawer, a turntable, etc. Each revisiting is more outrageous than the prior, repeating the general pattern of head-scratching, bewilderment, and mumbling claims of having one more question. The skit delivers a mildly hyperbolic version of Columbo's self-awareness as bothersome, interminable, and nerve-grating rhetorical inquiry, which drives villains to desperation. In fact, Carson's Columbo is even more antipotent than Falk's, based on the premise that the Lieutenant is a skill-less, inept but tenacious Inspector Clouseau. In other words, Columbo is as dumb as his persona, having to be rescued from capture by Robert Blake as television's tough New York City detective Tony Baretta and his sidekick cockatoo, Fred, from the hit series *Baretta* (1975–78).

A final example of successful parody of Columbo is by Peter Falk himself during his appearance on the Dean Martin Celebrity Roast in 1977, for which Lieutenant Columbo was an invited guest of Frank Sinatra's roast. When Dean Martin introduces the next guest speaker as being from the Los Angeles Police Department, Falk enters the auditorium, met with exuberant applause, whistling, and cheers of praise. Played with spot on precision, of course, Falk stays in the Columbo character, bothering the guest of honor with high-speed ramblings about trivial, irrelevant, off topic details. For example, he showers Martin and Sinatra with an over indulgence of humility and gratitude for his invitation to the important event and for the generous introduction. Then, his lack of social sophistication and his working-class cop persona manifest themselves in his unrelated interruptions of his own speech to ask millionaire Dean Martin whether his shoes are rented. With Columbo's characteristic physical imposition of crowding others, Falk again breaches social decorum among the Hollywood elites. Furthermore, he makes Columbo-esque requests of the other panelists such as borrowing Dean Martin's cocktail napkin and Don Rickles's pencil. Of course, Falk as Columbo obligates them ever so politely but insistently, just as the detective does in the series. In a game of disruption, characteristic of his show's leading detective, Falk asks Frank Sinatra to autograph Dean Martin's napkin with Don Rickles's pencil for his wife, of course. Acting as a fan of the fellow celebrities is incongruent with his role as one who is roasting Old Blue Eyes, not to mention that he is doing so during a television broadcast. Falk as Columbo further agitates the guest of honor by offering an unsolicited and unqualified critique of Sinatra's last musical recording. With even more gall, softened in the guise of unintentional mockery, the detective passes along his family's equally unqualified theories about the singer's retirement relating to his "tired voice," questioning if Jerry Vail had to dub his voice on the record. Of course, the suggestion is absolutely absurd on both a literal level and in terms of social decorum. Within the context of the Dean Martin Celebrity Roast genre, Falk uses Columbo methods to effect irritating antipotency and imposition, negotiating between the conflicting demands of praising and humorously insulting the notable celebrity in the spotlight.

12

Using Columbo's Method in Our Everyday Lives

This book argues for the relevance of studying Columbo's methods of rhetorical inquiry with resistant responders. To be clear, the resistant responders to which we could apply the Lieutenant's rhetoric of inquiry are not of the same violent caliber as the show's killers, *though* many of them are equally as resistant to acknowledging or expressing truths about themselves and certain situations. The reasons for individuals' resistance may be a symptom of perceived incompatible values, allegiances, personal histories, demographics, psychographics, preferences, beliefs, educational profiles, fear of change, and the like. Further, some people are simply unmovable, despite the awareness of conflicting information. Such illogical refusal to accept new information and change one's mind is a stubbornness demonstrated by Chuck Klosterman: "I know the truth, but I just don't care" (199). With individuals who are unwilling to adjust their perceptions and preferences due to a mysterious emotional connection or the like, they may never see things as reasonably argued and supported. Sales professionals, for example, apply a version of Columbo's antipotent rhetoric of inquiry as an approach of combative metaphors of "targets," "wins," and "victims" (Greene). In contrast, Columbo's antipotent rhetorical inquiry can apply in a range of interlocutor relationships from cooperative, collaborative, assertive, to agonistic (Berzsenyi, "Teaching Interlocutor Relationships"). Certainly, downplaying one's authority, power, and ability can facilitate self-serving and manipulative endeavors as well as cooperative and connective collaborations. Columbo's strategic questions under the persona of a good faith partnership can be utilized more broadly, as determined by each rhetorical inquirer.

In Steven Berglas's *Forbes* article "The Top 5 Ways to Manage Closed-Minded, Defensive, Truth-Resistant People," the psychiatrist and retired faculty of Harvard Medical School of Psychiatry defines the term "resistant" in terms of communicating with his private practice patients and his executive clients:

> These folks regularly interrupt or terminate coaching relationships with what I call *Ostrich Moments:* Hiding, avoiding, or ensuring they won't get touched by the reality-based feedback they ask coaches to provide[.] In psychiatry, the behaviors people engage in to ensure they will be spared the stress of handling the truth is called *resistance*; a complex form of shooting the messenger that blocks the delivery of hard, cold, facts to someone who fears them.
>
> (Berglas 1)

In his taxonomy of five types of resistant people, which he likens to animals (gorillas, owls, foxes, horses, and skunks), Berglas describes the nature of each type's resistance, their reactions to the truths presented to them, and some strategies for helping them to overcome their resistant barriers, when it is possible to do so. For example, "truth-evaders" react with defensiveness about their poor performance stats by challenging another's expertise or status in making the criticism that is a matter of preference but not necessity. Truth-evaders refuse to recognize the validity of facts and behaviors that contribute to their failure, refuting facts with prideful arrogance (not unlike *Columbo*'s villains), lack of cooperation, and threatening backlash for the "groundless" insult. With so many ways that people actively react to, deny, and avoid hearing the reality of their situation, mentors are frustrated in pursing their goal of helping their employees improve.

To enable a productive working relationship with these successful but resistant managers and executives, Berglas employs various techniques that include the inundation of facts to elicit their own critical thinking in a less personal way. Presenting a case study demands the managers exercise sound judgments about comparable issues and the benefits of making changes. Drawing on the resistant truth-evaders, Berglas disengages their personal defenses that were protecting their previous decisions and actions. This way they can recognize more objectively the problem-solving impasse of the situation at hand, which requires alternate actions. Similar to the detective's methods, rhetorically based questions solicit the intelligent viewpoint of the resistant supervisors. Together, in dialogue, the team of Berglas and the resistant manager recognize the complexities of the case scenario without blaming anyone or triggering personal defenses. Once the resistant responders are given authoritative responsibility to solve the problem, they discover procedures that serve the corporation. Instead of competing with the managers, Berglas bolsters their sense of authority and managerial acumen without a direct confrontation of who is right and wrong (similar to Columbo's technique with his suspects). By removing the one-on-one battle dynamics, Berglas facilitates the resistant manager's critical thinking, which is the aim. Many of these strategies can be combined with a question-based method, but not all of them. In any case, the goal is to elicit cooperation, openness, and communication.

Another type of resistant responder is the generally shy or socially anxious person. This nervousness can manifest from their being unaccustomed to feeling or having any agency to speak up, express their views, and/or argue for their positions. Subjectively feeling intimidation, lack of belonging to an organization, and inadequacy about one's contributions to a group project may lead to resistant behavior when confronted with their perceived betters in that team. In turn, these students may be inhibited or anxious about engaging in discussions, exploration, negotiation, and decision-making in a conversational or presentational context. However, such individuals will not entirely avoid nervous situations because their fear level is manageable. Those interacting with shy people would benefit from a less direct, argumentative, or interrogative persuasive approach. Using questions with purpose to draw out the individual's feelings, thoughts, goals, and the like in order to collaborate is a starting point that cannot be skipped or risk overwhelming, offending, or pushing too hard. The undesired outcome may be their shutting down to the dialogue or transaction, which defeats the purposes of engaging in the first place.

While many aspects of the Lieutenant's investigative methods are irrelevant or inappropriate for most people's everyday rhetorical situations, there are several tactics that merit examination and application:

- Instead of assuming that you know others and their concerns, ask them many questions, a variety of questions, purpose-driven questions, and well-timed inquiries.
- Listen carefully, observe, and get to know the interlocutor's vantage point, needs, and preferred style of engagement.
- Use general kindness and politeness, reasonable praise, appropriate apologies when applicable, and respect to foster mutual understanding and readiness to work.
- Solicit other's input and cooperation to learn respectfully from them, and, then, share your views, building a common goal.
- Offer your assistance on their project, not a debate or contradictions.
- Negotiate carefully to avoid undoing the goodwill you have established.

Specifically, professionals across fields and markets have recognized the value of applying Columbo's antipotent questioning style to numerous workplace communications. In particular, two individuals influenced the writing of this book: Adrian Sutton and Max Brandon. While performing patient psychoanalytic research for his book *Pediatrics, Psychiatry, and Psychoanalysis*, Adrian Sutton identifies direct comparisons between Georg Groddeck's theory about therapist–patient dynamics in psychological therapy and the detective–suspect inquiry. While the comparison is underdeveloped, Sutton articulates several points of similarity in doctor–patient relationships and therapist inquiry to assist the patient in self-discovery: "His persona is of being someone for whom only questions arise, not answers. ... In essence, he makes an art of 'not knowing and not-being-capable-of-becoming-knowing'"(168). Therefore, the patient supplies the answers to the questions from the clinician's raised awareness about the particular patient's needs and tolerances, rather than approaching all patients uniformly.

In the field of business management, the CEO of the pyramid-structured business Ca$hCard, Max Brandon, created a training and screening video for his employees, which he explicitly calls "The Columbo Tactic." Further, the method of interest to him is Columbo's "signature interrogation technique," which is "a wholesale departure from hard pressing, course heavy, tough guy investigators who try to bully their suspects with their badge or gun or gruff demeanor" (Brandon). He recommends using questions to get to know the potential employee, discover common ground and values, and cultivate a relationship of sharing information.

In addition to these two, other professionals have referenced the fictional detective's inquiry-based methods of encouraging cooperation with resistant responders: management of stubborn employees and anxious clients in finance (Roseman), ethical and bio-medical diagnostics with frightened patients (Ryan), sales training with tougher potential prospects (Davidoff), evangelical preaching to nonbelievers as "diplomacy rather than D-Day" (Koukl), rhetorical instruction on the Socratic Dialogue (Madigan), academic advising of insistent students, and so on. This list is far from exhaustive, and the full development of the query is beyond the scope of this work. In the meantime, professionals are reconsidering the efficacy of their standard approaches to working with supervisors, employees, clients, and the like that tell others what they should want or do with an authority that inhibits collaboration. Columbo's method has taken a few decades to enter into the mindset of career professionals, but, clearly, this is a rhetorical turn to think about people first versus idiosyncratic styles imposed in all situations with all people. Advantageously and more collectively, the rule of authoritative, hard sell, and competitive communication is being supplemented with antipotent demeanors and sophrosynic approaches to incite collaboration within communities of projects, missions, relations, transactions, and the like.

13

"Just One More Thing": *Columbo* and Spectatorship

In this triad of the wealthy and powerful villain, effective detective, and, generally, sympathetic victim, where does the audience stand? Viewers have firsthand knowledge of the villain's motives, *modus operandi*, and crafted alibi, but have minimal-to-no insight into the detective's hypotheses and strategies via dialogue with other characters or behaviors. A dozen or so cases from the 69 episodes have villains who are sympathetic to some degree, as their actions are designed to protect or avenge what they hold dear. In contrast, most are clearly unsympathetic killers from the start, deserving legal justice for their selfish greed for money, narcissistic avarice for power, or tactical violence or planting of false evidence on others in efforts to maintain their own self-preservation. There is a dozen or so who appear more sympathetic at the start, but devolve into calculating, self-protecting villains at anyone else's expense (Catz 228–51). In this case, perhaps familiarity does breed contempt from audiences who witness the heinous acts of which the slayers are capable, and on which the narcissistic priorities underlying these aggressive and objectifying conquests induce their desired situations. While the Lieutenant's method of rhetorical inquiry (ad nauseum) annoys villains and some viewers alike, the investigation is done in the line of duty with a dependable, predictable, and, therefore, reassuringly familiar course of action. In the end, Lieutenant Columbo's escalating verbal strangulation of villains with copious inquiries rouses viewers' anticipation for the best rhetorical game in town. Perhaps most remarkably, spectators continue to offer the fictional, strategic rhetorician their respect, loyalty, and, even, in some cases, obsession, across the globe, long after the originally aired broadcasts and deep into syndication.

Works Cited

Adams, Charles Warren (pseudonym Charles Felix). *Notting Hill Mystery*. Serialized in *Once a Week Magazine: New Series, 8 Sections*, vol. 7-8, 1862–63.

Akhmerti, Primasita Fitria, and Heddy Shri Ahimsa-Putra. "An Introduction to the Police Procedural: A Subgenre of Detective Genre." *Humaniora*, vol. 31, no. 1, 2019, pp. 33–40.

Ames, Christopher. *Movies about the Movies: Hollywood Reflected*. University Press of Kentucky, 1997.

Anderson, Bill. "He's a Dignified Working Man in a Wrinkled Raincoat Rumpled, but Brainy, Detective Columbo's Back." *The Globe and Mail (Canada)*, August 1988.

Aristotle. *Rhetoric: The Complete Works of Aristotle Volume Two*. Edited by Jonathan Barnes, translated by W. Rhys Roberts, Revised Oxford Translation, Princeton University Press, 1984.

Arntfield, Michael. "TVPD: The Generational Diegetics of the Police Procedural on American Television." *Canadian Review of American Studies*, vol. 41, no. 1, 2011, pp. 75–95.

"Ask Figaro." *Figures of Speech Served Fresh*, 2005, inpraiseofargument.squarespace.com ask-figaro/.

Barthes, Roland. *Mythologies*. Hill & Wang, 1972.

Bazerman, Charles. "Systems of Genres and the Enactment of Social Intentions." *Genre and the New Rhetoric*, edited by Aviva Freedman and Peter Medway, Taylor & Francis, 1994, pp. 79–101.

Berenstein, Rhona J. "It Will Thrill You, It May Shock You, It Might Even Horrify You: Gender, Reception, and Classic Horror Cinema." *Dread of Difference: Gender and the Horror Film*, edited by Barry Keith Grant, University of Texas Press, 1996, pp. 145–91.

Berglas, Steven. "The Top 5 Ways to Manage Closed-Minded, Defensive, Truth-Resistant People." *Forbes*, 11 January 2013, www.forbes.com/sites/stevenberglas/2013/01/11/the-top-5-ways-to-manage-closed-minded-defensive-truth-resistant-people/2/#63db0d7e35b7.

Berman, Marc. "Laughing Matters: Screwball Drama." *Mediaweek*, 17 November 2003, advance.lexis.com/api/document?collection=news&id=urn:contentItem:4B58-HSK0-01V4-X2MS-00000-00&context=1516831.

Berzsenyi, Christyne. "Teaching Interlocutor Relationships in Electronic Classrooms." *Computers and Composition*, vol. 16, no. 2, August 1999, pp. 229–46.

———. "'Evil, Beautiful, Deadly': Publicity Posters of Drive-in Horror's Monstrous Women." *Horror at the Drive-in: Essays in Popular Americana*, edited by Gary Don Rhodes, McFarland Publishers, 2003, pp. 169–85.

Bitzer, Lloyd. "The Rhetorical Situation." *Philosophy and Rhetoric*, vol. 1, Winter 1968, pp. 1–14.

Bounds, Dennis. "*Columbo*: U.S. Police Drama." *The Museum of Broadcast Communications—Encyclopedia of Television*, 5 October 2013, www.museum.tv/eotv/columbo.htm.

Brandon, Max. "Topic 11: Columbo-Style Questioning." *YouTube*, 13 July 2012, www.youtube.com/watch?v=i2xsymNTM9Q.

Brownson, Charles. *The Figure of the Detective: A Literary History and Analysis*. McFarland & Company, Inc., 2014.

Brune, Drew. Comment on "A Deadly State of Mind." *The Good Columbo Guide*, 25 May 2013, planetbods.org/columbo/series_4/.

Brunsdale, Mitzi. "Columbo: The Disheveled Detective." *Icons of Mystery and Crime Detection: From Sleuths to Superheroes*, Greenwood, 2010, pp. 199–228.

Buonanno, Milly. *Italian TV Drama and Beyond: Stories from the Soil, Stories from the Sea*. Intellect Books, 2012.

Burke, Edmund. *A Philosophical Enquiry into the Origin of Our Ideas of the Sublime and Beautiful (1757)*. Edited by James T. Bolton, Routledge and Kegan Paul, 1958.

Burke, Tom. "Peter Falk and the Real Story of Nick and Mabel and Why the Bars Stay Open for Mr. Columbo." *Rolling Stone Magazine*, no. 185, 24 April 1974, pp. 40–44.

Burns, Stephen, Bob Hoey, and Ted Kerin. "Columbo Parodies and Comedies." *The Ultimate Columbo Site!*, 2008, columbo-site.freeuk.com/parodies.htm.

Carson, Johnny, and the Mighty Carson Art Players. "Columbo Spoof." *The Tonight Show Starring Johnny Carson*, Carson Productions, 19 September 1975, www.youtube.com/watch?v=3W1TDnSITaQ.

Catz, Sheldon. *Columbo Under Glass: A Critical Analysis of the Cases, Clues and Character of the Good Lieutenant*. Bear Manor Media, 2016.

Chandler, Raymond. "The Simple Art of Murder." *Atlantic Monthly*, vol. 174, no. 6, December 1944, pp. 53–59.

ChangingMinds.org. "The Columbo Technique." *Techniques*, 2002–18, changingminds.org/techniques/questioning/columbo_technique.htm.

———. "The Power of Questions." 2002–18, changingminds.org/techniques/questioning/power_of_questions.htm.

Christie, Agatha. *Murder on the Orient Express*. Collins Crime Club, 1934.

Clark, Craig. "Sense of Humor by Damon Runyon." *Somebody Dies*, 7 August 2008, somebodydies.blogspot.com/2008/08/sense-of-humor-by-damon-runyon-broadway.html.

Clover, Carol J. *Men, Women and Chainsaws: Gender in the Modern Horror Film*. Princeton University Press, 1992.

Coates, Gordon. *Wanterfall: A Practical Approach to the Understanding and Healing of the Emotions of Everyday Life*. Wanterfall E-Books, 2012, www.wanterfall.com/Wanterfall-Contents-Page.htm

Cohen, Maurice H. "The Aporias in Plato's Early Dialogues." *Journal of the History of Ideas*, vol. 23, no. 2, 1962, pp. 163–74, jstor.org/stable/2708153.

Coletta, Lisa. *And in Our Time: Vision, Revision, and British Writing in the 1930s*. Rosemont Publishing and Printing Corp, 2003.

———. "The Dark Domestic Vision of Ivy Compton-Burnett: A House and Its Head." *Dark Humor and Social Satire in the Modern British Novel*, edited by Anthony Shuttleworth, Palgrave McMillan, 2013, pp. 59–80.

Collins, Max Allan. "The Hard-Boiled Detective." *Encyclopedia Mysteriosa*, MacMillan, 1994, pp. 153–54.

Collins, Paul. "The Case of the First Mystery Novelist: Before Hercule or Sherlock, There Was Ralph." *New York Times*, 7 January 2011, pp. BR23.

Collins, Wilkie. *The Moonstone*. Tinsley Brothers, 1868.

Columbo. Created by Richard Levinson and William Link, performance by Peter Falk, NBC 1968–78, ABC 1989–2003, Universal Television/Studios USA, 1968–2003.

"Columbo: A Cop Like No Other." *MysteryNet.com™: The Online Mystery Network*, 3 January 2015, MysteryNet.com/tv/columbo/.

Columbo Fans' Site: Cheap Cigar Club, 10 February 2020, www.clapstick.com/columbo/indexE.html.

Columbophile. "The Arguments For and Against a *Columbo* Reboot." *The Columbophile*, 9 August 2015, columbophile.com/2015/08/09/why-im-against-a-columbo-reboot-in-principle/.

———. "Top 10 Most Sympathetic Columbo Killers." *The Columbophile*, 16 August 2015, columbophile.com/2015/08/16/who-are-the-most-sympathetic-columbo-killers/.

Cook, Pam. *Screening the Past: Memory and Nostalgia in Cinema*. Routledge, 2005.

Cooper, John M. "Introduction to Plato's *Charmides*." *The Complete Works of Plato*, edited by John M. Cooper, Hackett Publishing Company, Inc., 1997, pp. 639–40.

Copeland, Edward. "After 40 Years, I Have Far More than Just One Thing to Say about Columbo." *Edward Copeland's Tangents*, 15 September 2011, eddieonfilm.blogspot.com/2010/09/after-40-years-i-have-far-more-than.html.

Corkin, Stanley. *Cowboys as Cold Warriors: The Western and U S History*. Temple University Press, 2004.

Creed, Barbara. *The Monstrous-Feminine: Film, Feminism, Psychoanalysis*. Routledge, 1993.

Daily Mail Reporter. "Columbo Star Peter Falk Leaves Bulk of Multi-Million Dollar Estate to his Devoted Wife Shera." *Daily Mail*, 24 June 2011, dailymail.co.uk/tvshowbiz/article-2007957/Columbo-star-Peter-Falk-leaves-bulk-multi-million-dollar-estate-devoted-wife-Shera.html#ixzz4i8othDI6.

Dan. "Wise Fool vs. Idiot Savant: *Columbo* vs. *Monk*." *Dislogue: Books, Culture, Fishing, and Other Games*, 15 August 2003, dislogue.dansch.net/archives/000024.html.

Danytė, Milda. *Introduction to the Analysis of Crime Fiction*. Vytautas Magnus University Press, 2011.

Davidoff, Doug. "The Five Lessons That Everyone in Sales Should Learn from *Columbo*." *Imagine Business Development*, 21 September 2015, blog.imaginellc.com/b2b-sales-lessons.

Davis, Flora. *Moving the Mountain: The Women's Movement in America Since 1960*. University Press, 1999.

Dawidziak, Mark. *The Columbo Phile: A Casebook*. Mysterious Press, 1989.

Del Drago, Antonio. "5 Characteristics for an Epic Villain." *Mythic Scribes: The Art of Fantasy Storytelling*, 23 July 2013, mythicscribes.com/character-development/5-characteristics-epic-villain/.

"Detective Robert Goren." *USA Network*, 2016, usanetwork.com/criminalintent/cast/det-robert-goren.

Dewitt, Amy J. "Integrating Rhetorical and Literary Theories of Genre." *College English*, vol. 62, no. 6, July 2000, pp. 696–718.

Dill-Shackleford, Karen E. *How Fantasy Becomes Reality Information and Entertainment Media in Everyday Life*. Revised and Expanded ed., Oxford University Press, 2015.

D'Onofrio, Vincent (@vincentdonofrio). "I wish I was that good. Peter Falk was an amazing actor." *Twitter*, 27 February 2017, 10:13 a.m. twitter.com/vincentdonofrio/status/836277972227211264.

———. "I loved Columbo and would sometimes celebrate that with adding a lil something from the iconic character." *Twitter*, 19 March 2017, 7:34 p.m, twitter.com/vincentdonofrio/status/843651813253545984?lang=en-gb.

Dostoevsky, Fyodor. *Crime and Punishment*. Translated by Constance Garnett, The Project Gutenberg EBook #2554, 2006.

Dove, George N. *The Reader and the Detective Story*. Bowling Green State University Popular Press, 1997.

Dowler, Ken. "Police Dramas on Television." *Oxford Research Encyclopedia, Criminology and Criminal Justice*, Oxford University Press, 2016, criminology.oxfordre.com/view/10.1093/acrefore/9780190264079.001.0001/acrefore-9780190264079-e-175?print=pdf.

Doyle, Sir Arthur Conan. *Hound of the Baskervilles*. George Newnes, 1902, n.pag.

Eisner, Manuel. "Modernity Strikes Back? A Historical Perspective on the Latest Increase in Interpersonal Violence 1960–1990." *International Journal of Conflict and Violence*, vol. 2, no. 2, pp. 288–316.

Emerson, Ralph Waldo. "Heroism." *The Complete Works: Vol. II. Essays*, First Series, 1904.

Etter, Jonathan. *Quinn Martin, Producer: A Behind the Scenes Look at QM Productions and Its Founder*. McFarland Press, 2013.

Fahraeus, Anna, and Kikmen Yakali-Camoglu. "Who Are the Villainous Ones? Introduction." *Villains and Villainy: Embodiments of Evil in Literature, Popular Culture, and Media*, Probing the Boundaries Series, edited by Anna Fahraeus and Kikmen Yakali-Camoglu, Ropodi, 2011, pp. vii–xii.

Fairbanks, Brian W. Comment on "*Columbo*: Exercise in Fatality." *International Movie Database*, 21 May 2003, imdb.com/title/tt0072802/reviews.

WORKS CITED

Falk, Peter. *Just One More Thing: Stories from My Life*. Carroll and Graf Publishers, 2006.

Ferguson, Christopher. "A History of Violence in Media." *Adolescents, Crime, and the Media: A Critical Analysis*, Springer, 2013, pp. 17–30.

Firestein, Stuart. "The Pursuit of Ignorance." *TED2013 Conference*, 25 February 2013, ted.com/talks/stuart_firestein_the_pursuit_of_ignorance.

Fisher, Nick R. E. "Hubris." *The Oxford Classical Dictionary*, edited by Simon Hornblower and Antony Spawforth, 3rd rev. ed., Oxford University Press, 2017.

Fishwick, Marshall W. "Introduction." *The Hero in Transition*, edited by Ray B. Browne and Marshall W. Fishwick, Bowling Green University Press, 1983, pp. 5–13.

Fiske, John. *Television Culture*. Routledge, 2006.

Freeman, Austin R. "Preface." *The Singing Bone (The Adventures of Dr. Thorndyke)*, First UK ed., Project Gutenberg Australia, Hodder & Stoughton, 1912, n.pag.

Frye, Northrop. *Anatomy of Criticism: Four Essays*. Princeton University Press, 1957.

Fukuyama, Francis. *The Great Disruption: Human Nature and the Reconstitution of Social Order*. Free Press, 1999.

Futon Critic, The. "USA Network Launches New Seasons of *Law & Order: Criminal Intent* and *In Plain Sight* Premiering Sunday, May 1." *The Futon Critic*, 2 February 2011, thefutoncritic.com/showatch/law-and-order-criminal-intent/.

Galbraith, Stuart, IV. "Review: Columbo—Mystery Movie Collection, 1989." *DVD Talk*, 10 May 2007, dvdtalk.com/reviews/27997/columbo-mystery-movie-collection-1989/.

Graham, Adam. *All I Needed to Know, I Learned from Columbo: Life Lessons from Great Detectives of Film, Radio, and Page*. Smashwords, 2011.

Greene, Robert. *The Art of Seduction*. Viking Press, 2003.

Groddeck, Georg, and Sigmund Freud. *The Meaning of Illness: Selected Psychoanalytic Writings*. International Universities Press, 1977.

Grundhauser, Eric. "Why Is There a Statue of Columbo in the Middle of Budapest?" *Atlas Obscura: The Definitive Guide to the World's Hidden Wonders*, 16 October 2018, youtu.be/-zZHEQLVyWE.

Guiley, Rosemary Ellen. "Lucifer." "Satan." "Mammon." *The Encyclopedia of Demons and Demonology*, Visionary Living, Inc., 2009.

Haden, Jeff. "10 Genuine Ways Anyone Can Be Exceptionally Charming." *Inc. Magazine*, 1 April 2014, inc.com/jeff-haden/10-genuine-ways-anyone-can-be-exceptionally-charming.html.

Harmon, Gary L. "Tarzan and Columbo: Heroic Mediators." *The Hero in Transition*, edited by Ray B. Browne and Marshall W. Fishwick, Bowling Green University Press, 1983, pp. 115–30.

Haskell, Molly. *From Revenge to Rape: The Treatment of Women in the Movies*. Holt, Rinehart and Winston, 1974.

Hastie, Amelie. "'Just One More Thing': Columbo's Investigation of Analog Technologies." *Media Res: A Media Commons Project*, 10 March 2010, mediacommons.futureofthebook.

org/imr/2010/03/10/just-one-more-thing-columbo-s-investigation-analog-technologies. [no longer available]

Haycraft, Howard. *Murder for Pleasure: The Life and Times of the Detective Story*. Mercury Publications, Inc., 1951.

Heather. "The 30 Best Fictional Detectives." *BackgroundChecks.org*, 21 July 2013, backgroundchecks.org/30-best-fictional-detectives.html.

Heinrichs, Jay. *Thank You for Arguing: What Aristotle, Lincoln and Homer Simpson Can Teach Us About the Art of Persuasion*. Three Rivers Press and Penguin, 2013.

Henne, B. G. "Enter the Amazingly Specific World of the Rockford Files Filming Locations." *A.V. Club*, 17 September 2015, news.avclub.com/enter-the-amazingly-specific-world-of-the-rockford-file-1798284413.

Hodgson, Philip. "What User Researchers Can Learn from Sherlock Holmes." *Userfocus*, 4 October 2011, userfocus.co.uk/articles/learn_from_Sherlock_Holmes.html.

Hoffmann, Josef. *Philosophies of Crime Fiction*. No Exit Press, 2013.

Holbrook, Stewart. "The Lady of Lynn, Mrs. Pinkham." *The Golden Age of Quackery*, Collier Books, 1959, pp. 63–70.

Horsley, Lee. "Parody of the Crime Film." *Crime Culture*, 9 March 2011, crimeculture.com/Contents/Parodies.html.

Hughes, Paul. *The Columbo Case Files: Season One*. Hughes, 2012.

Hurka, Thomas. *Virtue, Vice, and Value*. Oxford University Press, 2001.

"Huw Wheldon Meets Alfred Hitchcock." *Monitor*, starring Afred Hitchcock and Huw Wheldon, 5 May 1964, BBC Television, 1958–present, m.youtube.com/watch?v=c9PO-767D8I&autoplay=1.

Inciardi, James A. and Juliet L. Dee. "From the Keystone Cops to Miami Vice Images of Policing in American Popular Culture." *Journal of Popular Culture*, vol. 21, no. 2, 1987, pp. 84–102.

James, P. D. *Talking about Detective Fiction*. Alfred Knopf and Alfred Knopf Publishers, 2009.

Jaster, Margaret Rose. "The Earnest Equivocator: Columbo Undoes *Macbeth*." *Journal of American Culture*, vol. 22, no. 4, 1999, pp. 51–55.

Jenner, Mareike. *American TV Detective Dramas: Serial Investigations*. Palgrave MacMillan, 2016.

Jeramiah and Thad. "The Top 5 Reasons Why Columbo Is an American Paradox." *The Fandomentals*, 15 June 2018, thefandomentals.com/the-top-5-reasons-why-columbo-is-an-american-paradox/.

Jing Qiong, Zhou. *Raymond Carver's Short Fiction in the History of Black Humor*. Peter Lang Publishing, 2006.

Jung, Carl. *The Archetypes and the Collective Unconscious (Collected Works of C.G. Jung Vol.9 Part 1)*. Translated by R. F. C. Hull, 2nd ed., Princeton University Press, 1981.

Kahn, Victoria. "Machiavellian Rhetoric in Paradise Lost." *Religious Invention and Religious Inquiry*, edited by Walter Jost and Wendy Olmsted, Yale University Press, 2000, pp. 223–53.

Kalinina, Ekaterina. "The Flow of Nostalgia: Experiencing Television from the Past." *Journal of International Communication*, vol. 10, 2016, pp. 5324–41.

Karl, Frederick R. "Introduction." *The Moonstone*, Signet Classics, 2002, pp. 1–21.

Kaufman, Carolyn. "Three-Dimensional Villains: Finding Your Character's Shadow." *Archetype Writing: The Fiction Writer's Guide to Using Psychology*, 23 April 2013, archetypewriting.com/articles/articles_ck/archetypes2_shadow.htm.

Keen, Richard Keen, Monica L. McCoy, and Elizabeth Powell. "Rooting for the Bad Guy: Psychological Perspectives." *Studies in Popular Culture*, vol. 34, no. 2, Spring 2012, pp. 129–48.

Keene, Carolyn (collective pseudonym with Mildrid A. Wirt Benson as primary). *Nancy Drew Mystery Stories*. Created by Edward Stratemeyer, Grosset & Dunlop, 1930–53.

Kellermann, A. L., and J. A. Mercy. "Men, Women, and Murder: Gender-Specific Differences in Rates of Fatal Violence and Victimization." *Journal of Trauma*, vol. 33, no. 1, July 1992, pp. 1–5.

Kennedy, George A. *Aristotle: On Rhetoric*. Oxford University Press, 1991.

Kiss, Stephen. "On TV Westerns of the 1950s and '60s." *Mid-Manhattan Library at 42nd Street*, 1 December 2012, nypl.org/blog/2012/12/01/tv-westerns-1950s-and-60s.

Klosterman, Chuck. *I Wear the Black Hat: Grappling with Villains (Real and Imagined)*. Scribner, 2013.

Knight, Stephen. *Form and Ideology in Crime Fiction*. Indiana University Press, 1980.

____. *Crime Fiction, 1800-2000: Detection, Death, Diversity*. Palgrave MacMillan, 2004.

Kojak. Created by Abby Mann, performances by Telly Savalas, Dan Frazer, and Kevin Dobson, Universal Pictures and CBS, 1973–78.

Koukl, Greg. "The Columbo Tactic." *Stand to Reason*, 28 February 2013, str.org/articles/the-columbo-tactic#.WTXAbOvyvX4.

____. "The Columbo Tactic: Diplomacy Rather Than D-Day." *YouTube*, 10 December 2016, youtu.be/iFVktfjz4O0.

Laity, Kate. "Anglo-Saxon Charm for Bees." *WitchesAndPagans.com*, 23 July 2014, witchesandpagans.com/pagan-studies-blogs/history-witch/anglo-saxon-charm-for-bees.html.

Leibovitz, Anne. "Peter Falk as Columbo." *Rolling Stone Magazine*, no. 185, 24 April 1975, Cover.

Lenihan, John H. *Showdown: Confronting Modern America in the Western Film*. Illini Books ed., University of Illinois Press, 1985.

Levi-Straus, Claude. *Structural Anthropology*. Basic Books, 1963.

Levinson, Richard and William Link. *Stay Tuned: An Inside Look at Making Prime-Time Television*. Ace Books, 1983.

Lierberson, Stanley. *A Matter of Taste: How Names, Fashions, and Culture Change*. Yale University Press, 2000.

Link, William. *The Columbo Collection*. Crippen & Landru Publishers, 2010.

Loh, Yip Mei. "Socrates' Mythological Role in Plato's *Theaetetus*." *International Journal of Social, Behavioral, Educational, Economic, Business and Industrial Engineering*, vol. 11, no. 2, 2017, pp. 403–06.

Madigan, Tim. "Just One More Thing ...." *Philosophy Now Magazine*, no. 64, Nov/Dec 2007, philosophynow.org/issues/64/Just_One_More_Thing.

Martha the Mobile Librarian. "The Genre of Mystery." *The Mystery Corner: Books, Movies, and Games, WordPress*, 4 March 2011, booksmoviesandgames.wordpress.com/tag/inverted-mystery/.

Martindale, David. "A Touch of Class." *Armchair Detective*, vol. 26, no. 68, January 1993, n.pag.

McCarthy, Jerome E. *Basic Marketing: A Managerial Approach*. Irwin Publishing, 1964.

McGirr, Lisa. *The War on Alcohol: Prohibition and the Rise of the American State*. W.W. Norton, 2015.

Meyers, Ric. *Murder on the Air: Television's Great Mystery Series*. Mysterious Press, 1989.

Miller, Carolyn R. "Genre as Social Action." *Quarterly Journal of Speech*, vol. 70, May 1984, pp. 151–67.

Monk. Created by Andy Beckman, Mendeville Films, Touchstone Pictures, and USA Network, 2002–09.

Moore, Grace. "The Great Detectives: Dupin, Sergeant Cuff & Inspector Bucket." *The Strand Magazine*, 2018, strandmag.com/the-magazine/articles/the-great-detectives-dupin-sergeant-cuff-inspector-bucket-by-grace-moore/.

Mortensen, Klaus P. *The Time of Unrememberable Being: Wordsworth and the Sublime, 1787–1805*. Museum Musculanum Press, 1998.

Murder by Natural Causes. Directed by Robert Day, A Richard Levinson and William Link Production, Universal Studios, CA, 1979.

North, Helen. *Sophrosyne and Self-Restraint in Greek Literature*. Cornell University Press, 1966.

Nystrom, Derek. *Hard Hats, Rednecks, and Macho Men: Class in 1970s American Cinema*. Oxford University Press, 2009, pensu.eblib.com/patron/FullRecord.aspx?p=472338.

O'Brien, Geoffrey. "A Memory of *Columbo*." *Black Clock*, no. 4, 2005, pp. 52–55.

Odendahl-James, Jules. "Reflexivity and the Procedural." *In Media Res: A Media Commons Project*, 10 March 2010, mediacommons.futureofthebook.org/imr/2010/03/10/just-one-more-thing-columbo-s-investigation-analog-technologies#comment-1752.

Ousby, I. "Black Mask." *The Cambridge Guide to Literature in English*, Cambridge University Press, 1995, p. 89.

Pachmuss, Temira. "Dostoyevsky's Porfiry Petrovich: A New Socrates." *New Zealand Slavonic Journal*, no. 1, 1980, pp. 17–24.

Panek, Leroy L. "Post-War American Police Fiction." *The Cambridge Companion to Crime Fiction*, edited by Martin Priestman, Cambridge University Press, 2003, pp. 155–72.

Paris Motel. "Mr. Splitfoot (In the Darkest Night)." Hotel Records, 2005.

Pazak, Susan. "Healthy Emotions." *Ask Dr. Susan P*, 2 February 2011, www.askdrsusanp.com/healthy_emotions.

"Phantom." *Law and Order: Criminal Intent*, created by Wolf Films, performance by Vincent D'Onofrio and Kathryn Erbe, season 1, episode 16, USA Network, 2001–11.

Philbrick, Lisa. "Retro Hijinks: Dr. Robert Culpable—And the *Mad Magazine* Spoof of Columbo." *The Consummate Culp*, 6 March 2013, theconsummateculp.com/2013/03/retro-hijinks-dr-robert-culpable-and-the-mad-magazine-spoof-of-columbo.html.

Phillips, J. B. "Devil." *The New Testament in Modern English*. Harper Collins, 1962, ccel.org/bible/Phillips/CN054-Death.htm.

Phillips, Melanie Ann. "Hero is a Four-letter Word: The Villain." *The Writers Store Zine*, April 2013, writersstore.com/hero-is-a-4-letter-word-the-villain/.

Phillips, Nickie D., and Staci Stroble. *Comic Book Crime: Truth, Justice, and the American Way*. New York University Press, 2013.

Pinker, Steven. "Decivilization in the 1960s." *Human Figurations: Long-Term Perspectives on the Human Condition*, vol. 2, no. 2, 2013, hdl.handle.net/2027/spo.11217607.0002.206.

Plato. "Charmides." Translated by Rosamond Kent Sprague. *The Complete Works of Plato*, edited by John M. Cooper, Hackett Publishing Company, 1997, pp. 639–63.

Poe, Edgar Allan. "Murders in the Rue Morgue." *Graham's Magazine*, vol. XVIII, no. 4, April 1841, pp. 166–79, eapoe.org/works/tales/morgueb.htm.

Postrel, Virginia. *The Power of Glamour: Longing and the Art of Visual Persuasion*. Simon and Schuster, 2013.

———. "Trump Isn't Just Campaigning: He's Selling His Supporters a Glamorous Life." *The Washington Post*, 18 March 2016, washingtonpost.com/opinions/trump-is-selling-a-dream-his-supporters-are-buying/2016/03/18/5307698e-eb8f-11e5-bc08-3e03a5b41910_story.html?noredirect=on&utm_term=.2d956d771c5e.

Prudentius, Aurelius Clemons. *Psychomachia (The Battle for the Soul of Man)*. 410 AD, people.virginia.edu/~jdk3t/psychomachia.pdf.

Rademaker, Adriaan. *Sophrosyne and the Rhetoric of Restraint: Polysemy and Persuasive Use of an Ancient Greek Value Term*. Koninklijke Brill NV and Brill Academic Publishers, 2005.

Reilly, John M. "Inverted Detective Story." *A Companion to Crime and Mystery Writing: Oxford Reference*, Oxford University Press, 2005.

Ricoeur, Paul. "Evil." *Encyclopedia of Religion*, edited by Lindsay Jones, 2nd ed., vol. 5, McMillan Reference USA, 2005, pp. 2897–904, go.galegroup.com.ezaccess.libraries.psu.edu/ps/i.do?p=GVRL&sw=w&u=psucic&v=2.1&it=r&id=GALE%7CCX3424500977&asid=29b56da55571b26ed68ffc7da0b60b5d.

Rifleman, The. Created by Arnold Laven, performances by Chuck Connors and Johnny Crawford, Four Star Television and ABC, 1958–63.

Riviere, Joan. "Womanliness as a Masquerade." *Psychoanalysis and Female Sexuality*, edited by Hendrik M. Ruitenbeek, College and University Press, 1966, pp. 209–19.

Rockford Files, The. Created by Stephen J. Cannell and Roy Huggins, performances by James Garner and Noah Beery, Roy Huggins-Public Arts Productions, Cherokee Productions, and CBS, 1974–80.

Rollyson, Carl E. *Critical Survey of Mystery and Detective Fiction*. Vol. 1, Salem Press, 2008.

Rose, Marilyn, and Jeannette Sloniowski. "'Home Sweet Havoc': *Howard Engel's Niagara* in Print and Film." *Journal of Canadian Studies*, vol. 39, no. 3, 2005, pp. 85–104.

Rushing, Robert A. *Resisting Arrest: Detective Fiction and Popular Culture*. Cultural Studies Series, edited by Samir Dayal, Other Press, 2007.

Ryan, Christopher James. "Commentary. Dirty Blood: Case Study." *Hastings Center Report*, vol. 39, no. 5, September–October 2009, pp. 13–15.

Rzepka, Charles J., and Lee Horsley, editors. *A Companion to Crime Fiction*. Wiley-Blackwell, 2010.

Sabin, Roger. "Columbo: 1968–1978." *Cop Shows: A Critical History of Police Dramas on Television*, edited by Roger Sabin, Ronald Wilson, and Linda Speidel, McFarland Publishers, 2015, pp. 58–65.

Sanello, Frank. "Columbo's World: It's a Mystery to Peter Falk How His Detective Captured the Globe." *Chicago Tribune*, April 1989, articles.chicagotribune.com/1989-04-02/features/8903310956_1_peter-falk-bodyguards-gideon-oliver.

Santas, Gerasimos. "Socrates at Work on Virtue and Knowledge in Plato's *Charmides*." *Exegesis and Argument: Studies in Greek Philosophy Presented to Gregory Vlastos*, vol. 1, 1973, pp. 105–32.

Scharrer, Erica. "More Than 'Just the Facts?' Portrayals of Masculinity in Police and Detective Dramas over Time." *Howard Journal of Communications*, vol. 23, no. 1, pp. 88–109.

Seddon, Gem. "The Top 50 TV Detectives of All Time." *GamesRadar, PressReader*, 21 September 2015, gamesradar.com/top-50-tv-detectives-all-time/6/.

Sepinwall, Alan. "TV's Top Detectives: Small Screen Masters of the Whodunit." *Rolling Stone Magazine,* July 2018, p. 131.

Shannon, Adam R. *Seven Deadly Sins: Sins Virtues Tales*, deadlysins.com.

Shields, Christopher. "Imagination/Phantasia." *Stanford Encyclopedia of Philosophy*, Center for the Study of Language and Information, Stanford University, 2016.

Silverstone, Lou (writer), and Angelo Torres (artist). "Clodumbo." *Mad Magazine*, no. 156, January 1973, pp. 40–46.

Skaggs, John. *Crime Fiction: The New Critical Idiom*. Routledge, 2005.

Skogan, Wesley G. "Social Change and the Future of Violent Crime." *Violence in America, Vol. 1: The History of Crime*, edited by Ted Robert Gurr, Sage, 1989, pp. 235–50.

Slotkin, Richard. *Gunfighter Nation: The Myth of the Frontier in Twentieth-Century America*. University of Oklahoma Press, 1998.

Springer, John Parris. "*Daughter of Horror*: Low-Budget Filmmaking, Generic Instability and Sexual Politics." *Horror at the Drive-In: Essays in Popular Americana*, edited by Gary Don Rhodes, McFarland and Company, Inc., 2003, pp. 155–68.

WORKS CITED

Sternberger, Chad. "Mark Ruffalo to Play *Columbo*." *The Studio Exec.*, 17 July 2014, thestudioexec.com/mark-ruffalo-to-play-columbo/.

Sutton, Adrian. *Paediatrics, Psychiatry and Psychoanalysis: Through Counter-Transference to Case Management*. Routledge, 2013.

Symons, Julian. *Bloody Murder: From the Detective Story to the Crime Novel*. Faber & Faber, 1972.

TC. Comment on "Ask Figaro." *Figures of Speech Served Fresh*, 2005, inpraiseofargument.squarespace.com/ask-figaro/?currentPage=4.

"Television: Mystery/Detective Series." *Ultimate Mystery/Detective Web Guide*, 28 January 2002, magicdragon.com/UltimateMystery/tv.html.

Thomas, Ronald R. "Detection in the Victorian Novel." *The Cambridge Companion to the Victorian Novel*, edited by Deirdre David, Cambridge University Press, 2001, pp. 169–91.

Thompson, David. "David Thompson on Film: Why I Loved Peter Falk as Columbo." *New Republic Magazine*, 28 June 2011, newrepublic.com/article/90865/peter-falk-columbo-television-actor-cassavetes.

Tom. "Mark Ruffalo As 'Columbo'?....Yes Please!!" *The Last Reel*, 17 July 2014, thelastreel.blogspot.com/2014/07/mark-ruffalo-as-columboyes-please.html.

Trexler, Richard. "Introduction." *Gender Rhetorics: Postures of Dominance and Submission in History*, edited by Richard Trexler, Medieval & Renaissance Texts & Studies, 1994, pp. 1–14.

Tucker, Ken. "Peter Falk was Columbo and a Whole Lot More: A Career-Spanning Appreciation." *Entertainment Weekly*, 24 June 2011, ew.com/article/2011/06/24/peter-falk-columbo/.

"TV's Smartest Detectives." *Huffington Post*, April 2014, huffingtonpost.com/2011/11/28/tvs-smartest-detectives_n_1116516.html.

U.S. Justice Department. *Homicide Trends in the U.S.* U.S. Bureau of Justice Statistics, 2011, bjs.ojp.usdoj.gov/content/homicide/intimates.cfm.

USA Network. "Character Bio: Detective Robert Goren." *USA Network*, usanetwork.com/criminalintent/cast/det-robert-goren.

Vande Berg, Leah R. "Dramedy." *Encyclopedia of Television*, The Museum of Broadcast Communications, 1997, museum.tv/eotv/dramedy.htm.

Variety Staff Writers. " 'Columbo' Leads the Way Through French Primetime." *Variety*, English ed., 5 February 1995, variety.com/1995/more/news/columbo-leads-the-way-through-french-primetime-99124936/.

Virtue, Graeme. "A Reboot *Columbo* Is a Fantastic Idea—Apart from One Enormous Flaw." *The Guardian*, 18 July 2014, theguardian.com/tv-and-radio/tvandradioblog/2014/jul/18/reboot-columbo-fantastic-idea-apart-one-enormous-flaw.

Vlastos, Gregory. "The Socratic Elenchus." *Journal of Philosophy*, vol. 79, no. 11, 1982, pp. 711–14, jstor.org/stable/2026548.

Von Mueller, Eddy. "The Police Procedural in Literature and on Television." *The Cambridge Companion to American Crime Fiction*, edited by Catherine Ross Nickerson, Cambridge University Press, 2010, pp. 96–109.

Walker, Wren. "Runs with Bees." *Wren's Words, Wrants and Wramblings*, 8 April 2002, witchvox.com.

Walsh, Kay. "Comedy, Workplace." *Encyclopedia of Television*, Museum of Broadcast Communications, 1997, museum.tv/eotv/comedyworkp.htm.

Warshow, R. *The Immediate Experience*. Doubleday and Ancho, 1955.

Watson, Robert I. *The Great Psychologists: From Aristotle to Freud*. J. B. Lippincott Company, 1968.

Weil, Lisa. "Fidesz Clue in The Case of the Columbo Sculptor." *Budapest Times*, 6 April 2014, budapesttimes.hu/2014/04/06/fidesz-clue-in-the-case-of-the-columbo-sculptor/.

Wilkinson, Deanna L., Chauncey C. Beaty, and Regina M. Lurry. "Youth Violence – Crime or Self Help? Marginalized Urban Males' Perspectives on the Limited Efficacy of the Criminal Justice System to Stop Youth Violence." *Annuals of the American Association for Political Science*, vol. 623, no. 1, 2009, pp. 25–38.

Williams, Claire, and Margaret Hanson. "Just One More Thing. ….." *The Safety & Health Practitioner*, July 2013, cardinus.briefyourmarket.com/Newsletters/Safety-Risk-Management-newsletter---May-14/Just-one-more-thing-.aspx.

Wilson, James. *Thinking About Crime*. Basic Books, 1974.

Yancey, Richard. *The Highly Effective Detective*. Vol. 1, MacMillan, 2008.

"Yesterday." *Law and Order: Criminal Intent*. Created by Rene Balcer and Dick Wolfe, performances by Vincent D'Onofrio and Kathryn Erbe, season 1, episode 18, Wolf Films Production and NBC, 2001–11.

Zeng, Jessica. "Crime Fiction." *English Enrichment Crime Fiction*, 2 February 2020, sites.google.com/site/englishenrichmentcrimefiction/.

About the Author

CHRISTYNE BERZSENYI, Ph.D. is an Associate Professor of English, teaching Techno-Rhetoric and Professional Writing as well as Genre-Based Literature and Cultural Studies at Penn State University, Wilkes-Barre since 1998. Her courses draw upon classical texts as well as contemporary stories across media, while instruction varies in delivery formats from computer-assisted, to blended and hybrid learning, to web courses. Her research utilizes rhetorical discourse analysis of popular electronic interaction, analysis of genre as generative of applied communication with audiences, and the theorizing of contextualized, mediated rhetoric. Example texts include e-dating profiles and interactions; print, performance, web, and video promotions; and dialogue in terms of language choices and strategies employed to build identities and relationships among characters in fiction, students of professional writing, and real-time chat and asynchronous discussion board interlocutors.

Index

A

The Alienist (2018–20) 54
ambipathy 77–78, 89–90, 93–94, 100–01
American paradox 22
antipathy 78, 82, 89–90, 93–95, 99–100
antipotency 19, 30, 56, 71, 72, 73, 74, 75, 77, 131, 134, 154, 156, 166, 171, 173–74, 184–85, 191
aporia 20, 140–43, 171, 189

B

Baretta (1975–78) 38, 190
Barnaby Jones (1973–80) 36, 91, 179
bee charmer 50
Bonanza (1959–73) 12

C

cable networks 53
car (Columbo's) 154
Cassavetes, John 60, 95–96
Cassidy, Jack 46, 89, 93, 148
Charlie's Angels (1976–81) 36, 38
charm, charmer, charming (suspects and viewers) 19, 38, 48, 49–50, 57, 67, 78, 84, 99, 107, 112, 115, 126
children (villain's) 88–89, 105, 108, 123
Civil Rights Movement 20, 107, 127
Clark, Susan 87, 91, 112, 115
Columbo (1968–2003)
　"Agenda for Murder" (1990) 87

"Any Old Port in a Storm" (1973) 31, 55, 87, 90
"Ashes to Ashes" (1998) 57, 87, 88
"A Bird in the Hand" (1991) 108
"Blueprint for Murder" (1972)
"Butterfly in Shades of Grey" (1994) 87, 88, 94, 109
"By Dawn's Early Light" (1974) 40, 55–57, 87
"The Bye–Bye Sky Hight IQ Murder Case" (1977)
"Candidate for Crime" (1973)
"A Case for Immunity" (1975)
"Caution: Murder Can Be Hazardous to Your Health" (1991)
"Columbo and the Murder of a Rock Star" (1991)
"Columbo Cries Wolf" (1990) 87, 124, 126
"Columbo Goes to College" (1990) 88
"Columbo Goes to the Guillotine" (1989) 87, 94
"Columbo Likes the Night Life" (2003)
"The Conspirators" (1978) 87
"Dagger of the Mind" (1972) 17, 55, 83, 87, 92, 108, 110, 111, 123
"A Deadly State of Mind" (1975) 83, 99, 124, 170
"Dead Weight" (1971) 34
"Death Hits the Jackpot" (1991) 125
"Death Lends a Hand" (1971) 168, 188

"Double Exposure" (1973) 30, 110
"Double Shock" (1973) 62
"Étude in Black" (1972) 4, 60, 95, 101, 161
"An Exercise in Fatality" (1974) 64
"Fade in to Murder" (1975) 31, 71, 87, 143, 145
"A Friend in Deed" (1974)
"Forgotten Lady" (1975) 32, 58, 82, 90, 101, 108, 111, 112, 116, 167
"Grand Deceptions" (1989)
"The Greenhouse Jungle" (1972) 38, 41, 87
"How to Dial a Murder" (1978) 87, 94
"Identity Crisis" (1975) 87
"It's All in the Game" (1993) 32, 88, 90, 92, 112, 113, 138, 167
"Lady in Waiting" (1971) 87, 91, 94, 108, 112, 114, 115, 120
"Last Salute to the Commodore" (1976) 156–57
"Lovely but Lethal" (1973) 55, 56, 91, 107, 108, 110, 111, 112, 120, 127, 130, 144
"Make Me A Perfect Murder" (1978) 101, 108, 112, 118
"A Matter of Honor" (1976) 55, 87, 88
"Mind Over Mayhem" (1974) 87, 88, 90, 109
"The Most Crucial Game" (1972) 42, 43, 182
"The Most Dangerous Match" (1973) 87, 150
"Murder: A Self Portrait" (1989) 87
"Murder by the Book" (1971) 8, 138, 148
"Murder in Malibu" (1990)
"Murder, Smoke and Shadows" (1989)
"Murder under Glass" (1978) 87, 94
"Murder with Too Many Notes" (2001) 34, 38, 87, 152–55
"Negative Reaction" (1974) 41, 55, 74, 91, 140, 151, 154, 169
"No Time to Die" (1991) 48
"Now You See Him" (1976) 88

"Old Fashioned Murder" (1976) 90, 108, 112
"Playback" (1975) 87, 110
"Prescription Murder" (1968) 5, 7, 15, 68–69, 83, 108, 122, 137, 159, 160, 161, 168, 170
"Publish or Perish" (1974) 40, 42
"Ransom for a Dead Man" (1971) 5, 70, 83, 88, 103, 108, 109, 117, 118, 119, 120, 158, 170
"Requiem for a Falling Star" (1973) 108, 110, 111, 134–35
"Rest in Peace, Mrs. Columbo" (1990) 58, 87, 94, 108, 116, 121
"Sex and the Married Detective" (1989) 108, 112, 120
"Short Fuse" (1972) 87
"A Stitch in Crime" (1973) 94, 149, 158, 163–64
"Strange Bedfellows" (1996)
"Suitable for Framing" (1971) 87, 123, 136
"Swan Song" (1974) 90, 92, 167
"A Trace of Murder" (1997) 124
"Troubled Waters" (1975) 92, 101
"Try and Catch Me" (1977) 31, 78, 108, 109, 110, 111, 112, 162, 167
"Undercover" (1994)
"Uneasy Lies the Crown" (1990)
"Columbo and Dog" Statue in Budapest, Hungary 7
Comer, Anjanette 60, 95–96
Connolly, Billy 34, 87, 152, 154, 155
Conrad, Robert 46–47, 64, 89, 93, 94
cozy 9, 33, 34, 37, 45, 53, 60, 113
Culp, Robert 30, 43, 46, 89, 93, 168, 182, 188

D

daughter (villain's) 88, 90, 96, 109, 118, 126
Devil 19, 77, 84–85
dialectic 21, 27, 49, 67, 73, 141

INDEX

Dishy, Paul 38, 41
dissociation 93
Doctor Who (2005–present) 54
D'Onofrio, Vincent 180–81
Dog 2, 6, 7, 22, 39, 54, 57–58, 60–62, 90, 186
Dragnet (1951–59; 1967–70) 13, 37
Drew, Nancy 14
Dunaway, Faye 32, 46, 90, 109, 112, 113, 126, 138, 167
duping delight 116, 121, 130, 165, 168

E
Ellery Queen 9
Everyman Hero 15, 75, 173

F
false exit 29, 134, 146, 158, 160–61, 185, 190
Father Knows Best (1954–60) 12
The F.B.I. (1965–74) 37

G
glamour 52–54
Golden Age mysteries 10, 33, 34, 38
Grant, Lee 70, 103, 117, 119
Gunsmoke (1955–75) 12

H
hard–boiled detective 22, 33
hard–boiled mode 33, 36, 37, 45, 158
Harrington, Grant 181
Hec Ramsey (1972–74) 5
heroic mediators 15
heroification 141, 184
Holmes, Sherlock 14, 18, 19, 23, 32–33, 134, 167, 183, 187
Hound of the Baskervilles, The Strand, (1901–02) 32
hybris/hubris 19, 68, 80–81, 93, 97, 107, 147, 152, 168–69, 173

I
indirect *elenchus* (Socrates) 141–42
interlocutor 50, 71, 150, 192, 194
inverted mystery 4–5, 8, 16, 18, 23, 24, 26, 38, 39, 45–46, 77, 92, 180

K
kairos 139, 158
Kirby, Bruce (Sgt. Kramer) 39, 40, 55, 56
Kojak (1973–78) 36, 37

L
Law and Order: Criminal Intent (2001–11) 180–01, 186
Law and Order: Special Victims Unit (1999–present) 44
Leave it to Beaver (1957–63) 12
Lucifer 84

M
MacMillan and Wife (1971–77) 5
Mad Men (2007–15) 54
Marple, Jane 14
marriage (among villains) 65, 96, 100, 102, 104, 105, 106, 118, 137, 162
McClanahan, Rue 57
McCloud (1970–77) 5
McGoohan, Patrick 46, 55, 57, 87–88, 89, 93, 155, 157
Miles, Vera 55, 56, 85, 91, 96, 107, 112, 127, 130, 144
modus operandi (M.O.) 21, 32, 50, 72, 89, 90, 111, 116, 148, 170, 196
Monk (2002–09) 180
Mrs. Columbo (wife) 22, 38, 39, 44, 54, 59, 65–66, 70, 88–89, 120, 121, 130, 135, 137, 144, 149, 151, 153, 156
Murder on the Orient Express (1934) 34
Murder, She Wrote (1984–96) 9, 34
My Three Sons (1960–72) 12

N

nostalgia 17, 53–54

P

Peaky Blinders (2013–present) 54
Peter Gunn (1958–61) 13
Petrovich, Porfiry Magistrate 24, 26–31, 36 90
phantasia 79–80
Plato 19, 66, 141–42
Pleshette, Suzanne 34
Poirot, Hercule 14, 33–35
police procedural 5, 13, 16, 19, 20, 37, 38, 44, 45, 79, 88, 107, 168, 184, 186
Price, Vincent 56, 127
propathy 78

Q

Quincy, M.E. (1976–83) 5

R

Raskalnikov, Rodion 26–30, 31
ratiocination 5, 20, 21, 23, 28, 30, 32, 36, 39, 50, 56, 59, 65, 71, 134, 143, 148, 159
resistant responder 3, 18, 21, 49, 62, 64, 81, 192–95
rhetorical genre 16, 18
rhetoric of inquiry, rhetorical inquiry 3, 8, 18, 20–21, 29, 81, 131, 138, 139, 141, 146, 151, 174, 180, 184, 190, 192, 196
The Rifleman (1958–63) 12, 13
The Rockford Files (1974–80) 38, 170
Ruffalo, Mark 186–87

S

Satan 84
Schadenfreude 83, 86, 93, 96, 120

Shenar, Paul (Sgt. Young) 40, 42
Sherlock (2010–present) 54
sidekick 7, 22, 23, 32, 38, 39, 57, 171, 186, 190
Socrates 20, 21, 27, 51, 66–67, 72–73, 141–42, 171, 172
son (villain's) 78, 88
sophrosyne 19, 66–68, 70, 71, 80, 142
standard *elenchus* 142
Steinem, Gloria 52, 105
Strong, Michael (Sgt. Hoffman) 41

T

Tarzan/*Tarzan* (1966–68) 15, 16
Theaetetus 141
trench coat/raincoat (Columbo's) 2, 74, 96–97, 177, 187, 190

U

underestimated detective 2, 14, 19, 30, 72, 92

V

Van Devere, Trish 101, 112
Van Dyke, Dick 41, 74, 91, 140, 180
Vaugh, Robert 93, 101, 157
video streaming services 53
villainy 19, 79, 81, 83, 85, 87, 89–90, 93, 95, 100, 105–06, 118, 120–21, 123–24, 174

W

Watson, John (Sherlock Holmes) 23, 32, 39, 187
the western (genre) 12–13, 15, 23
women's movement 104–05, 128

Z

Zodiac (2007) 187

Ingram Content Group UK Ltd.
Milton Keynes UK
UKHW030416230623
423792UK00025B/624